ROUGH JUSTICE

MICHAEL J. PFEIFER

Rough Justice

LYNCHING AND
AMERICAN SOCIETY,
1874–1947

UNIVERSITY OF ILLINOIS PRESS

URBANA AND CHICAGO

First Illinois paperback, 2006
© 2004 by the Board of Trustees
of the University of Illinois
Manufactured in the United States of America
∞ This book is printed on acid-free paper.

1 2 3 4 5 C P 5 4 3 2 1

The Library of Congress cataloged the cloth edition
as follows:
Pfeifer, Michael J. (Michael James), 1968–
Rough justice : lynching and American society,
1874–1947 / Michael J. Pfeifer
p. cm.
Includes bibliographical references and index.
ISBN 0-252-02917-8 (cloth : alk. paper)
1. Lynching—United States—History. 2. Culture conflict—
United States—History. 3. Social control—United States—History.
4. Capital punishment—Social aspects—United States—History.
5. Discrimination in capital punishment—United States—History.
I. Title: Lynching and American society, 1874–1947. II. Title.
HV6457.P44   2004
364.1'34—dc22   2003022987

PAPERBACK ISBN 0-252-07405-X / ISBN 978-0-252-07405-9

*This book is dedicated
to the victims of lynching
and of legal execution*

*In memoriam,
Rowland Berthoff*

Contents

Acknowledgments

This work is extraordinarily indebted to the late Rowland Berthoff. From Professor Berthoff's lectures, books, and thesis direction, I acquired an appreciation for the complexity of the American past and an agnostic respect for the flawed people who lived it. Berthoff was a terrific mentor whose intellectual acuity and curiosity powerfully inspired a young historian. He directed my undergraduate senior thesis on lynchings in Missouri at Washington University in St. Louis. That project set in motion the research and conceptual agenda that culminated many years later in this book.

This book would have been a much lesser work without the generous support offered by other scholars in the burgeoning field of lynching studies. Fitz Brundage read full drafts at various stages, and his comments immeasurably improved the work. Fitz's encouragement and mentoring from the earliest stages of the dissertation were extremely valuable. Chris Waldrep also read complete drafts on several occasions, and his rigorous critiques pushed me to make the most of this material. Bill Carrigan and Clive Webb shared their important research and offered good fellowship.

Allen Steinberg oversaw this work when it was a dissertation and offered many useful suggestions. Also at that stage, Leslie Schwalm lent a close reading and sharp eye. State archivists and librarians in Louisiana, Iowa, Wyoming, Wisconsin, Washington, Minnesota, California, Missouri, Mississippi, and New York and district court employees in St. Landry, St. Mary, and Ouachita Parishes, Louisiana, offered fine help as I conducted research. I would like to especially thank Carl Hallberg in Cheyenne and Keith Fontenot in Opelousas, who went well out of their way to find sources that aided my inquiry. Marvin Bergman, Woody Beck, Terrence Finnegan, Roberta Senechal de la Roche, Carl Brasseaux, Rocky Sexton, David Baldus, Quintard Taylor, Kabby Mitchell III, Carlos Diaz, Jacinta McCoy, and James Lowe also provided scholarly assistance. Earlier versions of some of this material appeared in *Louisiana History* 40.2 (Spring 1999), *Western Legal History* 14.2 (Summer/Fall 2001), and *Pacific Northwest Quarterly* 94.2 (Spring 2003). I am grateful to the editors of those journals for granting permission to reprint portions of those articles.

I thank Richard Wentworth of the University of Illinois Press for his strong support for the project and his patience during the process of revision; Laurie Matheson and Matt Mitchell provided fine assistance through the final stages of making a book out of this work.

My colleagues at the Evergreen State College, David Marr and Sam Schrager, offered superb backing and helpful advice. Babacar M'Baye offered not only those things but also some excellent ideas as I wrote the epilogue. The Provost's Office at the Evergreen State College awarded a sponsored research grant that helped me complete several important portions of the manuscript in the summer of 2001.

My friends Father John Boyle, Bill Thomas, Michael Smith, Scott Grau, Daniel Honey, and Martin Jardon provided encouragement and shelter. Ginger Vehaskari offered lodging in Louisiana and a careful reading of a full draft of the manuscript. Coleen Maddy read an early draft and offered crucial moral support throughout. My family tolerated my insatiable curiosity for a morbid topic and my absence from Wisconsin for Christmas 2002 as I completed the manuscript. I alone am responsible for any errors herein.

Introduction

The crimes of this man were most cruel and wanton, and his
death at the hands of an indignant and outraged populace was
an extreme though inadequate penalty. Eastern philanthropists
may lift their hands in horror at this violation of the written
law, but they must remember that there is an unwritten law
that in many cases is more just than the written law. In the
east, foul and brutal murderers are saved from the gallows by
the interposition of the law, trial after trial, and oftentimes acquittal being had upon flimsy technicalities. . . . Cold-blooded
murders may be committed in the east and the people let the
matter pass with a mere comment. The murderer may be arrested and brought to trial. If his crime is of an extra heinous
character he will be petted. His prison life may be brightened by
the visits of fair women bringing bouquets and delicacies. He
may be convicted and by some quibble secure a stay of proceedings and a new trial. Perhaps he may be acquitted on the emo-
tional insanity plea, or some other thin excuse, and go free to
kill again. The people of the west will not stand any such non-
sense. They are both of a sympathetic and practical turn of
mind.

—*Fort Collins (Colo.) Express*, reprinted in the *Cheyenne Daily
Leader*, September 22, 1883, commenting on the September
17, 1883, lynching of Henry Mosier in Cheyenne, Wyoming

Almost every week the people in some part of the country take
vengeance on lawbreakers. They rise above statutes and courts,
and, by their acts declare the inefficiency of such agencies for
the punishment of offenders.

—*Santa Rosa (Calif.) Republican*, quoted in the *Yreka (Calif.)
Journal*, September 10, 1895, commenting on the August 26,
1895, lynching of William Null, Lawrence H. Johnson, Luis
Moreno, and Garland Stemler in Yreka, California

Now what will Iowa authorities do about it? Nothing. Up north they are always lecturing us for not punishing our lynchers, but when were northern lynchers ever punished for hanging a rapist? Human nature may wear different frills in different sections, but is the same after all.

—*Atlanta Constitution*, quoted in the *Ottumwa (Iowa) Daily Democrat*, December 9, 1893, commenting on the November 21, 1893, lynching of Frank Johnson, alias Gustaveson, in Ottumwa, Iowa

Lynching occupies a unique place in American history and culture. Its special resonance is consonant with Americans' long-term preoccupation with violence, a still-pervasive mythology of the frontier, the unsettled legacy of a brutally racist past, and a long-standing skepticism of the law and legal mechanisms. Only recently have historians devoted careful attention to southern mobs, discovering that the ubiquitous practice of lynching African Americans was intimately bound with the oppressive "free" labor cultures of cotton cultivation that replaced slavery. The distinct but related practice of mob violence in the West has not yet received careful scholarly attention, with the exception of the vigilante movements in San Francisco in the 1850s. Mob killing in the West is even more encrusted in mythology in the popular mind; it has been traditionally defended as a necessary activity on a violent frontier lacking effective legal institutions. Recent scholars have chiseled away at the positive reputation of western lynching but have not sufficiently explained its meaning or social context after the mid-nineteenth century. With a few exceptions, historians have not noticed that extralegal violence also flourished in the Midwest into the late nineteenth century. In fact, only the states of New England and the mid Atlantic in the Northeast escaped a significant encounter with lynching.

The omnipresence of collective killing in three diverse American regions, the Midwest, the West, and the South, from the mid-nineteenth century through the early twentieth century requires some explanation. I believe that lynching can best be understood as an important aspect of a process of legal change that had far-reaching social and cultural ramifications throughout the United States. The response of midwesterners, westerners, southerners, and northeasterners to the evolution of the formal law is the key to understanding the social and ideological underpinnings of mob violence.

Lynching in postbellum America was an aspect of a larger cultural war over the nature of criminal justice waged between rural and working-class supporters of "rough justice" and middle-class due-process advocates. Lynchers failed to assimilate conceptions of an abstract, rational, detached, and antiseptic legal process that urban middle-class reformers wrote into statutes, particularly those pertaining to capital punishment, and that state appellate courts increasingly enshrined in rulings pertaining to legal procedure in capital cases. Mobs were impatient with the inevitable delays of legal process and disdainful of the alleged leniency of legal solutions and the seeming distance of a newly professionalized and bureaucratized criminal justice apparatus. They instead enforced racial and class goals through ritualized, communally based punishment. Postbellum mobs did not respond to an *absence* of law but rather to a *style* of criminal justice that was careful and deliberative, ostensibly impersonal and neutral, in which the rights of the defendant, the reform of the criminal, and humanitarian considerations were factored in beyond the punitive demands of communal opinion.

To rough-justice advocates, real justice was lodged in the community. It was administered face-to-face with a measure of retribution that matched the offense, and it sought to "preserve order," that is, to uphold the hierarchical prerogatives of the dominant residents of the locality. These might be prerogatives of race, class, ethnicity, or the differences between men and women or adults and children. For many rural and working-class people, law only had value as far as it served this understanding of justice. They came to believe that a "higher law" could be invoked to justify lethal violence that served the purposes that formal law would not. Criminal justice in the British Isles, Western Europe, and the American colonies had in fact largely matched their vision until the early to mid-nineteenth century, when reformers arose who sought to make the criminal justice system's avowed commitment to due process, inherited from English common law and enshrined in the Fifth Amendment to the U.S. Constitution, into a meaningful one.[1] Local criminal justice continued to match the rough-justice vision south and west of the Alleghenies well after the rise of the reformers. But as local criminal justice perceptibly altered, sometimes under the influence of great changes in social arrangements, such as emancipation and Reconstruction in the South, rough-justice enthusiasts revolted against due process through lynching.

Midwestern, western, and southern lynchers shared a commitment to this notion of rough justice, a cultural complex that demanded the harsh, personal, informal, and communally supervised punishment of what was perceived as serious criminal behavior. The understanding of what was serious criminal behavior was heavily mediated by factors of race, gender, class, and circumstance. Murders of whites by blacks pro-voked a harsh response, as did murders of women, murders of law offic-ers or of "well-known" residents of a locality, and homicides that seemed especially heinous because of the brutal method or relative defenseless-ness of the victim. Alleged sexual assaults of white women by black men could provoke a lethal reaction, as could the challenge posed by margin-al landholders or the landless to the property-holding of the landed elite. In addition to its requirement that serious crime be adequately redressed and thus crime deterred,[2] rough justice had an important performative quality. Punishment required a communal and often ritualistic dimen-sion. Rough-justice advocates, who were usually rural residents or mem-bers of the urban petty mercantile or working class, flocked to legal exe-cutions, hoping to witness the death rite. They argued strenuously for a prolific and merciless application of the death penalty. And they partic-ipated in or apologized for lynchings. Members of the rural gentry, includ-ing southern planters and wealthy cattlemen in the West, aligned with the rough-justice camp. Support for rough justice from urban elites was less common, but there were exceptions that included businessmen vig-ilantes in New Orleans and Tampa, Florida, and occasional editors and jurists in every region.[3]

Rough-justice enthusiasts in the Midwest, West, and South were opposed by middle-class reformers who advocated for due-process law as a guarantor of social order and the free flow of capital. This middle-class reform element was composed of lawyers, entrepreneurs, clergy, and some editors. The reformers evinced a significant humanitarian impulse and inclination toward social engineering. They also sought the amelioration of the death penalty through abolition or at least the physical segrega-tion of executions behind four walls and before limited witnesses. The statutory physical concealment of executions occurred in most states and territories by 1900, although in western and southern locales the law often was disregarded in rural jurisdictions in favor of continued public access to executions. The middle-class intention in statutory reform was to place executions beyond the primal, morally depraved fascination of working-class people and their potential disorder as an aroused crowd.[4] For their part, due-process advocates bitterly attacked lynchings as ata-vistic, prone to miscarriages of justice, and destructive to the cause of law and order.

Only the states of New England and the mid Atlantic avoided this prolonged cultural conflict, which was waged everywhere else in news-paper columns and courtrooms by day and on tree limbs outside court-houses by night. In the Northeast, concentrated capitalist transformation in the antebellum period created powerful middle classes who reshaped legal institutions and public opinion in such a way that by the late nineteenth century, rough-justice sentiments could be channeled into a reformed and allegedly sanitized but nonetheless prolific death penalty.[5] Eventually the rural and working-class rough-justice enthusiasts who endorsed mob murder in the Midwest, West, and South compromised with the bourgeois advocates for due-process law. In the early twentieth century, states in those regions, aping the punitive innovations of northeastern states, revamped the death penalty into a comparatively efficient, technocratic, and highly racialized mechanism.

Southern historians have richly elaborated our understanding of lynching as a critical aspect of regional culture and social relations in the postbellum period.[6] Beyond the South, Richard Maxwell Brown's work since the 1960s has identified many of the key dynamics of violence in American society and in the American West. Brown has detailed signal patterns of collective and individual violence and their relation to deeply rooted values and ideology. His work has helped to correct and problematize the work of the West's initial historians, such as Hubert Howe Bancroft, who had legitimated and indeed sanctified vigilantism as the appropriate response of democratic citizens to frontier disorder.[7] Although Brown considers lynching violence throughout the country, few other historians have analyzed mob violence as more than a regional phenomenon.[8] This has led to two oddly provincial literatures on American collective violence.

Understandably concerned with how violence enforced prerogatives of race, southern historians have focused little on how lynching reflected a perspective on law. In his pathbreaking, superbly contextualized 1993 study of lynching in Georgia and Virginia, W. Fitzhugh Brundage observes that white southerners often talked about the supposed failures of the criminal justice system, especially when they lynched whites. But Brundage argues that the multivariate phenomenon of lynching was much more about imposing racial control in a rigid cotton economy than about a vision of law.[9] In their fine cliometric analysis of southern lynchings published in 1995, Stewart E. Tolnay and E. M. Beck found little basis for a "popular justice" thesis in which lynchings substituted for legal executions and a weak legal system in the South. However, as Tolnay and Beck acknowledge, comparing the actual rate of lynching to that of legal execution does not reveal popular attitudes and practices concerning law, which take shape in a shady sphere of impression, ideology, and experience. Moreover, lynching occurred in highly localistic cultures of authority, community, resistance, deviancy, and punishment. Statistics for the entire South or entire states simply cannot convey the nuances of the social relations that are embedded in local experiences of social control, violence, and law.[10]

Meanwhile, western historians have been too obsessed with refuting Bancroft's distasteful apology to take the ideology of lynching as seriously as they should. This ideology revolved around the American notions of popular sovereignty, self-preservation, and the right to revolution, a belief inherited from the American Revolution that government was ultimately rooted in the people and could, if threatening circumstances dictated, be reclaimed by them.[11] Western historians have dated the decline of lynching too early, arguing that the widespread mid-nineteenth-century collective violence was a short-lived phenomenon and that the mob killings that followed were socially insignificant aberrations.[12] Furthermore, the still widespread notion that distant or corrupt law enforcement caused the violence indicates the persisting explanatory appeal of Bancroft's defense, which echoed that of the vigilantes themselves. However, competent law enforcement and courts were usually in place when collective violence occurred in the early West of the mid-nineteenth century as well as in the developing West of later decades. Thus explanations for the violence must be found elsewhere. Caught up in still trying to argue that lynching was wrong, which is irrefutable, or that the West was or wasn't violent,[13] a debate in which the carefully controlled collective violence of lynching can be read in contradictory ways, western historians have been, oddly, more haunted by the ghosts of their region's past than have southern historians.

This analysis defines a lynching as experts on southern mob violence did at Tuskegee, Alabama, in 1940: "'there must be legal evidence that a person has been killed, and that he met his death illegally at the hands of a group acting under the pretext of service to justice, race, or tradition,'"[14] with a "group" defined as three or more persons. The Tuskegee definition, while historically contingent and imperfect,[15] remains useful. Its emphasis on the collective, purposeful, ideological, lethal, and unlawful nature of lynching is consistent with the popular usage of the term as well as the actual praxis of violence from the mid-nineteenth century through the present day.

Western historians (but not southern historians) have often distinguished between vigilantism and lynching. They have asserted that vigilantism was more organized, lynching more impulsive. It is true that most of the lynchings in the late nineteenth-century West were perpetrated by temporary groups rather than preexisting organizations. It is also true that some mob killings in the earlier period in the West involved short-lived, nearly spontaneous gatherings of people who sought to kill an alleged offender, as in Pierce County, Washington Territory, in the 1860s (analyzed in chapter 4). Vigilantism also connotes a certain validity grounded in communal authority. "Lynch law" once had the same connotations, before the discrediting work of the antilynching campaigns waged in the early twentieth century. "Vigilantism" in the contemporary usage need not be lethal; it refers to an illegal or extralegal act of collective force. Strangely enough, as late as 1912 lynching had a similarly fluid definition, one that coexisted with a usage referring unambiguously to lethal violence. In that year, Paul Walton Black published an extensive analysis of lynchings in Iowa. He defined lynching as Ohio legislators did in crafting an 1896 antilynching law: "Any collection of individuals assembled for any unlawful purpose intending to do damage or injury to anyone, or pretending to exercise correctional power over persons by violence, and without authority of law, shall for the purpose of this act be regarded as a 'mob,' and any act of violence exercised by them upon the body of any person, shall constitute a 'lynching.'"[16]

The voluminous sources from the West, Midwest, and South in the late nineteenth and early twentieth centuries employed in this book consistently used the term "lynching" to describe the lethal collective violence that they chronicled. In sum, the distinctions that are made between these terms in the western literature are not meaningful, and they reflect the parochialism of regional histories of violence. In this book I adopt the definition employed by recent southern historians of collective violence, which has the virtue of precision and consistency across regions.

Investigation of the relationship between lynching and the law is critical because of what it reveals about a seminal moment in state and legal formation in the United States. In the late nineteenth century, many rural and working-class midwesterners, westerners, and southerners sought to impose communally based solutions to the dilemmas of social order ostensibly provoked by serious criminal acts. Collective violence most often served the goals of white supremacy, as lynchers especially targeted alleged African American offenders. Lynchers responded in part to a middle-class reform movement, present in all regions, that stressed due process and attempted to rid the performance of criminal justice of its popular trappings. The advent of the modern death penalty can be discerned in the eventual compromise, in the early twentieth century, of the rough-justice and due-process camps. By the 1910s, 1920s, and 1930s, as lynching quickly declined, capital punishment was administered systematically and "scientifically" by state governments. In the

Midwest, West, and South, which were anticipated by the Northeast, the death penalty now symbolized the social and especially racial control of crime once expressed by lynching.[17] The brutal, racialized excesses of urban police forces in the twentieth century and after also assumed some of the functions of rough justice.

One might argue that lynching and the transformation of the death penalty were not necessarily related. It could be asserted that lynching reflected temporary communal anger at serious crimes, private retribution, and racial and class animosities that had little to do with a broader understanding of the criminal justice system. Perhaps lynching would have died out anyway, as dramatic cultural shifts (for example, the impact of commercialism and advent of mass culture) swept the Midwest, West, and South. Maybe the rate and mode of capital punishment would have changed regardless of lynching, as the result of political trends and as a by-product of the application of technological fervor to the process of state-administered death. Crucially, it is attractive to dismiss the notion of a close relationship between lynching and notions of law because the idea that lynchers were acting out an understanding of law seems to confer their actions legitimacy, a legitimacy that they and their apologists at the time coveted and that antilynching advocates and western historians fought long to debunk. Yet a particular understanding of law can be tragically misguided, racist, oppressive, and brutal. It need not be seen as legitimate.

To dismiss the relationship between lynching, law, and the death penalty is to ignore a debate that constantly ignited fin-de-siècle midwesterners, westerners, and southerners as well as lynching's first historians.[18] It is also to neglect the very contexts within which mob killings and legal hangings occurred. Lynching emerged in the mid- to late nineteenth century at precisely the moment when reformers sought to revise the criminal justice system in line with bourgeois capitalist values. Concerns over the alleged inadequacy of the administration of capital punishment for the purposes of retribution and racial control infused lynchers' motivations and the rhetoric of their supporters in the Midwest, the West, and the South. Opponents of lynching in all three regions believed that the haphazard administration of criminal justice spurred mob executions. Legislators renovated the death penalty in the early twentieth century out of direct concern for the alternative of mob violence. With the remaking of capital punishment beyond the Alleghenies, lynchings declined and then ceased.

Legal anthropologists offer a useful concept for the analysis of the relationship between lynching and the criminal justice system. Refining the work of early twentieth-century social theorists such as Max Weber, legal anthropologists suggest that we disregard the notion of a monolithic, static, abstract legal system or "law" that applies to all subgroups within a society. Instead we should recognize the existence of a "multiplicity of legal systems," a set of social-control mechanisms that complement and sometimes circumvent the established law.[19] This book traces the shifting formal and informal arrangements, or legal systems, through which dominant social groups in Iowa, Wisconsin, Wyoming, Washington, California, Louisiana, and New York sought to punish what they defined as serious criminal behavior.

These seven states embodied key aspects of the legal systems of their regions. Iowa manifested characteristics of the lower Midwest, where upper-southern cultural skepticism of formal law competed with Yankee cultural traits that stressed order and legal regularity to produce an extensive popular conversation over law and lynching. Wisconsin fit the pattern of the upper Midwest, where Yankee origins and a robust capitalism promoted advocacy of due process, but particularly heinous crimes also occasionally led to lynching. Wyoming, Washington, and California encompassed the diverse socioeconomic experience of the West, including economies and social orders revolving around ranching, maritime, railroad, and extractive industries. Each of these three western states had a substantial encounter with the postbellum revolt against due process. In each, lynch mobs protested the reform of capital punishment, and property holders unleashed lethal vigilantism against the rural proletariat. Racially motivated mobs killed Mexicans in California, Native Americans in all three states, and African Americans in Wyoming and California.

Louisiana was the most diverse southern state, encompassing the Cotton Belt of northern Louisiana, the Sugarland and Cajun areas of southern Louisiana, and the postbellum South's largest city, New Orleans. The various regions of Louisiana participated in different ways in the postbellum revolt against due process. Northern Louisiana whites disavowed formal criminal justice agencies in favor of frequent mob killings reasserting white supremacy; northwestern and north central parishes became some of the most lynching-prone jurisdictions in the South. Southern Louisiana whites acted out rough-justice values through occasional lynchings and by precociously adapting legal agencies—namely, capital punishment and a brutal police force in New Orleans—for the enactment of a highly racialized but orderly and formalized administration of criminal justice. New York was the largest, most urbanized, and most economically dynamic northeastern state, lying between the mid-

Atlantic states and New England. Lynchings were exceedingly rare in the Empire State, as New York authorities crafted instead a prolific, technocratized death penalty that melded a bourgeois preference for social order and the centralization of state authority with the functions of racialized retributive justice.

Through newspaper accounts and coroner's inquests, I have collected information concerning virtually all postbellum lynchings in these seven states and composed case studies and aggregate profiles of mob violence. These flawed sources, when read carefully and in combination with other sources, yield much information concerning the circumstances and motivations of mob executions. After reading extensively in county and parish criminal court records, state government correspondence on criminal justice matters, and accounts of legal executions, I have also attempted to identify the role of lynching within the broader context of regional legal systems. This approach is obviously experimental and nonscientific, but I believe that it has produced a much fuller understanding of the significant relation between lynching and the criminal justice system.

Recent historians of southern lynching have argued that the practice involved great variation and that its causes and motivation were extremely complex.[20] The analytical and organizational problem posed by the "multifarious" nature of lynching is all the more apparent when examining collective violence in disparate regions of the United States. Reductionistic interpretations that ignore the particularity of the historical evidence across time and place would obscure understanding of an already misunderstood phenomenon. Therefore, the chapters that follow are organized on a topical basis and examine a wide range of collective violence and styles of criminal justice. The first chapter surveys the temporal and geographical dimensions of lynching across the country, examining how the violence flowed from particular regional contexts. The second chapter traces how lynching manifested the deeply held values of its advocates in its organization, practice, and ritual and how it acted out social relations of class, ethnicity, religiosity, and gender. The third chapter analyzes the varied contexts in which white supremacy offered lynchers their greatest inspiration. The fourth chapter discusses the extensive debate in the West, Midwest, and South among lynchers and their adversaries over law. The final chapter analyzes the decline of lynching and the rise of a death penalty that sustained the goals of rough justice across the United States.

The chapters unveil the contradictory effects of capitalist transformation on Americans' perceptions of criminal justice. The extension of the market into rural areas illuminated class and racial tensions that heavily informed lynchings. Similarly, urbanization and industrialization created unique social spaces that raised questions about racial order and encouraged the formation of working-class white mobs. Yet capitalism also created middle classes whose distaste for public disorder led them to reform criminal justice in a manner initially unacceptable to many rural and working-class persons. The energetic efforts of middle-class reformers undercut lynchers in the early twentieth century and resulted in a new mode of capital punishment. The newly remade death penalty combined the middle-class disdain for public disorder and stress upon legal forms with the racial, class, and punitive emphases of rough justice.

As a prelude to the nineteenth-century battle between rough justice and due process, the revolution had unshackled Americans from traditional, hierarchical constraints through its radical invocation of the people as the font of political authority and their right to reclaim that authority when exigencies dictated.[21] The revolutionary era bequeathed influential precedents for particular modes of collective violence, usually nonlethal, with which a populace might summarily punish social enemies, whether they be criminals, contenders for backwoods resources, or loyalists to the crown. These included "Regulator" movements in the Carolinas and the thirty-nine lashes upon the bare backs of Tories that the fortuitously named Col. Charles Lynch administered in his "court" in the Blue Ridge Mountains of Virginia.[22] The revolution also spawned constitutional reform impulses that sought to abolish a vast array of capital offenses. Before the revolution, the monarchy and local elites had exerted their authority in highly public executions that were rich in the ritual and symbolism of power and punishment that held together a hierarchical society. Seeking to create a new society upon Enlightenment and humanitarian perfectionist principles, some postrevolutionary reformers went as far as to seek to abolish capital punishment entirely, or at least to conceal it behind four walls. Reformers sought to keep executions from plebeians who might be degraded or demoralized by the brutal violence and orgiastic celebrations that had for centuries accompanied public punishments.[23] As these impulses were manifested in statutory reform in the early to mid-nineteenth century, they surged far beyond the customary notions of criminal justice that rural and working-class people had acquired from tradition in the backwoods, in the village, on the plantation, on the farm, and increasingly in towns and cities.

Moreover, in the early to mid-nineteenth century, immigration and westward expansion created new communities where social order and questions of respectability and political power were especially unsettled and contested. The land beneath the Ohio River saw the spread of chattel slavery, with its severe racial ideology and underlying threat of overpowering force, to the Mississippi River and beyond. In these novel and shifting antebellum circumstances, popular sovereignty wedded to collective violence proved an intoxicating, elastic, and highly instrumentalist ideology. Popular sovereignty was most useful for pulling into definition the moral sensibility of an ever-shifting community versus its erstwhile enemies. These social enemies sometimes were antagonists of class through transgression of property, such as horse thieves and counterfeiters. They sometimes were violators of racial codes, such as participants in slave rebellions or abolitionists. And they sometimes were offenders against moral economy, such as murderers whose act of homicide was distinguished by brutality or the honored social status of its victim, such as a wife, child, law officer, or otherwise prominent member of the community. Between the 1820s and 1850s, in a process that historians have not yet systematically examined, traditions of nonlethal popular violence against those who transgressed social norms transmuted on the midwestern, western, and southern frontiers into the deadly collective violence that came to be known as lynching.[24]

Today's debate over the death penalty, in which some Americans argue that only state-sponsored execution can adequately fulfill a societal need for appropriate retribution while others argue that capital punishment too often fails the requirement for fairness in due process, carries on in milder form the cultural war between rough justice and due process waged through most of the nineteenth century and well into the twentieth century. This book initiates its analysis as the immense mid-nineteenth-century American social convulsion over the meaning of freedom—so pivotal in the Civil War and Reconstruction but also, however perversely, in every lynch mob's insistence on popular sovereignty in usurping legal authority, as well as in the unjust, arbitrary fate of their victims—resolved into the social, economic, and legal consolidation of the postbellum period.

1   Mobs across Time and Space: The Chronology and Geography of Lynching

The era of the Civil War and Reconstruction marked a turning point in lynching violence across the United States. The war upset prevailing economic, social, racial, legal, and constitutional orders. It precipitated racial leveling, centralization of state authority, and the ascendancy of the North's dynamic industrial and agricultural capitalism. The war's result also inspired profound questions about the shape and role of law and the meaning of freedom in the newly remade nation.[1] Beyond the Alleghenies, many Americans responded to these questions with collective violence that reasserted white supremacy and a vision of criminal justice lodged in localistic prerogatives.

In the South, Union army occupation and the emancipation of the slaves destroyed slavery and the physical prerogatives of white supremacy, including the slaveholder's recourse to corporal punishment and the slave patrol's police power. In the late 1860s and early 1870s a vast wave of homicidal violence swept the South as whites, often through paramilitary organizations such as the Ku Klux Klan and the Knights of the White Camelia in southern Louisiana, reclaimed political power from enfranchised African American men.[2] Although historians have yet to systematically study lynching across the South during Reconstruction, evidence suggests that episodic collective violence reinforcing white masculine authority in all walks of southern life accompanied the political violence.[3]

It seems likely that during Reconstruction white southerners honed lynching into a weapon for sustaining their authority. Whites employed collective violence to brutally and effectively deny African Americans' claim to a freedom that would encompass meaningful political, economic, social, and legal autonomy. In turning to lynching, white southerners drew on antebellum precedents from the vigilante movements with which landed whites had suppressed landless whites, the brutal suppression of slave revolts, and the relatively rare (because slaves were property and their lives thus valuable) ferocious mob punishment of an alleged rape or murder by a slave.[4] After "Redemption" and the return to power of conservative white southern state governments in the 1870s, lynching remained a valuable device for the sustenance of white power amid the periodic crises of a continuously contested racial order. White elites in Cotton Belt areas such as the river valleys of north central and northwestern Louisiana allowed formal legal agencies to languish in favor of extralegal violence punishing black resistance and criminality. An anemic criminal justice system was the legal heritage of slavery,[5] but this weakness only threw into relief the muscular authority of postbellum planters.

Meanwhile, in the Midwest and West, the struggle for authority and respectability that had accompanied settlement in Iowa and California in the 1840s and 1850s and in Wyoming and Washington Territories in the 1860s evolved in succeeding decades into a more stable set of social and legal relations. Lynching for transgressions of property—the collective violence perpetrated by the landed against the landless or marginal landholders as they fought over the disposition of valuable natural resources—became far less significant than it had been before the Civil War, when extensive vigilante movements had erupted on the midwestern and western frontiers. For instance, in eastern Iowa between April and December 1857, landed vigilantes had collectively murdered sixteen white men whom they accused of horse theft, counterfeiting, and murder.[6] Instead, postbellum rural and working-class midwesterners and westerners, drawing on memories of the history of popular violence in their regions, revived the elastic doctrine of popular sovereignty as an antidote to changing practices of criminal justice in an era of economic and social consolidation.

Midwestern and western lynchers articulated a critique of the adjudication of homicide cases. This critique was rooted in a rejection of the purportedly lenient and "sentimental" approach of middle-class reformers, who sought to abolish or ameliorate the death penalty through humane reforms and to ensure the safeguarding of the individual defendant's rights through the observance of due-process safeguards. The due-process reform of criminal justice crystallized in the Northeast in the mid- to late nineteenth century and spread slowly and unevenly throughout the country, sometimes carried by Yankee emigrants who became elites in their new regions.[7] The rough-justice advocates who participated in or apologized for lynching in the Midwest and West waged a kulturkampf against due process. Midwestern and western lynchers stressed instead the deterrent and morally enobling effect of the harsh physical punishment of serious crime and the community's customary interest in participating in that punishment.

Beyond these general tendencies, the frequency and character of lynching violence varied substantially within and among regions due to factors of demography and social and ideological relations. The analysis that follows suggests the geographical and chronological contours of mob violence across the country after the Civil War and Reconstruction.

The South

In September 1893 Henry Coleman, a black cotton worker in Bossier Parish, Louisiana, allegedly shot a white planter, Captain Thomas Lyles, because he feared that Lyles was about to seize his crop. A mob of eighty to one hundred men broke into the parish jail at noon. Probably anticipating a lynching, Coleman had been reportedly baptized by a "colored preacher" that morning. Mobbers allowed him a moment of prayer before "starting" the horse upon which they had placed him, having tied one end of a rope to a tree limb and the other around his neck.[8] Coleman's death at the hands of Bossier Parish whites represented a terrifyingly characteristic aspect of northern Louisiana's racial regime. Lynchers killed 263 persons, at least 219 of them black, in northern parishes between 1878 and 1946. More than 40 percent of the mobs charged their victims with murder, large mobs perpetrated nearly one-fourth of lynchings, and a majority of collective killings occurred before 1900.

Northern Louisiana cotton planters utilized lynching to assert their unconditional authority over black laborers, claiming prerogatives of white power that they claimed the institutions of formal law could not sufficiently support. They were backed by a white consensus favoring racial hierarchy and the drastic enforcement of the social control of African Americans. The incidence of mob killing was heavily concentrated in particular Cotton Belt areas: the Red River Delta in the northwest and the Ouachita River Valley in north central Louisiana. Eleven parishes accounted for almost 60 percent of the lynchings.[9] The mob murders

Map 1. Lynchings by parish in Louisiana, 1900–31,
from data compiled by the Tuskegee Institute. In 1931,
the Commission on Interracial Cooperation, an antilynching organization, published a sociological study
of lynchings. The report was accompanied by a map
displaying the distribution of lynchings by county in
the forty-eight United States. The map offered a good
sense of the geographical distribution of mob violence
in the early twentieth century, although some of the
data plotted were inaccurate or incomplete. (Adapted
from "Lynchings by States and Counties in the United
States, 1900–1931." Southern Commission on the
Study of Lynching. *Lynchings and What They Mean.*
Atlanta: Southern Commission on the Study of Lynching, 1931.)

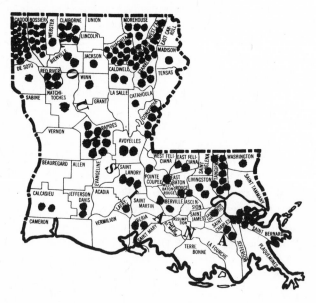

Map 2. Lynchings by county in Iowa and Wisconsin, 1900–31, from data compiled by the Tuskegee Institute. The lynching displayed in Muscatine County, Iowa, represents what was actually a near lynching in that county in March 1903. The lynching displayed in Dane County, Wisconsin, erroneously represents an incident that occurred in Madison, West Virginia, rather than Madison, Wisconsin. (Adapted from "Lynchings by States and Counties in the United States, 1900–1931." Southern Commission on the Study of Lynching. *Lynchings and What They Mean.* Atlanta: Southern Commission on the Study of Lynching, 1931.)

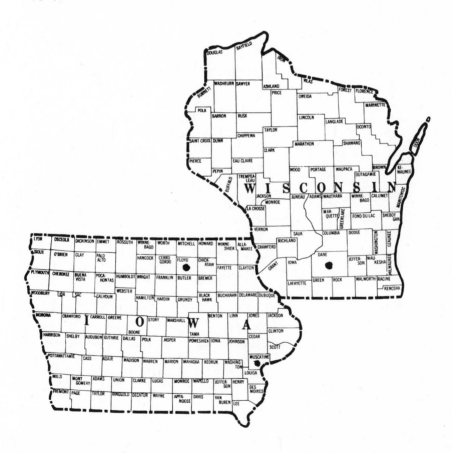

Map 3. Lynchings by county in Wyoming, 1900–31,
from data compiled by the Tuskegee Institute. The
map does not include four lynching victims collectively murdered in Weston County, one from Sweetwater
County, and two from Big Horn County. (Adapted
from "Lynchings by States and Counties in the United
States, 1900–1931." Southern Commission on the
Study of Lynching. *Lynchings and What They Mean.*
Atlanta: Southern Commission on the Study of Lynching, 1931.)

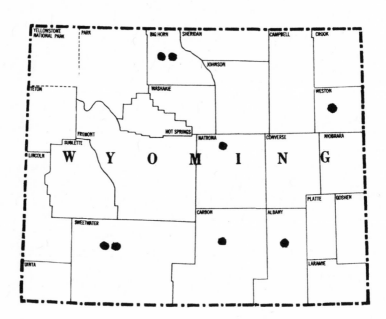

Map 4. Lynchings by county in Washington State,
1900–31, from data compiled by the Tuskegee Institute. The map does not include a lynching victim collectively murdered in Asotin County in August 1903.
(Adapted from "Lynchings by States and Counties in
the United States, 1900–1931." Southern Commission
on the Study of Lynching. *Lynchings and What They
Mean.* Atlanta: Southern Commission on the Study of
Lynching, 1931.)

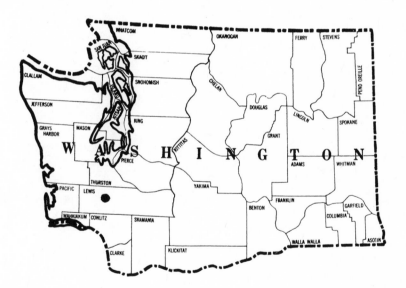

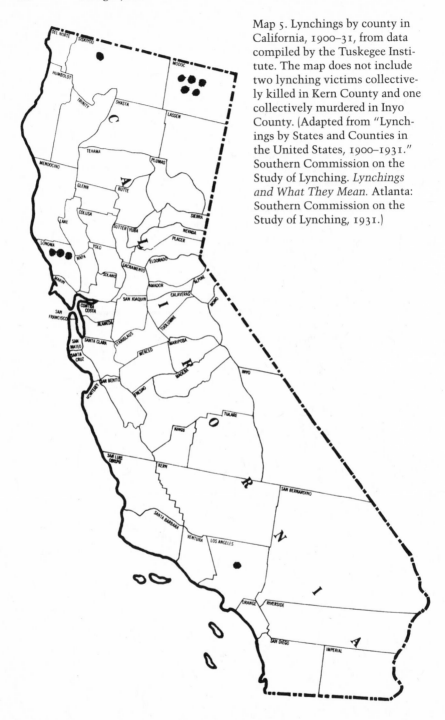

Map 5. Lynchings by county in California, 1900–31, from data compiled by the Tuskegee Institute. The map does not include two lynching victims collectively killed in Kern County and one collectively murdered in Inyo County. (Adapted from "Lynchings by States and Counties in the United States, 1900–1931." Southern Commission on the Study of Lynching. *Lynchings and What They Mean.* Atlanta: Southern Commission on the Study of Lynching, 1931.)

Map 6. Lynchings by county in New York, 1900–31, from data compiled by the Tuskegee Institute. As the map plots incidents beginning in the twentieth century, it does not include the lynching of Robert Lewis in Port Jervis, Orange County, in June 1892. (Adapted from "Lynchings by States and Counties in the United States, 1900–31." Southern Commission on the Study of Lynching. *Lynchings and What They Mean.* Atlanta: Southern Commission on the Study of Lynching, 1931.)

that occurred in these subregions drew their meaning from the tensions that underlay exploitative arrangements in the rural cotton economy, domestic service, and the credit-based mercantile system. An undercurrent of black racial consciousness that protested the constriction of African American rights fueled collective white violence. In lynching-prone Cotton Belt parishes, planter-class whites disabled the formal legal system and imposed informal police powers to punish deviant black laborers. In areas where mob violence was deeply entrenched in local conceptions of jurisprudence and punishment, even African Americans utilized lynching to retaliate against blacks who committed serious crimes such as homicide and rape against blacks. In the late nineteenth century, upcountry whites and African Americans from the Cotton Belt migrated to the growing urban centers of Monroe and Shreveport. Working-class whites unleashed frenzies of collective violence with which they sought to define the parameters of racial and gender interaction in these novel urban spaces. But this planted the seeds for the decline of lynching, as a growing urban middle class strove to preempt the social disorder of lynching violence with legal segregation and highly racialized criminal justice.

Elsewhere, in the Mississippi River Delta parishes with overwhelming black majorities, lynchings were rare, occurring instead at particular and infrequent moments of racial crisis. White planters, who controlled the Delta's economy and politics, realized the practical limitations of repressive violence in parishes where whites comprised merely a fifth of the population. Instead, planters manipulated the administration of the formal legal system, especially the gallows, for the social control of an African American labor force. By contrast, in northern Louisiana's predominantly white central and western upcountry, lynchings usually expressed private vengeance or the class and racial frustrations of lowerclass white farmers. Articulations of honor among whites and impatience with the vagaries of due-process law typically informed mob killings that claimed white victims. Additionally, hill-country whites were especially catalyzed by allegations that black men had transgressed sexual boundaries by pursuing white women.

Lynchings also occurred in southern Louisiana. At ten A.M. on March 14, 1891, a crowd estimated at twenty thousand gathered at the statue of Henry Clay on Canal Street in New Orleans. Attracted by placards and newspaper announcements and quickly inspired by fervent oratory at the mass meeting, the mob soon descended on the Orleans Parish Prison a few blocks away. Forcing entry into the prison, mob members fatally shot and hanged eleven Sicilians charged with murdering the chief of police,

David Hennessy, in October 1890. A jury the previous day had failed to convict nine of the Italians accused in the murder, acquitting six and disagreeing on the fate of three. Amid allegations of jury tampering and reputed "mafiosi" involvement in the assassination of Hennessy, prominent white New Orleans residents, including John M. Parker Jr., a future governor of Louisiana, led the lynch mob.[10] New Orleans newspapers lauded the mass killing. In defending the lynching, the *New Orleans Picayune* invoked the alleged failure of the criminal justice system and cited the justification of popular sovereignty: "Yesterday the people of this city rose in wrath and indignation at the corruption and perversion of the machinery to which was delegated the administration of justice. They did not overwhelm and sweep away the officials, but, brushing them aside, they took in their own hands the sword of justice, and they did not lay it down until they had executed vengeance upon the criminals whom the corrupt ministers had excused and set free."[11]

Vehement protests by the Italian government led the U.S. government to agree a year later to pay indemnities to the families of those lynched.[12] However, a grand jury investigation of the affair returned no indictments against those who participated in the collective killing.[13]

The 1891 lynching of the eleven Sicilians was an important event in the history of New Orleans that indicated the depth of class and ethnic antagonisms in the midst of significant Italian immigration to the region in the late nineteenth century. The multiple killing also displayed the collective consciousness of the city's American entrepreneurial elite and the salience of the ideology of vigilantism in the fin-de-siècle era. But in other respects the mob execution varied greatly from general tendencies in extralegal violence and legal systems in southern Louisiana. The killing of the Sicilians received unequivocal support from the New Orleans press and elite whites. Few other lynchings in the southern portion of Louisiana engendered such vocal and unqualified support. A mass mob performed the lynching. Yet smaller, secretive, and well-organized private mobs were most common in the southern parishes. Furthermore, the mob murder occurred in New Orleans, the South's largest city, where popular violence usually took the form of riots directed against particular segments of the population, not lynchings that targeted individuals. Finally, and most importantly, the 1891 mob violence claimed Sicilian lives, not African American lives. Yet the overwhelming majority (83 percent) of lynching victims in southern Louisiana were black.[14] African American leaders who campaigned against lynching noted the irony that the federal government compensated Italians for mob violence in Louisiana. By contrast, black Louisianans, who were American citizens, never obtained redress, monetary or otherwise, when mobs acted against them.[15]

Overall, lynchers in southern Louisiana claimed slightly more than a third of the 422 lives lost to lynch mobs in Louisiana between 1878 and 1946.[16] Mob violence in the southern portion of the Pelican State concentrated in the late nineteenth century, and collective killings in southern parishes became rare after 1900.[17] The Sugarland was a vast, ethnically and racially diverse region of sugar plantations that formed the heart of southern Louisiana. Sugarland elites generally enforced their racial dominance over an African American labor force through frequent use of the gallows, not with extralegal violence. Heavily Cajun southwestern Louisiana was a marginal cotton area where lower-class white farmers sometimes targeted their African American competitors in the rural economy. But in Acadiana, where a prolonged experience with vigilantism had marked the years of the Civil War and Reconstruction, a highly informal style of criminal justice mitigated impulses toward collective murder after Redemption.

Two areas in the southern half of the state saw anomalous patterns of racial violence and elevated rates of lynching comparable to those in northern Louisiana. The eastern Florida Parishes were located in a piney-woods subregion north of New Orleans that experienced rapid industrialization and in-migration after Reconstruction. In the eastern Florida Parishes, a period of rapid social and economic change disrupted political and legal authority. In this atmosphere, plainfolk whites unaccustomed to the racial arrangements of the Cotton and Sugar Belts unleashed their fury on African Americans. Jefferson Parish, immediately south and west of the Crescent City, also acquired a virulently racist white subculture that endorsed the profligate mob murder of African Americans in the 1890s.

In sum, southern Louisiana was easily the most racially, politically, and ethnically varied region in the American South. Like most white southerners, Creole, Cajun, and Anglo-American whites constantly sought to ensure their racial superiority over blacks. Southern Louisiana whites also subscribed to a rough-justice philosophy that advocated ritualistic retribution for serious crimes such as homicide and rape. Yet Creole and Anglo-American elites usually found legal hangings the appropriate means for punishing alleged African American offenders. Lynching was an exceptional measure in a region where Gallic cultural influences strengthened respect for legal process.

The Midwest

In 1910 Paul Walton Black, a graduate student in sociology at the University of Iowa, set out to research the history of lynching in the Hawkeye State. With an early twentieth-century faith in the truths to be revealed through a scientific study of society, Black read voluminously in old issues of newspapers and wrote hundreds of letters to persons who might shed light on Judge Lynch's activities. Correspondents included county attorneys and county clerks in most of Iowa's ninety-nine counties and old-timers who had lived in the state since the antebellum period. Black received revealing comments as to whether lynchings had ever occurred in a particular place. Some elderly writers happily recounted their participation in mobs and in vigilante committees and suggested that vigilance and collective violence were at one time necessary for the protection of citizens from criminals: "a want of faith in courts was the prime cause." A long-term resident and lawyer in Marengo suggested that his locale had remained free of lynching because "there has been no complaint of dilatory criminal procedure in cases of grave offenses in this county." Another writer argued that in his district they had a tradition of "using the courts not lynching."[18]

These statements tell us much about how midwesterners perceived an institution, the lynch mob, that had survived into the new century but was rapidly losing its popular underpinning and declining in incidence.[19] Black's findings underline the significant relationship between lynching and the criminal justice system in Iowa. Lynchings punctuated an extensive popular conversation over the nature of criminal justice and, particularly, the punishment of homicide. Mobs murdered twenty-four and unsuccessfully sought at least fifty-two persons between 1874 and 1909. Most lynchings and near lynchings involved white victims[20] and charges of murder. Collective killings were much more likely to occur in the southern portion of the state than in northern Iowa, with only twenty-seven counties seeing mob activity. Iowa's last lynching, of a white man accused of murdering his wife and stepson, occurred in Charles City in northern Iowa in 1907, although mobs gathered in the years that followed.[21]

In the late nineteenth century, rural and working-class Iowans in southern counties lynched in retribution for crimes that offended collective notions of moral order, particularly homicides that were exceptionally aggravated or transgressed the accepted relations between men and women. This preponderance of lynchings following homicide allegations marked a decisive shift away from the tendency of antebellum Iowans to collectively murder those accused of property violations. While some postbellum mob killings were more overtly ritualistic than others, most lynchings served in some fashion as performances of communal vengeance. Victims of mob murder tended to be individuals on the margins of the rural economy, and their low status may have accentuated the repercussions for their alleged actions. Several factors made southern Iowans more skeptical toward formal law and more inclined toward extralegal violence than northern Iowans. These included yeoman cultural traditions brought from upper southern states and "Butternut" border regions of northern states in the Ohio River Valley and a relatively slow pace of capitalist transformation. By contrast, many members of a growing middle class in expanding towns and cities and in agriculturally prosperous northern counties, where the descendants of Yankees, Germans, and Scandinavians predominated, regarded due-process law as a dependable regulator of social problems.[22]

A profound clash emerged between these competing cultural factions by the late nineteenth century. Rural southern Iowans and members of the growing urban working class emphasized the moral imperatives of communally based retributive justice through lynching and legal execution. Their opponents, bourgeois reformers, stressed humanitarian principles and the sustenance of public order. Middle-class due-process advocates denounced lynching and sought the amelioration of capital punishment through commutation of individual death sentences, privatization, and abolition. By 1900, accrual of power in the state government undermined the pervasive localism that had permitted mob killing in earlier decades, and governors increasingly intervened to prevent lynchings. Mob executions ended in the early twentieth century, as state officials intensified the pace of legal hangings. Rural and working-class Iowans acquired a respect for the state's novel role as technocratic executioner, stripped of the older customs of communal supervision and retributive ritual.

Following an 1893 lynching for rape in Ottumwa, Iowa, the *Atlanta Constitution* stated its expectation that Iowa authorities would do nothing to punish mobbers, despite northerners' constant refrain that southern officials should be more aggressive. The *Constitution* concluded with satisfaction that the Ottumwa lynching proved that "human nature" was the same everywhere.[23] Almost as if in response, a Louisa County resident wrote that the failed lynching of A. D. Storms in Burlington in 1898, thwarted by the sheriff and his deputies, proved that "Iowa is not Mississippi."[24] Nonetheless, commentators sought to explain how Iowa, with social and legal conditions ostensibly more stable and harmonious than those in the South or the West, could produce lynch mobs. Commonly, they argued that the aberration of lynching was the result of a lack of public confidence in a changing criminal justice system and its ability to deal with the perpetrators of serious crimes against persons. Detailing local examples of the "laxity" of law, Iowa's literati proposed legal reforms that would ensure efficient justice.[25]

An assumption of a progressive development of society and law, demonstrated in the process of settlement in the western states, was ubiquitous among midwestern literati. A midwestern bourgeois faith in progress driven by capitalist development, evident in the increasing complexity and profitability of agricultural operations, retail establishments, and manufacturing plants, interpreted vigilantism as archaic and incongruous. In a typical statement, a letter writer in a Des Moines newspaper in July 1883 equated lynch law with "barbarism," a regression for a midwestern state advancing into an elevated level of civilization. Recourse to collective violence was perhaps understandable in frontier communities, where legal and social institutions were not mature, but it was inexcusable and a cause for "demoralization" in a sophisticated and vanguard society such as Iowa.[26]

Unlike Iowa, the upper midwestern state of Wisconsin was not a magnet for southern border-state emigrants and their Butternut culture. The Yankees, Irish, Germans, and Scandinavians that peopled Wisconsin resorted less often to mob killings. Despite the intense communalism and the substantial defense elicited by the five lynchings in Wisconsin in the last two decades of the nineteenth century, the practice was never as deeply rooted in the Badger State as it was in the lower Midwest. A political culture rooted in the Yankee heritage of the state's most influential residents and a farm and industrial economy characterized by a vibrant capitalism meant that respect for due-process law and the promise that it might ensure social and economic order were strong countercurrents to the temptations of Judge Lynch. The abolition of the death penalty in 1853 signaled that Wisconsin stood at the vanguard of the legal reforms that originated in the humanitarian and perfectionist tendencies of a growing middle class in the Northeast.[27] Yet Wisconsin was not immune to a characteristic nineteenth-century American disease. In peculiarly traumatic circumstances of aggravated homicide, especially in western counties, Wisconsinites sometimes brutally acted out a rough-justice ideology shaped with reference to ethnic solidarities and to their state's abolition of capital punishment. However, after what would become the state's last lynching in September 1891 in the southwestern

town of Darlington (in which a German American farmhand, Anton Sieboldt, was accused of murdering an Irish American farmer, James
Meighan), Wisconsin authorities increasingly acted to avert lynching.

The West

In Casper, Wyoming, on March 28, 1902, a masked mob of sheepworkers, cowboys, and ranchers hanged Charles Woodard, a white sheepworker who had murdered the sheriff, W. C. Ricker, in January. The lynching followed weeks of speculation by the town's leading newspaper and
the judge in Woodard's trial, C. W. Bramel, that only a speedy trial, conviction, and execution might prevent a mob killing. Three days earlier
the Wyoming State Supreme Court had granted a stay of Woodard's execution, scheduled for March 28, so that they could review his conviction
and sentence. The mob hanged Woodard on the scaffold erected for his
execution.[28]

Charles Woodard's assassination of the Natrona County sheriff had
particular resonance for residents of Casper and east central Wyoming.
Casper had a population of around a thousand, half of vast Natrona County, which it served as county seat. Founded in the late 1880s, the town
functioned as a market and social center for an extensive sheep-raising
and cattle-ranching hinterland.[29] Casper and Natrona County in the winter of 1902 amplified national trends in their reaction to the shooting of
Ricker. The murder of a law officer in the rural United States frequently
drew intense communal anger and, occasionally, threats to the life of the
person accused of committing the offense. A sheriff and his deputies often were the only agents of law enforcement familiar to countryside and
village residents. These personal, powerful representatives of abstract
legal institutions tended to be deeply involved in regional social networks,
including informal institutions of patronage and politics. The murder of
a county law official was thus an affront to the local social hierarchy, the
larger social order, and the formal law and informal forces of social control that regulated that order.[30]

All of these tendencies can be seen in the rapt and angry communal
response to Ricker's murder, aggravated by the details of Woodard's act
of homicide: he finished off the sheriff with a blow to the head after he
lay wounded and helpless and then robbed his corpse.[31] In the communally conceived moral geography of serious crime, some offenses occupied more dangerous regions than others. The circumstances of Woodard's
crime marked it as peculiarly heinous and, in fin-de-siècle parlance, "cold-
blooded."[32]

A resident of Rock Springs succinctly captured the philosophy of the lynchers and their supporters when, after the killing of Woodard, he expressed the need for "[m]ore justice and less law."[33] In the late nineteenth and early twentieth centuries, many in Wyoming echoed the Rock Springs opinion. Rural and small-town Wyomingites expressed considerable frustration with a style of criminal justice that they believed failed to punish homicide rapidly or severely enough. Those who promoted the principles of rough justice rationalized lynching, attacked the state's allegedly haphazard and infrequent application of the death penalty, and enthusiastically gathered around scaffolds when executions were scheduled. Influential landholders promoted an analogous brand of vigilantism that lambasted supposedly ineffectual courts and sought the extermination of lower-class range residents who appropriated ranchers' property.

The complaints of the rough-justice camp were rooted in a rural cultural perspective unsympathetic to the deliberative nature of due-process law and to the legal reforms promoted by a rising middle class in Wyoming's towns and cities. Besides defending due-process procedures as the basis for an orderly society, bourgeois Wyomingites strove for a death penalty stripped of popular excesses and passions. Urban middle-class Wyomingites similarly condemned lynching as barbaric and inconsistent with civilized values. Conflicts over property rights, driven by the class tensions intrinsic to the incorporation of the range, provoked a substantial proportion (60 percent) of mob killings in Wyoming. In the early twentieth century, as the state underwent significant urban and industrial growth, the rough-justice and due-process factions compromised with capital punishment that was more frequent but concealed and centralized in the state penitentiary at Rawlins. By the 1910s, the clamor over the nature of criminal justice lowered considerably, and mob killings of whites ceased.

Lynching in Wyoming emerged from the cultural war waged between rough-justice and due-process camps and can be divided into five chronological phases. The first phase occurred with the initial stages of white settlement in the early territorial period (late 1860s). The activities of vigilante committees in the boomtowns of Cheyenne, Laramie, and Bear River City most fully correspond with conventional notions of the necessity for extralegal policing of a lawless frontier but also display the complexities of mid-nineteenth-century western vigilantism.[34] A second phase, beginning in the late 1870s, saw lynch mobs punish charges of homicide. These collective killings asserted a regional vision of punitive justice that exposed class and cultural strains in an increasingly differentiated territorial society.[35] A third phase began in the mid 1880s and lasted through the first decade of the twentieth century, as powerful cattle operators employed terrorist lynch mobs to intimidate their lower-class competitors, small ranchers, farmers, and sheepworkers for resources on the range. A fourth phase of collective murder erupted in the early twentieth century, when rural and small-town Wyomingites, who had not assimilated bourgeois, reformist notions of deliberative legal procedure and orderly and concealed capital punishment, temporarily rejected the state's limited death penalty. The final phase emerged by the first two decades of the twentieth century, when lynching became a tool for white Wyomingites to assert racial hierarchy in industrializing and urbanizing settings. White Wyomingites lynched four African Americans between 1904 and 1918. Overall, lynchers killed thirty-six persons in Wyoming from 1874 through 1918. Sixty percent of lynching victims (twenty-one persons) were accused of property crimes; 31 percent (eleven persons) faced homicide allegations; and 9 percent (three persons) were alleged to have committed rape.

West of the Rocky Mountains, almost to the Pacific Ocean, Washington State experienced a process of legal and cultural change similar to Wyoming's. In January 1882 in Seattle, for example, a "committee of safety," angered by the death of George B. Reynolds after he was shot by "foot-pads" who sought to rob him, transmogrified into a mob of four hundred that hanged James Sullivan and William Howard, pulled from their preliminary examination, and Benjamin Payne, the murderer of a police officer, extricated from jail. Congratulatory telegrams arrived from Olympia and Port Townsend, and a coroner's jury issued an exonerating and adulatory verdict: "We, the jury summoned in the above case, find that they came to the death by hanging, but from the evidence f[u]rnished, we [a]re unable to find by whose hands, and we are satisfied that in their deaths substantial and speedy justice has been subserved."[36]

Lethal vigilantism was not new to the Northwest—vigilantes had killed two murderers and two claims jumpers in southern Puget Sound in the decade after 1860, for instance—but it was transformed in the last two decades of the nineteenth century. Contrary to the popular understanding, early territorial lynching usually did not flow from an absence or distance of law enforcement but rather from the social instability of early communities and their contest for property, status, and the definition of social order. As it did elsewhere in the West, early territorial vigilantism established a blueprint for a cultural perspective on law that remained influential even as the "Old West" was fondly memorialized amid an evolving social landscape. The contest over land and resources between landed and marginal settlers played a far larger role in the earlier collective violence than it would after 1880. The earlier phase, in which definitions of property loomed large, persisted longer in the sparsely settled areas east of the Cascade Mountains, however. For instance, in a lynching for property crime, around twenty settlers in the vicinity of Rockford near Spokane, Washington, hanged a nineteen-year-old horse herder, "Oldie" Neal, in June 1882. The "citizen's committee" that performed the lynching asserted that Neal was implicated in the theft of horses in the locality and that his uncle ran a horse-theft ring ranging from Oregon to Canada. Collective memory disputed Neal's guilt and fashioned varying versions of the incident.[37]

After 1880, as railroads remade the Northwest with immigrants from "back east," lynching signaled an uneasy transition among rural and working-class northwesterners from customary notions of criminal justice that had been grounded in communal supervision of the social control of crime and harsh retribution for serious offenses.[38] Washington lynchers murdered at least seventeen men, fifteen after allegations of homicide, between 1882 and 1903. Unlike the Northwest's most well-known mob killing—the hanging and mutilation of Wesley Everest, an Industrial Workers of the World (IWW) labor radical, after a shootout with Legionnaires in Centralia in November 1919—most collective murders involved few political overtones or overt class antipathies. Washington's lynchings occurred east and west of the Cascade Mountains, in ranching and maritime settings, and in small towns and cities. However, small-town lawyers, some petty entrepreneurs, and occasional editors denounced lynchings and stressed the priority of due-process safeguards, legal regularity, and professional law enforcement for the promotion of social order and the flow of capital. Racial ideologies also sometimes played a role in mob violence in the lynchings of Native Americans in Washington Territory and State. Washington whites collectively murdered two Native Americans and two mixed-race Native Americans between 1873 and 1896.

Lynching in California fully displayed that state's racial complexity. Slightly more than half of the sixty-five victims of mobs between 1875 and 1947 were white, but nearly a fourth (fifteen victims) were Mexican, nine were American Indians, three were Chinese, and two were African Americans. Many rural residents and working-class and petty-mercantile elements in California's towns and cities questioned the efficacy of what they characterized as overly deliberative and careful legal process. Advocates of rough justice instead stressed the importance of swift, harsh punishment of heinous crime and communal participation in the rites of justice. For instance, Thomas and William Yoakum allegedly murdered two men in a mining dispute. William Yoakum's trial ended in a hung jury, Thomas Yoakum's in a first-degree murder conviction. Thomas Yoakum successfully appealed to the California Supreme Court, which ordered a new trial and a change of venue. Seventy-five masked men hanged the Yoakum brothers on May 28, 1879, after taking them from the Bakersfield jail.[39] Bakersfield editors offered contrasting perspectives on the mob killing and on law. The *Kern County Gazette* highlighted the participation of the county's "best citizens" and asserted that "[l]ynch-law is always to be deprecated, but the people believe that under the circumstances it is the only road that leads to safety." The *Kern County Courier* rebutted its rival, arguing that "[n]o respectable journal can encourage the execution of mob law. The danger to society and the public peace is vastly greater than in the escape of criminals through the machinery of the courts."[40]

A second trend in California mob violence involved a more spontaneous, less articulated sense of working-class grievance, one that was fueled by ethnic, racial, and sexual anxieties. Communities of miners and railroad laborers collectively murdered alleged deviants in the passionate hours that followed allegations of crimes that fell short of murder. For example, B. H. Harrington, a printer and upholsterer, allegedly raped the eight-year-old daughter of a railroad shop machinist in Dunsmuir, near Mount Shasta and the Oregon border. The girl's father chose not to press charges to avoid the trauma of a trial, and Harrington agreed to leave town. News circulated through the railroad hamlet, and twelve men seized Harrington, beat him, and placed him on a southbound train. The growing mob, estimated at a hundred, took Harrington off the train and injured him severely. Reports indicated that Harrington's corpse was found in the Sacramento River, although mobbers would not confirm how Harrington died.[41] Mob killings of Chinese and African Americans by working-class whites also expressed the ready and combustive, if unstable, social cohesion of the wageworkers' frontier. California landholders' hatred of marginal landholders and the landless and their competition for resources could also channel into organized lethal violence, as it did in the hanging of a white man, two mixed-race Indians, and two Indians accused of theft from ranchers at Lookout in northeastern California in May 1901.[42]

Postbellum lynching in California was concentrated in two areas of the state, reflecting cultural tendencies in interior counties that may have inclined toward collective murder. Coastal counties, with their urban and maritime orientations, saw limited mob violence after 1880. Three counties immediately south of the Oregon border, Siskiyou, Shasta, and Modoc, claimed sixteen victims between 1875 and 1904. A central corridor of eight northern counties contributed more than a third of the sixty-five lives lost to lynch mobs in California between 1875 and 1947. This remote southern Cascades mountain-range district experienced a localized syndrome of mob violence, propelled by the rough-justice perspective of miners, ranchers, and railroad laborers. The Central Valley and nearby mountain and desert areas added thirteen lynching victims, a fifth of the state's total. Kern County (seated at Bakersfield) at the southern end of the valley was the site of five lynchings that killed ten. There, participants in the region's industrialization, including miners and railroad workers, along with rural denizens such as ranchers and mountaineers, contended with agricultural interests and town builders over the area's future. Amid the tensions of the region's development, racial, ethnic, sexual, and personal animosities easily led to bouts of communal violence. Retribution following homicides dominated California's mob violence. Sixty-five percent of the state's lynching victims from 1875 through 1947 were accused of murder. A mere 26 percent of lynching victims (seventeen persons) faced property-crime allegations. Less than 10 percent (five persons) had purportedly committed rape or other sexual crimes. Eighty-nine percent of postbellum lynching victims were murdered by mobs before 1910. Yet several lynchings in the 1920s and 1930s connected the Golden State's heritage of collective violence with the "modern" traumas of urban gangster crime and the notorious Depression-era crime of kidnapping for ransom. Away from the urbanized Bay Area, mob killings persisted in the southern Cascades near the Oregon border into the 1940s.

The Northeast

On the evening of June 2, 1892, a mob of more than a thousand seized an African American, Robert Lewis, from law officers in Port Jervis, New York. Lewis had allegedly assaulted a young white woman, Lena McMahon, that afternoon along the Neversink River. Drawn to the village lockup by rumors of Lewis's capture and imminent arrival, the crowd overpowered a wagon that carried Lewis, and ringleaders placed a rope around his neck. As the crowd shouted, "Lynch him! Lynch him!" the mob dragged their captive down several streets, resisting entreaties from the village president, a county judge, and other prominent persons. The mob responded to the numerous efforts of Simon Yaples, a police officer, and another citizen, William Boner, to remove the noose from Lewis's neck by placing the rope around their necks. After dragging him a half mile while hitting and kicking him and tearing away his clothes, the lynchers hanged Lewis from a maple tree that was illuminated by an electric streetlight. When Lewis briefly regained consciousness several minutes later, lynchers yanked him into the air again until he was dead. His corpse remained hanging for a half-hour, and "hundreds" hurried to the lynching site to see his body. Afterward, "men, women, and children" hacked apart the lynching tree and cut up the rope for distribution among the crowd. Port Jervisites proudly displayed their "morbid relics" in the following days.[43]

Details that soon emerged cast considerable doubt upon the Port Jervis mob's apparent understanding that this was a simple case of an African American man attacking a white woman. Law officers arrested Peter J. Foley, a young white man who allegedly had arranged the assault as retaliation against Lena McMahon and her family. McMahon's stepparents, who operated a store, had forbade her consensual relationship with Foley. Foley was formerly an insurance salesman who reputedly gambled and associated with African Americans in an interracial subculture in the town of nearly ten thousand situated near the New Jersey border. Lewis, the mob's victim, had lived in Port Jervis and Paterson, New Jersey, and was a porter at the Delaware House, a hotel from which Foley had been evicted for unpaid bills. Law officers circumvented the possibility that Foley might be lynched by taking him to Goshen, New York, for safekeeping. The regional press lamented that Lewis's death removed the only substantial witness to Foley's complicity in the attack.[44]

The response in the region to the mob killing in Port Jervis was divided, although many locals voiced strong support for the lynchers. Of the town's three newspapers, one condemned the lynching, another was silent, while a third regretted "the lynching but [forgave] the lynchers." Papers in nearby towns and in New York City criticized the lynching but expressed some sympathies for the mob and its harsh retaliation for the alleged assault upon a white woman by a black man. W. E. McCormick, the area's representative in the New York State Assembly, was similarly equivocal. McCormick expressed dismay at the mob's violation of law and order but stated that Lewis, if he was guilty, had "met with summary and exact justice." Pastoral opinion was similarly mixed. Some ministers reportedly approved of the lynching, and others strongly opposed it. "Rector Evans" sermonized that "irregular methods served, while regular methods would have defeated, the ends of justice. . . . But on the other hand the sacred Majesty of the Law has been insulted." The Orange County district attorney admonished a coroner's jury that there "must be no white washing of the men who took the law into their own hands." The inquest called numerous witnesses, including police officers, a physician, an editor, a rail manager, and an ex-postmaster. Only a police officer, Simon Yaples, was willing to name the most active lynchers, identifying eight persons, including a railroad engineer, the former chief of police, a grocer, a switchman, and an undertaker. Despite this, the coroner's jury found that Lewis had been hanged "by person or persons unknown."[45]

An Orange County newspaper claimed that race relations in southern New York were unaffected by the mob murder of Lewis and that if he had been white he would have received the same punishment. Blacks in the county did not share this opinion. Local African Americans scored whites for their hypocrisy in breaking the law in retaliation for a "criminal assault." In a letter to the *Middletown Daily Press*, an African American, M. C. W., deplored "unlawful acts of all kinds—including lynch law and criminal assault on virtuous women, whether they be white or black women, or whether the hellish offense is committed by black or by white men." The letter writer argued that the lynching had besmirched the county's reputation but also counseled African Americans to avoid "threats of political retaliation" and to allow the authorities time to respond to the matter. A similarly measured but angry tone can be discerned in the resolutions adopted by the Afro-American League in Newburgh, New York, about forty miles from Port Jervis. The league lamented the handling of Lewis before his death and "the crime that resulted in the taking of his life without a trial by jury." The Newburgh organization also praised Special County Judge William H. Crane's attempt to intervene to avert the lynching and asked New Yorkers "to grant them the same protection that is accorded the white citizen." African Americans in southern New York thus sought the equal protection of the law that the racially motivated lynching of Lewis had denied. Moreover, blacks in Port Jervis demonstrated their solidarity in the face of the lynching by collectively purchasing a burial plot and by unsuccessfully seeking to conduct the funeral themselves, independent of the authorities.[46]

The regional press recognized the oddity and irony of the lynching occurring in New York State, in the Northeast. The editor of the *Port Jervis Union* admitted the "disgrace" of the episode, requesting understanding from the rest of the country. The *New York Times* noted the similarity to the circumstances of some southern lynchings. But the *Times* found lessons as to "the dangers of lynching" in the affair, particularly in the remaining uncertainty concerning the respective guilt of Lewis versus that of Foley. A number of southerners opined in letters to the Port Jervis village president. One from Texarkana sought the demonstration of Foley's guilt and then his lynching. Another southern letter writer hoped that the mob killing in Port Jervis might teach the North "charity and mercy" toward the South.[47]

The 1892 collective killing of Robert Lewis in Port Jervis was one of a handful of lynchings in New York State in the second half of the nineteenth century. Cultural and legal factors in the states of the mid Atlantic and in New England strongly militated against lynch law. However, the mob murder of Lewis demonstrated that, given the power of southern example and northeastern whites' racism, in exceptional circumstances—for example, in the intense moments following the allegation of a particularly offensive crime perpetrated by an African American against a white person—a lynching could ensue.[48] One of the striking things about the Port Jervis mob killing was its sheer spontaneity and how quickly matters spiraled out of control despite the efforts of several community leaders. Another important and distinctive factor in the episode was the heritage of race relations and collective violence in Orange County. Twenty-nine years earlier, in Newburgh in 1863, a mob had broken into the jail, dragged out and brutally beaten, and then hanged an African American accused of "assault upon a white girl." A grand jury found indictments against "25 of Newburgh's citizens for riot" and convicted and imposed fines against eleven of them. Whites in Orange County vividly remembered the Civil War–era lynching, and this memory may have helped to loosen the constraints that typically overrode the modest inclinations toward collective violence in the rural Northeast.[49]

Why were lynchings so rare in the mid Atlantic and New England, yet comparatively prevalent in the Midwest and West and abundant in the South?[50] The answer is a complicated one and can only be tentative and speculative. It is much easier for historians to explain why something happened than why something did not. But most likely a mixture of cultural and legal elements disinclined northeasterners from lynching and acted as effective constraints on communal behavior in the inevitable moments of legal crisis that occur in all societies. The foremost of these elements were the heritage of a Yankee culture that stressed social regularity and probity and a rapid capitalist transformation in the antebellum period, which created substantial middle classes that backed due-process reform. Furthermore, New York and Pennsylvania employed a prolific death penalty, tied to the social relations of urbanization, in the late nineteenth and early twentieth centuries. The northeastern death penalty, at once urban, ethnic, racial, private, technocratic, and routinized, represented an alternative path toward the social control of crime. The innovative tendencies in capital punishment in the Northeast would be replicated in other regions as lynch law ebbed in the early twentieth century.

Thus the Northeast, from which due-process ideology emanated across the country as an accompaniment to capitalist transformation, anticipated the eventual and uneven transformation of criminal justice in the South, Midwest, and West. Despite the tragedy of Robert Lewis's death at the hands of a racist mob in Port Jervis, the Northeast never underwent the prolonged cultural conflict experienced west and south of the Alleghenies as Americans moved from an understanding of criminal justice grounded in the local prerogatives of communal authority to one lodged in abstract principles administered by state agencies.

2 The Making of Mobs: The Social Relations of Lynchers

As acts of collective violence, lynchings were deeply rooted in the social arrangements of the late nineteenth- and early twentieth-century Midwest, West, and South. Many mob killings were performed or condoned by communities. In other cases, elements of a local populace, particularly rural and working-class people, supported lynching, while others, for instance a developing middle class or an ethnic or racial group targeted in the mob murder, condemned the violence. All postbellum lynchers rejected due process in favor of deadly collective punishment, but lynchers were diverse in motivation, organization, and the ways in which they used lethal violence to act out understandings of race, social class, sexuality, and gender in crime and punishment. Some collective killings were more overtly ritualistic than others, but all lynchings constituted performances enacting the values of mob participants. Racial, class, and ethnic solidarities and antagonisms and strongly held notions of gender and sexuality animated lynchers and separated them from their victims.

The Varieties of Mobs

Categorizing mobs is important because of the wide range of lynching activity.[1] To ignore differences like circumstance, size, motivation, and ritual in the ways mobs sought to perpetrate rough justice is to underappreciate the complexity and the particularity of the lynching phenomenon.[2] For example, a rapidly assembled mob of several hundred that attempted to spontaneously overwhelm a jail with its numbers cannot be considered identical to a well-organized, masked mob of twenty-five that staged a careful attack on a jail. The first mob would have been less likely to succeed in lynching a victim because of poor planning and lack of leadership, but if it did succeed it would have been more likely to indulge in extensive ritual. The first mob would probably have represented a greater degree of popular support for a collective killing; the second, perhaps, would have had less popular backing.

In general terms, mass mobs evoked broad participation and approval, were spontaneous and possessed little if any formal organization, and were highly ritualized in practice. Posses were groups of men, sometimes authorized by the sheriff, who searched for fleeing suspects. But these often large crowds occasionally killed the persons they were seeking to apprehend. Posses could legally kill if suspects were armed or resisted arrest.[3] Two additional categories of mobs drew far less popular support. Private lynchings constituted secretive, small-scale but collective enactments of vengeance, often by relatives and friends of someone allegedly harmed by the mob's victim. Terrorist mobs were long-lasting, well-organized groups that perpetrated extralegal violence, often for economic goals.[4]

Sometimes, substantial proportions of western, midwestern, and southern communities participated in collective violence. For instance, a mass mob hanged an alleged rapist, Frank Johnson, alias Gustaveson, in Ottumwa, Iowa, in November 1893. The crowd, estimated at a thousand, attacked the Wapello County courthouse as Johnson was being arraigned for assaulting the young daughter of Jonas Sax. Apparently led by the mother and several male relatives of the alleged rape victim, this mob intent upon ritualistic punishment hanged Johnson from the courthouse balcony. When law officers carried Johnson's corpse to jail, lynchers demanded that they be allowed to inspect the body to ensure that he was dead, a request that the officers granted. Most newspapers condoned the lynching, and only the Swedish community in Ottumwa protested.[5]

Smaller towns might also be the settings for communal murders. In August 1885 in Eureka in northwestern California, a crowd estimated at a hundred seized Henry D. Benner, accused of murdering his alleged mistress. In an informal rite of justice, the mob took Benner to the corpse of Amanda M. Towne, where he reiterated his innocence. The mob then hanged him from a tree and filled his body with bullets.[6] Mass mobs killed 25 percent of lynching victims in Iowa and 15 percent of victims of mob murder in California.[7] In Shreveport, Louisiana, in May 1914, a mass mob estimated at several thousand dragged Earl Hamilton, an African American, from jail and stabbed and hanged him after accusing him of raping a white girl at a downtown movie house. Although some recent scholars have stressed the elaborated ritual and notoriety of mass spectacle lynchings, such collective killings constituted a minority of southern lynchings and were associated with the urbanizing trends of the early twentieth century. Mass mobs such as the one that murdered Hamilton killed 23 percent of northern Louisiana's 263 lynching victims.[8]

Sometimes, however, it is hard to distinguish between a mass mob and the posse in which it originated. In March 1893 in Monroe County, Iowa, William Frazier, a miner, fatally stabbed his sister-in-law and seriously wounded his wife and sister-in-law's child. When news spread to the mines at Hiteman, more than a hundred miners formed a posse and scoured the southern Iowa countryside for Frazier. Finding him, they briefly turned him over to the sheriff but then quickly seized him again and dragged him to the scene of the murder. As a crowd that included women and children watched, mobbers hanged him from a tree facing the house where the murder had been committed. Opinion in the mining community unanimously favored the lynching, although the larger state newspapers decried the act.[9]

Posses were an intrinsic cultural tradition not only in the South, where posses killed 11 percent of those who died at the hands of lynch mobs in Louisiana's northern parishes, but also in the Midwest and West into the early twentieth century.[10] As citizens deputized by a sheriff, posses were rural law enforcement at its most basic and traditional. Besides an exciting communal event, posses also had a strongly gendered component. The posse afforded men and boys in a rural locality the opportunity to enact the masculine duty and prerogative of physically protecting and defending their community. In 1883, newspapers lauded the bravery of the men and boys who pursued William and Isaac Barber, outlaws and brothers, through the timbered northeastern Iowa countryside. Male relatives of a murdered deputy sheriff eventually led the mass mob that lynched the Barbers at Waverly.[11]

Most posses that caught their victims did not end up killing them.[12] Or, if they did kill, posse members could claim that they merely did so in self-defense. Posses occupied a gray area between legal and illegal activity. While legally constituted, posses that killed unarmed or surrendering suspects crossed the line into lynching. Of course, posses seldom faced repercussions for their actions, and evidence is often ambiguous.[13] The stature of the posse as a staple of Iowa law enforcement in the late nineteenth and early twentieth centuries says much about the limitations of the county law-enforcement apparatus and corresponding communal efforts at social control. A sheriff and his several deputies on a limited county budget were not up to the task of capturing dangerous criminals, and the males in a rural county were not reluctant to offer their aid. The posse satisfied the rural communal enthusiasm for participation in law enforcement but presented the twin dangers of overzealous posse members killing suspects and of dangerous suspects killing posse members untrained in law-enforcement techniques.

Lynchings that were most likely to provoke division in community opinion were those perpetrated by private mobs. Small mobs utilized careful planning and tended to delay their vigilantism for some time after the commission of the supposed crime they were punishing. Private lynchers also tended to kill victims that were in the custody of legal authorities. For instance, a jury in Ellensburg, Washington, acquitted five men charged with participating in the murder by lynching of Samuel Vinson early on the morning of August 14, 1895. A mob of between fifty and two hundred, including "prominent farmers and business men," had overpowered deputies, broken into the Kittitas County jail, and taken Samuel and Charles Vinson to a nearby street corner, where they hanged them from a tree. The Vinsons, a father and son, had killed two men in a saloon quarrel, and Charles had previously conspired with but then betrayed a robber gang that sought to hold up a Northern Pacific train.[14] Opinion was sharply divided over the lynching in and beyond the Cascade Mountains ranching town. Judge Humes highlighted the fracture in the community over the efficacy of lynching versus due-process law in his charge before a crowded courtroom to the jury that would eventually acquit the accused lynchers on a third ballot: "'Some jurors in examination upon their voir dire have declared that in certain cases they believed in lynching and that in certain cases it was justifiable. There is no doubt others in this community and also other communities are of the same opinion. That men can be found in this community who sustain such opinions is to be regretted. For let me say to you that lynching, so-called, cannot be justified, nor is it under any circumstances justifiable. Every person's conduct in this state is regulated by law. The constitution of the state provides that no person shall be deprived of his life, liberty, or property without due process of law.'"[15]

Most deaths by lynching in the West and Midwest occurred at the hands of private mobs, and the mixed response to their actions indicated the uneven transition in perspectives on criminal justice in those regions. Private mobs murdered 75 percent of lynching victims in California, 62.5 percent of mob victims in Iowa, and 61 percent of victims of lynching in Washington Territory and State.[16]

In southern Louisiana's Sugarland, whites also failed to evince strong support for lynching. Private mobs predominated over mass mobs and posses in the region, killing more than a third of all victims there.[17] Private mob killings were sometimes insular affairs that elicited condemnation from other sectors of white Sugarland society. For instance, a band of thirty-five masked men overpowered a constable and seized and hanged William Carr, an African American accused of stealing a calf in Iberville Parish in March 1906. A newspaper reporter wrote that "[g]reat indignation is felt at this crime," and a district judge rapidly convened a grand jury to investigate the mob murder. The expression of disapproval reflected conflicting class interests among Sugarland whites. Lower-class whites competed with African Americans for their economic livelihood and sought to avenge the infringement of their small property holding. Planter- and mercantile-class whites held judicial and other parish offices and were not sympathetic to vigilantism that threatened the supply of black labor.[18]

With its strong class overtones, lynching in retaliation for transgressions of property failed to receive the popular support that collective murder avenging homicide and rape sometimes elicited. Small and well-organized terrorist mobs of less than fifteen persons performed sixteen lynchings for property crime in Wyoming, contributing 44 percent of the territory and state's lynching victims.[19] Terrorist mobs were usually disguised and acted in isolated areas where crowds could not gather and where the collective murders would initially remain secret; they drew on existing social alliances and organizations. In one example, a small mob of "cowowners" hanged an alleged horse and cattle thief, Tom Waggoner, in Crook County in northeastern Wyoming in June 1891.[20] In several instances, local opposition arose after news of lynching spread. An east central Wyoming newspaper printed a report that "a party of enraged men are scouring the Greybull Country" in pursuit of the lynchers of the reputed horse thieves Jack Bedford and "Dad" Burch, hanged in October 1892 near Bonanza. The dispatch suggested that the posse intended to lynch Bedford and Burch's "assassins." The posse seeking to avenge the lynching of Bedford and Burch may have been a reflection of the resentment that the violent incorporating efforts of wealthy ranchers engendered within the rural proletariat in north central Wyoming.[21]

At least one-third of the lynchings in southwestern Louisiana, where terrorist mobs killed seven (27 percent of the region's victims),[22] were part of a periodic and systematic effort by lower-class whites, especially Cajuns, to intimidate the black Creoles with whom they competed in the cotton economy. The unwillingness of black Creoles to passively accede to the racial superiority asserted by lower-class whites heavily informed a whitecapping episode that occurred in Avoyelles Parish in the fall of 1892. According to a newspaper report, a black teacher made an offensive remark about some white women. When a mob of whites visited his home and attempted to take him out and flog him, the man fired into the crowd and killed a white man. A black Creole politician, Ed Laurent, helped the teacher escape and threatened to kill four whites. A mob of whites responded by hanging and shooting Laurent. After a black Creole preacher, Gabriel Magliore, purportedly called for vengeance against the mob at a church meeting, a band of whites hanged him.[23]

As it did elsewhere in the upper and lower South, whitecapping, the lethal violence that white yeoman farmers directed against those they perceived as their economic and social antagonists, provoked a sharply divided reaction in southwestern Louisiana.[24] Whites in Avoyelles Parish drastically differed on whether the actions of the lynchers were acceptable. The sheriff arrested five whites involved in the collective killings, and they were taken to Natchitoches Parish for safekeeping. But night riders continued a campaign of intimidation against African Americans in the weeks that followed, apparently seeking to drive blacks out of the parish. White planters fretted over the loss of their labor supply, and parish authorities quickly suppressed the whitecap organization, arresting forty-seven participants.[25] The press, controlled by elements sympathetic to the planters' perspective, derided the "Regulators." The parish newspaper, the *Bunkie Blade*, argued, "'Every White Cap should have the noose adjusted and be strung up.'"[26] Equally scathing, a Baton Rouge editor castigated the Avoyelles whitecappers, with their avowed intention of leveling conditions for whites by banishing blacks from the area, as evidence of incipient "socialism," which "must be rooted out at any cost."[27]

Recent scholarship has taught us much about mobs that successfully procured and killed a victim. In many instances, though, persons gathered in mobs, made threats to lynch, and even used physical force to obtain a victim but ultimately did not murder the individual(s) they sought. In Iowa, for instance, these "near lynchings" were far more common than actual lynchings. I have documented twenty-four lynchings in the state from 1874 through 1907 and fifty-two near lynchings between 1878 and 1909. The reasons for the failure of mobs to achieve their objective were varied, from the efforts of law officers to protect a victim to

the fact that these usually large and hastily organized mobs lacked "will"
or leadership. Near lynchings say a great deal about the lynching phenomenon itself. They involved a failed but often vigorous articulation of extralegal authority, they cast light on the strength (or lack thereof) of lynching in a particular region, and they reflected the level of commitment by
law enforcement to the prevention of mob murder. The majority of the
near lynchings in Iowa involved mass mobs, and observers often suggested
that these groups failed in their objective because they lacked leadership
and were easily outwitted by law officers.[28] In a case of failed lynching
in February 1898, a crowd reported at five thousand stormed the jail in
Burlington, Iowa, seeking A. D. Storms, the alleged murderer of Fannie
Rathbun and her daughter Mary. On the way to the jail, the mob appoint-
ed several leaders, who were identified publicly, but in this delay the
sheriff managed to secrete Storms far out of town. The Burlington mob
apparently consisted largely of men and boys coming off of work in the
industrial working-class district.[29]

Lynching and Ritual

Lynchings had profound cultural significance. Terrorist mobs, private
mobs, posses, and mass mobs in the Midwest, West, and South engaged
in practices that amplified the meaning of punishment of particular offenses for an avid audience of local residents. In a sense, mob executions
were performances enacting what some persons perceived as the values
of a community. Through gratuitous, patterned practices, lynchers could
broadcast a message, and a larger segment of the population could in some
measure participate. Ritual allowed for broad communal participation,
at times imitated or mocked formal legal ceremony, and offered the sense
that lynchings were a valid cultural alternative to the criminal justice
system. But ritual was specific to context and to the kind of mob perpe-
trating the collective homicide.[30]

By the 1880s, legal executions in Iowa were private affairs, concealed
from public view and limited to a select group of witnesses. This reform
sanitized the public spectacle that had attended the gallows in antebellum Iowa, when thousands from a surrounding region sometimes observed what was a popular event rich in implications of public justice.[31]
In contrast, lynchings more fully indulged a communal fascination with
death, the spectacle of execution, and the consequences of terrible crimes.
Large crowds, representative of a cross-section of a local population,
watched mob killings in the Iowa counties of Bremer and Shelby in 1883,
Wapello in 1884, Taylor in 1889, Monroe and Wapello in 1893, and Har-

rison in 1894. In several of these incidents, the crowd watched a small and select group of disguised men execute a victim. We cannot conclude that all witnesses to a lynching wholeheartedly endorsed the act. But it is unlikely that a private mob with a large audience was acting against the will of a majority of the persons in a community or that there was little relationship between the attitudes and values of aggressive participants and their witnesses.[32]

The spectacle of an Iowa lynching event had greater dimensions than merely the presence of an audience. Theatrical elements in these acts of collective homicide linked diverse incidents. The site chosen for the execution often was important, emphasizing the values lynchers wished to enforce. Most strikingly, mobs sometimes took their victims to the places where they had allegedly committed crimes. For example, a private mob in Wapello County lynched Pleasant Anderson from a tree facing the house where he had allegedly murdered Christopher McAllister. A mass mob in Monroe County hanged William Frazier near the spot where he had killed his wife and injured his daughter. In other instances, a lynching in view of a courthouse may have signified a defiance of legal institutions and the invocation of popular authority, as in the lynching of a Native American called "Olaf" for rape in Taylor County in 1889.[33]

Lynchers also imitated the custom of legal executions in affording a victim the opportunity to make a confession, or at least to say some final words or a prayer. A confession had potential for drama and could serve a salutary purpose for lynchers either way: by confirming the guilt of the accused or by demonstrating the accused's unworthiness through a belligerent denial. A mob's victim might also turn the table on lynchers by asking God to forgive them for their actions. In any case, the confession held an important place in the lynchers' protocol. Constrained by a modicum of decency and tradition, the confession heightened the lynching event's power as an enactment of social control for serious crimes.[34]

Ritualistic trappings were also obvious in the final phases of Iowa lynchings. The method of killing was important. Modes of execution ranged from simple hanging to riddling a body with bullets fired by many individuals. The latter embodied a desire for communal participation and satiated communal vengeance in an act of overkill expressing power and prowess through the exercise of excessive force. Collective shooting also avoided individual responsibility for the murder of a mob victim. More rudimentary killing, such as a hanging, satisfied some Iowa lynchers' stated preference for "orderly" proceedings, a process as smooth as clockwork and ostensibly as systematic and legitimate as the judicial authority of the county district court. Hanging also mimicked the procedure in legal executions.[35]

In several instances relatives played instrumental roles as extralegal executioners in Iowa. This occurred in Wapello County in 1884, when a slain man's cousins participated in a private mob that first conducted a mock trial of Pleasant Anderson, and in 1893, when the mother and uncles of an alleged rape victim led a mass mob that besieged the courthouse. Obviously, the kin of a crime victim had the greatest interest in the enactment of retributive justice. Their role in a public spectacle of vengeance highlighted for participants and witnesses the personal nature of retribution and the conception of communal order, disturbed by a heinous crime, that many lynchers wished to restore.[36]

What happened after the death of a victim was also an integral part of the lynching event. In a common feature, county authorities in Iowa left a corpse hanging for a number of hours afterward, allowing large crowds, sometimes thousands, to come and view the victim's body. This occurred after private lynchings in Madison and Shelby Counties in 1883, Audubon and Hardin Counties in 1885, and Harrison County in 1894. We cannot easily discern what this meant for the mixed groups who flooded in from surrounding regions. Curiosity was certainly a strong motive, and the opportunity to gawk at a lynched corpse may have been a diversion in remote areas of southern and western Iowa that saw little professional entertainment in the late nineteenth century. Viewing the aftermath of a private lynching may also have offered for some a vicarious role in a spectacle of retributive justice. A private mob execution could become quite public once a victim had expired. In Harlan in 1883, for example, a courthouse guard summoned townspeople by bell. If the message of a mob killing was not explicit enough, some lynchers tried to clarify their broadcast by affixing signs to a site. A private mob in Harrison County attached a sign to Reddy Wilson's corpse that read "Public Library." But the recreational aspect of the lynching event was obvious in Bremer County in 1883, when vendors sold out of mass-produced photographs of the hanged outlaws, the Barbers.[37]

Ritual also contributed meaning to the few lynchings that occurred in upper midwestern states. In Vernon County, Wisconsin, in May 1888, for instance, a mob of a thousand hanged twenty-four-year-old Andrew Grandstaff for the shooting deaths of Reuben Drake, a farmer, and his wife, Matilda, and the stabbing deaths of their grandchildren, Laura and Granville.[38] Approximately two thousand people from Viroqua and the surrounding Coulee region flocked to see the lynched man's corpse the next day.[39] A familiar communalistic ritual ensued, a Viroqua newspaper reported, as the hanging tree was "nearly ruined by people who have a determination to get a piece of bark, limb or leaf from it. The authorities find it impossible to preserve the tree without placing a guard over it day and night. The rope, thirty feet long and an inch in diaracter [*sic*] has been cut into small shreds. People have a mania for gathering up such things as a reminder of the most tragic event and uncivilized procedure that took place in Vernon county."[40]

No simple conclusions can be drawn about the proclivity for ritual of different kinds of mobs in the Midwest. By their very nature, mass mobs and posses involved larger amounts of people and appealed to a broader spectrum of the population than private mobs. Their formulaic behavior most fully met the requirements of communally enforced retribution, although a tendency toward haste and improvisation in some cases hindered the potential for ceremonialism. Private mobs also emphasized symbolism, if merely for the sake of a potential audience afterward. As a vivid performance and projection of popular, extralegal authority in a locale, the lynching event mustered familiar custom in ways that satisfied some midwesterners and appalled others, depending upon their class and cultural perspectives.

A characteristic element in lynching in the West was the appearance of sadism in the ritualistic mistreatment of victims' bodies and in the morbid curiosity devoted to artifacts associated with a victim's death. The degradation of a corpse apparently signified the victor's privilege in the satisfaction of western masculine honor, the ultimate humiliation of a personal foe or communally defined villain. Examples of this kind of behavior abounded in Wyoming, as rural and working-class people participated in lynchings and flocked to legal executions. Following a coroner's inquest on "Big Nose" George Parrott, hanged by a mob on March 22, 1881, in Rawlins, Dr. John E. Osborne, who was later elected governor and congressman from Wyoming, placed Parrott's corpse in a salt solution and eventually skinned it to make shoes and a skull cap.[41] When a private mob of landholders murdered the poachers Nathan L. Adams and Charles Putzier in the "Snake River Country" of Carbon County in October 1888, they gouged out their eyes and mutilated their bodies.[42] At the legal execution of Charles Miller in Cheyenne in April 1892, a witness made a modest proposal to Sheriff Kelley: he wished to skin Miller's corpse. The sheriff angrily refused.[43] In March 1902, Natrona County residents also cut up the rope used to lynch Charles Woodard, who had murdered the sheriff, and spliced tags from his effects to carry home as mementoes.[44] The crowd that viewed Benjamin Carter's publicly displayed corpse after his execution in Rawlins on October 26, 1888, sliced the rope that had suffocated him into innumerable trophies.[45] Several showmen offered the brother of Tom Horn, the western legend legally executed in Cheyenne in November 1903, five hundred dollars for his corpse so that they might take it on tour.[46] In this respect, western lynching and legal executions bore a significant resemblance to southern lynch-mob practice, with its occasionally sadistic, participatory tendencies.[47]

California mobs, like midwestern ones, acted out a performance in which the injustice of a terrible crime could only be rectified by adhering to a particular blueprint of communal vengeance instead of awaiting the unpredictable results of formal legal process. For instance, in August 1881, Oroville lynchers took T. J. Noakes, awaiting trial for the murder of a disabled elderly man, to the elderly man's ranch, where they suspended him from a tree limb and pulled a wagon from under him.[48] The 150 men who lynched four whites and a Mexican, all accused of murder, in Yreka in August 1895 announced their purpose with a sign attached to the back of William Null, awaiting trial for the murder of his wife: "Caution—Let this be a warning, and it is hoped that all cold-blooded murderers in the county will suffer likewise. Yours respectfully, TAX-PAYING CITIZENS. P.S.—Officers—Ask no questions; be wise and keep mum."[49] A large crowd reportedly watched this "well-masked mob" in the courthouse park; a contentious crowd later thronged the engine house, where the coroner took the lynched men's bodies. Yreka residents "gobbled up . . . pieces of the ropes and other articles" as "souvenirs," and an entrepreneur sold many photographs of four of the lynched men hanging from a railway bar suspended between locust trees.[50] These actions may have intensified the experience and memory of mob executions in the West.

Some southern lynchings were far more ritualistic than others. Although scholars interested in a cultural analysis of lynching have focused on several well-known, highly public, and ritualistic mob killings, such as the lynching of Sam Hose near Newnan, Georgia, in April 1899,[51] the many collective killings performed by smaller southern mobs tended to be less elaborate. Like midwestern and western collective killings, virtually all southern lynchings, whether explicitly ritualistic or not, entailed a performance in which the white populace actively or vicariously participated and from which African Americans were supposed to apprehend the terrible consequences of breaching white supremacy. Certain performative patterns are discernable in southern lynchings. In testimony to the salience of the white yeomanry's racial-sexual phobias, collective killings following accusations of rape were among the most ritualistic of all mob executions in northern Louisiana.[52] In September

1891 near Arcadia in Bienville Parish, an African American man allegedly kidnapped and raped a white female schoolteacher. A posse of whites
captured the alleged perpetrator and decided to torture him to death. The
mob tied the black man, skinned him alive, and then cut up the corpse.[53]
In February 1906 in the same parish, cross-tie cutters from a lumber camp
formed a posse and arrested an African American, Willis Page, for the rape
of a white girl. District Judge B. P. Edwards and several others pleaded that
the law should be allowed to proceed unhindered. Mobbers ignored these
protests, took Page to the site where the crime allegedly occurred, and
forced a confession. The crowd, estimated at seven hundred, then hanged
Page and shot him with hundreds of bullets. Before leaving, lynchers
obtained souvenirs from the lynching and burned the corpse.[54]

The performance of sadistic retribution upon the bodies of African
American men who had allegedly sexually transgressed the color line
signified the explosive potential of the conflation of race and sex for upcountry whites. The district judge's unsuccessful objections underlined
the growing cultural divide between middle- and lower-class whites. The
frenzy of a mass lynching may have seemed to the rural white proletariat a cathartic expression of their racial and sexual anxieties. Some bourgeois whites in parish seats viewed it as a disorderly rejection of the values of decency and decorum that, along with reliable means of ensuring
racial hierarchy, ought to undergird southern society. This class and cultural conflict over styles of criminal justice and punishment, nascent in
the postbellum upcountry, would intensify amid the urbanization of
northern Louisiana.[55]

Lynching, Social Class, Ethnicity, and Religiosity

For all of the complexity of lynching, certain patterns of social relations that sustained it are discernable. Class, ethnicity, and culture contributed to the penchant for lynching. As noted above, planter elites opposed the terrorist whitecapping violence of the white yeomanry. By the
early twentieth century, a growing urban middle class derided the ritualistic violence of white working-class mobs in northern Louisiana and
championed the legal segregation of Jim Crow to head off what they
viewed as the social anarchy of lynching violence. Midwestern and western lynchers sometimes united across differences of status in their revolt
against due process, but they enjoyed more stable social standing than
the marginal landholders and landless that they lynched. Lynching for
property crime, which had plagued the antebellum South, Midwest, and
West in contests over respectability and social order in newly settled

locales, persisted into the late nineteenth century in Wyoming, where wealthy cattlemen employed vigilante violence in a deadly campaign against range settlers with smaller holdings and sheepmen. Ethnic allegiances and differences contributed to the solidarity of lynch mobs in the Midwest and to the ways in which their actions were interpreted. And religious theologies and cultures bolstered and contradicted lynching impulses throughout the country. Sometimes, however, broad sectors of the population, tied together by racist ideology or common residence in a neighborhood, united in lynching. For instance, in areas of the Cotton Belt South, including the Red River and Ouachita River Valleys of northern Louisiana, white planters and small farmers often united in vivid extralegal demonstrations of the consequences of defying white supremacy.

In midwestern posses and mass mobs such as the several hundred persons that gathered outside a jail in Anamosa, Iowa, seeking the alleged murderer Jerome West in October 1880, ties of kin and neighborhood brought together a cross-section of the rural population. In fact, a localistic sense of identity derived from common residence in the midwestern country district where a crime had been committed sometimes temporarily overrode differences in wealth and status.[56]

Local apologists for Iowa lynchers commonly insisted that mobs included "good men," that is, men of considerable property and social standing. Evidence suggests that rural property holders did participate, especially in private lynchings where their identity was usually concealed, for instance in the 1883 Shelby County hanging of William Hardy. Private lynchers might style themselves as the guardians of a community by virtue of their social status and good judgment. By the 1880s, however, Iowa mobs nearly exclusively punished individuals who had triggered the moral economy of crime by committing the most egregious offenses, murder and rape. Some of these incidents were deeply enmeshed in class antipathies, but they differed in substance from the more naked efforts at class control common in antebellum Iowa. The older variety of extralegal violence, lynching for property crime, particularly horse thievery, thrived in the 1850s and 1860s but was nearly extinct by the late nineteenth century. An increasingly sophisticated rural agricultural economy and well-developed transportation networks in the Midwest ended the landed-class prerogative expressed in property-crime vigilantism.[57]

Iowa's urban settings, towns of more than ten thousand, provided the landscape for mob activity of a different social basis. Mob participants in the lynchings and near lynchings that occurred in midwestern towns and cities tended to be from the working class, employed in skilled and unskilled manufacturing jobs and in retail establishments. Urban mass mobs sometimes collected as news of a crime spread through a manufacturing or working-class residential district. Recreational patterns could also aid mob formation, as downtown shoppers and evening strollers joined a gathering crowd. In Sioux City in 1904, a well digger named Harry Thompson shot the mayor, who had charged him with disorderly conduct. A mob reported at one hundred rapidly assembled, catalyzed by the attack on the senior municipal official. The sheriff of Woodbury County succeeded in sneaking Thompson on a train, which took him safely out of town. Similarly, the urban context of Council Bluffs was crucial in January 1894 when a large crowd sought to lynch a "well-known sprinter," Leon Lozier, accused in the rape of a young girl. The mob dispersed only after the dispatch of the Dodge Life Guards and speeches by local officials. Ethnic and racial tensions were also sometimes pivotal in the formation of urban mobs.[58]

The pressures of midwestern city expansion and class formation, and perhaps the transformation of rural folkways among Iowans who had only recently become urbanites and members of the working class, may have played a role in the urban mob phenomenon. In the most notable example, Des Moines grew from 22,408 in 1880 to 50,093 in 1890 and 62,139 in 1900. Des Moines experienced five near lynchings between 1891 and 1905. Ottumwa, with its one lynching and four near lynchings between 1893 and 1910, was another city with a large working-class population that seemed especially susceptible to the assembly of mobs. Nearly half of the near lynchings in Iowa occurred in cities; 60 percent of these urban mobs gathered after 1895.[59]

Working-class solidarity provided the crucial ingredient of social cohesion in several Iowa lynching incidents. The posse and mass mob that lynched William Frazier drew its members and its victim from the coal-mining community of Hiteman in Monroe County. Newspapers and the Methodist minister conducting Frazier's funeral in the nearby town of Albia condemned this insular and proletarian affair.[60] Working-class collective identity also led several hundred railroad workers to gather outside a Des Moines jail on the afternoon of May 23, 1894, after petty thieves from the city's Tenderloin district allegedly murdered and robbed a freight conductor. By that evening several thousand persons, including many women and some drawn by "curiosity," joined a throng dominated by a community of skilled workers. The sheriff swore in a dozen deputies, and plainclothes detectives encouraged the crowd to disperse, as small groups of railroad men continued to discuss lynching in their assembly hall and near railroad tracks. Middle-class and elite opinion derided the brutal methods and uncouth style of working-class mobs and, while acknowledging the validity of popular anger over an outrageous crime, criticized this idiom of expression as the behavior of "excitable and ignorant classes."[61]

In urban and rural Iowa, a class-linked cultural chasm developed over mob violence and, more generally, concerning the merits of due-process law versus crime-control efforts. The strongest defenders of due-process law were members of the legal culture, judges and lawyers. The triple lynching of Cicero Jellerson, John Smyth, and Joel Wilson in Audubon County in 1885 followed a decision to grant a change of venue in a murder trial. The editor of the *Council Bluffs Nonpareil*, joined by other crime-control advocates, attacked the actions of Judge Loofbourow and praised the objectives of the lynchers as not "influenced by any other motive than a desire for fair play and even-handed justice." In contrast, another district judge strongly condemned the lynching in a charge to the Audubon County grand jury. The judge suggested that criminals orchestrated the affair, perhaps leading more respectable men who were "excitable" into the mob action. In 1887, the Adams County attorney wrote to Governor William Larabee asking for a reward for the arrest and conviction of the lynchers of John Mckenzie, because a certain "class of men" were threatening the investigation of the lynching, an investigation supported by the "better class of citizens." In several instances, prominent local officials also made speeches to mobs, attempting to discourage them from lynching, an act mandated by state law.[62]

More prominent persons, especially in rural areas, sometimes supported mob activity. A Waverly editor castigated "bankers, capitalists, leading lawyers, officers, editor and in fact members of all class[e]s" for giving lynchers encouragement, although the most active members of the mob that killed the Barbers "were not the best citizens."[63] Rural Iowans often merged class issues with moral ones, viewing harsh justice as a means of controlling the dissolute on the edges of the social order. Construing lawbreakers as "desperadoes" or "ruffians," prolynching rhetoric contrasted upstanding citizens in the tradition of republican proprietors against parasitical, dangerous criminals who threatened the body politic. Lumping together three victims of Iowa lynch mobs in early June 1883, the *Council Bluffs Nonpareil* argued that they were "known to be dangerous men and notoriously bad citizens and the state was powerless to put a check upon them."[64] Lynching, then, invested authority in a vaguely defined community of "citizens" enacting morally charged punishment.[65]

Most midwestern lynching victims were lower-class whites, often marked with the stain of previous criminal activity or with disreputable social ties. Many midwestern victims of lynching were on the margins of the fin-de-siècle economy. In terms of social structure and culture, they were distant from the more well-established rural or working-class whites who participated in lynch mobs. In at least five lynchings of whites in Iowa, observers characterized the victims as "desperadoes" and pointed to long records of criminality that included theft, burglary, arson, attempted murder, and murder.[66] Other whites targeted by mobs, although perhaps not involved in explicitly criminal activity, were discredited by their peripheral role in community life and association with stigmatized residents. John Hamner, lynched for murder in Madison County in 1883, allegedly frequented local houses of prostitution and saloons, drank whiskey, and spent free time with other men who made a living from odd jobs and seasonal unskilled labor. John Mckenzie, lynched for murder at Corning in April 1887, supposedly had a "rough" past, working on "Mississippi Steamboats and on the plains."[67]

As in the Midwest, lynchers in the West were usually either rural residents or members of the growing urban mercantile or working class. Rural lynchers might be farmers, ranchers, cowboys, sheepworkers, or fishermen, but they generally enjoyed middling or lower-to-middling status in agrarian, range, or maritime society. They were socially distant from the marginal folks—vagrants, hired hands, professional criminals—who most often ended up the victims of lynching. Similarly, urban lynchers were usually members of the petty mercantile class or the nascent working class. Western lynchers may have been recent emigrants from the countryside, eastern states, or Europe, but their socioeconomic position was less precarious than that of the individuals from the urban underclass, who worked as day laborers, in lowly service professions (for example, as porters), or who made a living in criminal enterprises. Frank Wigfall, an African American lynched in October 1912 by inmates at the state penitentiary in Rawlins, Wyoming, after he was placed there for protection from a lynch mob of townspeople angered by his alleged rape of an elderly white woman, was an itinerant laborer and ex-convict.[68] Sam and Charles Vinson, a father and son lynched by "prominent farmers and business men" in Ellensburg, Washington, in August 1895 for murdering two men in a saloon quarrel, had worked around Puget Sound building houses and had previously been accused of participating in a robber gang that held up a Northern Pacific train.[69] There were exceptions to this pattern of class and status relations. In August 1903, a mob of approximately a thousand in Asotin County in southeastern Washington hanged

William Hamilton, a wealthy young rancher who had attempted to rape and then murdered a twelve-year-old girl.[70]

Sometimes collective killings in the West were performed by groups of working-class men suddenly aroused by news of a crime that seemed to offend wageworkers' sense of moral order.[71] Working-class men might respond with nearly spontaneous lethal violence to alleged violations of sexual and gender etiquette, especially those tinged with racial and ethnic overtones, as well as to homicides that seemed particularly threatening to the unstable social order of the remote outposts of the extractive economy. In April 1908, residents of the mining camp of Skidoo in Inyo County, California, near the Nevada line, seized Joe Simpson from jail and hanged him from a telegraph pole. A former soldier, saloon owner, and one of the first residents of Skidoo, Simpson had murdered James Arnold, a butcher and a former magistrate who had prosecuted him. In the culmination of a three-day drunken spree, Simpson reportedly shot Arnold in the heart after declaring that "his time had come." In the face-to-face society of the mining camp that stressed personal reputation and masculine honor enforced by violence, the miners viewed the killing of Arnold as an act of "cold-blooded murder" that merited lynching.[72]

A group of stockmen, asserting that local law enforcement had been ineffectual, hanged five petty thieves, including two Indians, Daniel Yantis and Martin Wilson, two "half-breed" Indians, James Hall and Frank Hall, and a white man, Calvin Hall, who had allegedly stolen barbed wire, a harness, and forks in Modoc County in northeastern California in May 1901. The northern California press condemned the Lookout lynching, and authorities prosecuted mob participants.[73] However, the quintuple lynching in Lookout in 1901 was something of an anachronism. The use of lethal collective violence by property holders to consolidate control over natural resources had marked the first several decades of white settlement in the West, but it had faded in California and the Pacific Northwest by the 1880s.

Yet lynching for property crime endured into the twentieth century in Wyoming, as the range war there produced a lively and prolonged contest over rural resources. Four Wyoming lynching victims—James Averill and Ella "Cattle Kate" Watson, who were hanged by six prominent cattlemen in Carbon County in 1889, and Nate Champion and Nick Ray, killed by an armed force of Texas mercenaries and influential Wyoming ranchers in April 1892 in Johnson County—loom large in western legend and literature. These cause célèbre lynchings epitomized the class conflict that pitted "nesters" (farmers), small cattle ranchers, and rustlers (cattle thieves) against the powerful cattlemen who dominated Wyoming politics. Wyoming's experience with lynching for property crime was an aspect of a late nineteenth-century western process of economic, environmental, cultural, and political consolidation that Richard Maxwell Brown has termed the "Western Civil War of Incorporation." The longer-term analysis that follows probes the social and cultural matrix of class relations on the range, ruling-class vigilante ideology, and the role of legal and political authority in episodic range violence. Like the southern planter class, the range gentry disavowed the unpredictability of the criminal justice system in favor of collective killings that would dramatically assert their domination of the local social order.[74]

Brown persuasively argues that wealthy Wyoming cattle operators joined "the consolidating authority of modern capitalistic forces" in the deployment of violent and nonviolent coercive means in ensuring their control of the region's resources. A rural working class that sometimes helped itself to stock and other goods claimed by ranchers resisted the cattle barons' attempt to dominate the range. Brown suggests that the conflict was largely fought between "incorporation gunfighters" with conservative principles, ties to the Republican party, and northern origins and "resister gunfighters," who tended to be Democrats, southern, and hostile to the intentions of large capital. In broad terms, the Republican-backed Johnson County Invaders rank with the "incorporation gunfighters," their enemies in the "anti-incorporation stronghold" of Johnson County with the "resister gunfighters."[75]

The struggle for control of the range lasted far longer than the dramatic years of the late 1880s and early 1890s, when increasing rural settlement, overstocking of the range, and depression in the cattle industry temporarily intensified the turmoil.[76] The record of collective murder with economic motivations in Wyoming illustrates the parameters of the battle over incorporation. Between 1885 and 1909, one private mob and eight terrorist mobs murdered fifteen persons whom they accused of horse theft, rustling, poaching, or grazing sheep on the range. After 1892, the feud between large and small cattle ranchers shifted direction, as cattle magnates began to employ paid assassins to eliminate alleged rustlers. The incorporation gunfighter Tom Horn, accused of murdering a number of members of the rural proletariat and legally executed in 1903, exemplified the transition from collective murder to contract killing. However, the advent of terrorist mob activity, in which cattle ranchers targeted sheepowners and sheepherders in the early twentieth century, marked the final phase of property-crime vigilantism. The public outrage following the Tensleep Raid in April 1909, in which fifteen masked men murdered three sheepworkers, effectively ended the lethally violent phase of range incorporation in the state.[77]

A profile of the social relations between several property-crime lynching victims and their mob executioners illuminates class and status distinctions. Si Partridge apparently immigrated from Kansas to Colorado in the early 1880s and joined a gang of horse thieves active in southern Wyoming Territory. His fifteen masked lynchers in August 1885 were probably members of a northern Colorado and southern Wyoming stock association, an outfit representing range property interests.[78] Charles Putzier and Nathan L. Adams infuriated their neighbors by living off the profits from the hides of the elk and deer they hunted on disputed lands along the Colorado border in Carbon County. One landholder along the Little Snake River, William Findlay, orchestrated retaliation against these marginal settlers, leading a lynching party of property holders in October 1888.[79] Tom Waggoner owned a horse ranch in Crook County in northeastern Wyoming. The "cow owners" that hanged Waggoner in June 1891 charged him with stealing horses and assisting cattle thieves over several counties. Local newspaper reports asserted that neighbors disliked the "shrewd" and "penurious" Waggoner, who failed to display proper rural hospitality or "good fellowship" despite his comparative wealth.[80]

From these examples, we can see that mobbers and their targets were distinguished by their respective roles in the range economy and social structure. Lynchers controlled natural resources of land, stock, and game and resented lower-class settlers' alleged appropriation of those commodities. Ruling-class landholders also expected particular folkways, such as treating and mutualistic but property-conscious land-use and stock practices, from their propertied comrades.[81] Failure to abide by these protocols or suspicion of rustling or horse theft meant loss of respectability and possible social and physical sanctions.

Property-crime mobs invoked a common mode of self-representation, the notion that an ineffectual criminal justice system dominated by sympathetic, rural working-class juries would not punish property violations. This schema morally coded lower-class individuals as threats to ranchers' livelihoods who were subject to collective, if illegal, remedies.[82] In the propertied-class explanation, the malevolent property transgressor often became an exoticized figure whose darkness of character, while thrilling, contrasted sharply with the virtuous stockowner bravely defending his holdings. The lynching of Si Partridge in 1885 set in motion these familiar themes. The *Laramie Boomerang* declared that Partridge had led a life "full of romance" and that despite his youthful and tender features, he "was 'game,' however, and showed that to the last." Meanwhile, the stock association detective nicknamed "Grit" who apprehended Partridge displayed "the courage of a lion."[83] The *Cheyenne Sun* deplored the Albany County coroner's inquest in the case: "'How far lynch law may be given the support of public opinion is going to be a question for the western country to determine some day. The coroner's jury, sitting on the body of Si Partridge, the man lynched at Fort Sanders, found in its verdict "that the evidence shows that he was a notorious desperado, criminal, and horsethief," and then exculpates the sheriff from any blame for entrusting the man to an irresponsible party to take to Cheyenne, when it was known threats were made openly against his life.'"[84]

The verdict of the coroner's jury represented the mob murder of Partridge in partisan, laudatory terms, simultaneously encompassing a ruling-class representation of the lynching event and an abandonment of the nominal neutrality of the state. The Cheyenne editor's denunciation of the Albany County coroner's inquest signaled two other characteristics of property-crime vigilantism in Wyoming: the collusion of officials with the activities of propertied vigilantes and the mixed popular response that lynchings by the range elite typically evoked.

In the Johnson County War, Republicans holding state and federal office shielded ranchers from prosecution. The intersection of the interests of officials and propertied lynchers was more often a local affair, as county law officers and the rural elite orchestrated the circumstances for the collective murder of a lower-class enemy and then circumvented legal redress. In the 1885 lynching of Si Partridge, Albany County officials collaborated with the stock association in arranging the mob murder and then defended the hanging as justified by Partridge's record of criminality. Three years later, the territorial governor, Thomas Moonlight, prodded Carbon County officials to investigate the lynching of Nathan L. Adams and Charles Putzier and to bring charges, and in correspondence with them he chided their lackadaisical approach. Moonlight conceded that the county attorney and district court possessed the sole authority to prosecute the individuals responsible. In fact, the governor could only make an official offer of a reward for the arrest and conviction of guilty parties. By territorial statute, the county attorney had to request that a reward be offered, and the county even provided the funds for the payment of a reward. When a landholder implicated in the lynching, Alfred McCargery, wrote to Moonlight protesting his innocence, the governor equivocated. In reply, Moonlight agreed that the lynched men had violated the game law and expressed the desire that he would "have the pleasure of meeting you all face to face in your homes."[85] The territorial and early statehood arrangement of powers thus guaranteed that countryside grandees could safely retaliate against their enemies in the rural working class. The range elite usurped the criminal justice system with the connivance of office holders who may have shared their ideological and political preferences.

Ethnocultural loyalties and differences also motivated lynchers and those who responded to their actions. The sociologist Paul Walton Black discovered in his early twentieth-century survey of Iowans with firsthand knowledge of lynching that most lynchers were of "American" (that is, Anglo-American) stock, whose families had migrated from upper southern, Old Northwest, or mid-Atlantic states. But the ethnic identity of more recent immigrants sometimes also played a role. Participation in a lynch mob constituted an interesting measure of assimilation. German farmers joined lynchers in Bremer County in 1883 and in Audubon County in 1885, targeting individuals who had murdered members of German farming communities. In Bremer County, a newspaper reporter remarked that the Germans' unfamiliarity with revolvers prevented them from killing the Barber brothers when, as members of a posse, they encountered the outlaws. Working-class Germans were also among the thousand who gathered to lynch a Swede, Frank Johnson, alias Gustaveson, in Ottumwa in 1893. Gustaveson had allegedly raped the daughter of Jonas Sax, a German. Ottumwa's Swedish community pressed for a fair investigation and argued in a mass meeting that Gustaveson had not been given the same protection as an "American." Other Ottumwans dismissed these concerns, exposing ethnic tensions in the city.[86] Sometimes ethnic solidarity played a role in the West as well, for instance, when Finns and Scandinavians gathered in "the Upper Town" of Astoria, Oregon, in late July 1893 to demand the lynching of John Hansen, a wife-murderer. Lacking a leader and faced with the Clatsop County sheriff's vow to wound or kill if need be to defend his prisoner, this crowd of "the unfortunate Mrs. Hansen's fellow countrymen" dissipated.[87]

The complex ethnic and class landscape of late nineteenth-century Wisconsin similarly shaped collective violence and the response to it. In September 1891, Anton Sieboldt, a twenty-six-year-old hired hand born to Prussian immigrant parents, murdered a young farmer of Irish descent, James Meighan, in a drunken quarrel. A mob of fifty, perhaps half of them Irish American farmers, seized Sieboldt from a jail and hanged him in front of a thousand men, women, and children in Darlington.[88] Underlining a cleavage of class and culture, the *Milwaukee Sentinel*'s correspondent reported that in the town's stores and saloons people believed that the lynching would "serve as a timely warning to other persons with murderous intentions." Yet "the more conservative citizens" deplored the affair. "Mr. Warren Gray, a well-known citizen and church member," stated, "'[I] regard it as one of the worst things for the county that ever happened. . . . There is no doubt that Sieboldt's crime was an atrocious one but that was no excuse for the lawless manner of his death.'"[89]

Wisconsin's diverse array of ethnic loyalties factored into the interpretation of the mob killing of Anton Sieboldt. A Milwaukee German Catholic newspaper, the *Seebote*, underlined the fact that a lynching party of Irish Americans had murdered a German and argued that Sieboldt would not have been lynched if he had not been, in the colloquial parlance, "a Dutchman." The *Milwaukee Sentinel*, representing the state's Yankee establishment, denied that "race feeling" had anything to do with it and asserted that racial and ethnic allegiances and antagonisms had never played a role in the Badger State's heritage of mob violence.[90]

But ethnic identities and nativism had influenced lynchings as well as the response to acts of collective violence in Wisconsin's history. On September 26, 1868, for example, the ethnic solidarity of Irish in and around Richland Center transformed an overflowing crowd of mourners gathered at the cemetery for the funeral of twenty-year-old, recently married Anna Wallace into a mob that soon descended on the nearby Richland County jail. Pulling fifteen-year-old John Nevel from the jail, women stoned him and men hanged him from a tree until he was dead. Nevel, whose father farmed near the town of Dayton, had allegedly shot Wallace and then decapitated her with an axe, supposedly to obtain the twenty-five dollars she had earned picking hops. The *Richland County Republican* noted that the "Rev. J. M. Reid, Col. Hasentine, Dist. Attorney Wilson, Judge Fries, Sheriff McMurtry, Esq. Lovelas, Constable Barrett, and many other worthy citizens" had tried to dissuade the mob; but "the people of the outraged settlement" ten miles from the county seat could not be dissuaded.[91]

Twenty years later in Trempeleau County, Wisconsin, the strength of communal ties among Norwegians led them to lynch a Norwegian farmer, Hans Jacob Olsen, in the town of Preston on November 24, 1889. Olsen had made threats of violence against his family. When the *Milwaukee Sentinel* castigated the *Seebote*'s supposed attempt "to sow dissensions between the people of this state of different national origins" in its commentary on the 1891 lynching of Anton Sieboldt, it denounced this 1889 mob killing by Norwegians as "the worst outrage, probably, in the whole list" of lynchings in Wisconsin. However, a recent historian argues that the eventual conviction of Olson's wife, Bertha, her son, and two other men and their sentence to life in prison for their participation in the lynching resulted from Yankee nativism in league with "liberal legalism and American gender ideals [that] privileged the rights of the individual man over those of his wife, family, and community."[92]

As with ethnic identities, regional religious cultures sometimes assisted and sometimes undercut collective killing. The "blood sacrifice" and "vindicatory justice" of lynching as a scapegoating ritualistic atonement for sin resonated strongly with some elements of fundamentalist Protestant symbolism and theology, which predominated in the South. Moreover, for many white Americans in the late nineteenth century, including white southerners, notions of racial boundaries had become sacralized.[93] Southern Louisiana, which was predominately Catholic, saw far less lynching than fundamentalist Protestant northern Louisiana, and segregation arrived in Catholic Louisiana later and ended earlier. But a myriad of cultural differences, including the social relations of a cotton economy versus those of a sugar economy and the impact of an Anglo-American legal heritage versus a Gallic one, also contributed to the divergence among the regions of Louisiana in their approaches to race and law.[94]

Whether Christianity served as context or contradiction for lynching, primary sources are generally silent on how the religiosity of lynchers and their opponents may have influenced the performance and understanding of collective murder.[95] Occasionally, Christian churchmen openly endorsed mob murder. The Reverend Robert A. Elwood, pastor of the Olivet Presbyterian church in Wilmington, Delaware, incited the June 1903 lynching by several thousand of George White, an African American who had allegedly raped and murdered a young white woman, Helen Bishop. Elwood wedded a scriptural understanding of the necessity of punishing wrongdoers with a rough-justice critique of the criminal justice system. In his open-air sermon, which was publicized in the *Wilmington Morning News*, the minister cited 1 Corinthians 5:13, "Therefore put away from yourselves that wicked person," and the Sixth Amendment to the U.S. Constitution, guaranteeing to the accused "the right to a speedy and a public trial."[96] The Presbyterian Church (U.S.A.) censured Elwood for "dishonoring the word of God." Helen Bishop's own father, also a clergyman, had pursued another strain of Christian theology, arguing in a letter to the mob that the best punishment for George White was not lynching but "'his guilty conscience, a hell of itself.'"[97]

Discord among Christian clergy over the validity of mob violence occurred in other cases. Following the January 1907 lynching of James Cullen, a white man who had murdered his wife and stepson in Charles City, Iowa, the Reverend J. R. Hargreaves, minister of the First Baptist church in nearby Iowa Falls, backed the lynching by citing popular sovereignty in the need to ensure harsh and rapid justice: "The people after all are the law makers and enforcers while jurists and other court officials are but delegated authorities. If those to whom the work is delegated are repeatedly remiss in duty, it might seem as though the original power must at times take matters in hand. . . . The murdering of women and children at the hands of degenerate men has become so common in our fair state that the people have reason to become desperate when, with pretty good reason, they have reason to fear further miscarriage of justice."[98]

However, Charles City's "ministerial alliance" of clergymen strongly excoriated the lynching's infringement of due process, a position summarized by a Methodist minister, the Reverend Nathaniel Pye, at a mass meeting of six hundred: "'When that mob (many of them under the influence of liquor) gathered in front of the jail and forced that railway iron through its door they did more! [T]hey drove it through the purity, the fidelity and the heroism of the Stars and Stripes and tore it to tatters. For over every jail, confining prisoners of every degree throughout our fair land, floats the invisible and indissoluble flag of our nation sheltering the poor wretch within until he shall have had a fair trial from his peers and have been proven guilty.'"[99]

In Duluth, Minnesota, in June 1920, two Catholic priests, Frs. William Powers and P. J. Maloney, determinedly tried to dissuade their young working-class male parishioners from joining a lynch mob of several thousand that would lynch three African American circus employees on a spurious accusation of rape. But most of the young men rejected the entreaties, one exclaiming, "Stay out of this, Father. This has nothing to do with God." Catholic and Presbyterian ministers also sermonized against the Duluth lynching after it happened.[100] In short, the theologies, symbols, and clergy of the various Christian denominations in the South, Midwest, and West—ranging from liberal mainline Protestantism, with its reformist and humanitarian perfectionist tendencies, to conservative fundamentalist Protestantism, with its emphasis on atonement for wrongdoing, to the Catholicism of rural and working-class people of French, Irish, German, and Polish extraction that stressed the sinfulness of man and the opportunity for redemption through clerical intercession—both undergirded and undermined the ritualistic collective homicide of lynching.

Lynching and Gender

Considerations of gender also inspired the revolt against due-process law. A participant in the lynching of William Hardy, the alleged murderer of two local officials, in Shelby County, Iowa, in July 1883, expressed that private mob's masculinist view, as well as that of the posse of over a thousand that lynched Hardy's partner, Simpson Tyler Crawford, when he stated that the lynchers were "good citizens, indulgent fathers, kind husbands." This masculinist perspective saw the collective enactment of violent social control as an extension of masculine prerogative and authority from home and workplace to the policing of a locale and the supervision of its legal institutions. The notion of masculine role activated the posse of five hundred men and teenage boys, "the flower of Logan's manhood," that pursued burglars who had shot a town marshal in Harrison County, Iowa, in 1894, an episode that eventually led to a mob execution. Women and children often attended lynchings by mass and private mobs in the Midwest, West, and South, and they played essential roles by offering aggressive moral support and cheers, but they usually did not physically participate.[101]

On rare occasions women fell victim to lynching, particularly African American women whom white southerners excluded from the deference and protection they accorded to white femininity.[102] Some of these women were accused of committing crimes against whites; others were caught in the indiscriminate violence of white rage. In March 1892, a private mob in Richland Parish, Louisiana, killed Ella, a teenage black domestic who had allegedly poisoned the family that employed her. Ella reportedly had intended to poison a black male house servant, but her employer's family consumed the coffee she doused with "rough on rats."[103] Eight other African American women died at the hands of lynch mobs in Louisiana. One of these, lynched in Catahoula Parish in November 1892, was the daughter of John Hastings, the alleged murderer of a constable. Another black woman, Charlotte Morris, lived with a white man in Jefferson Parish, where a mob shot them and set their houseboat alight in January 1896.[104]

On July 20, 1889, six cattlemen in Carbon County, Wyoming, hanged Ella Watson and Jim Averill, homesteaders whom they accused of rustling. Seeking to justify their lynching of a white woman, stockmen and their apologists conflated Watson with a local prostitute, "Cattle Kate," in newspaper accounts and invented stories about her past, including a variant in which she had poisoned her husband and shot a "colored boy" who had stolen her jewels.[105] The *Salt Lake Tribune*, while accepting the apologists' characterization of Watson as an unfeminine, degraded woman, stressed how the lynching of Watson defied western norms of gender relations. The *Tribune*'s editor underlined why white women so seldom fell victim to lynchings in the Midwest, South, and West: because prevailing chivalric notions protected them from lethal collective violence.

> "The men of Wyoming will not be proud of the fact that a woman—albeit unsexed and totally depraved—has been hanged within their territory. This is about the poorest purpose a woman can be put to! The woman may have been all that she was pictured. If that was true, it was clear that her proper place was a madhouse, and certainly there were methods by which she might have been made to leave the region without hanging her. This is so certain that we do not believe the men who strangled her are just the class of men that decent people would like to make their homes among. There is many a tragedy on the frontier: there is much that is rough and wild, but there is generally, withal, a crude chivalry which protects the most abandoned of women. This is a tough business in Wyoming."[106]

Much more often than they lynched women, mobs sought to punish the supposed perpetrators of particular crimes resonant with ideas of gender and sexuality. Lynchers who targeted alleged rapists most bluntly enforced their understandings of sexuality and the relations between men and women. A group of fifty masked men lynched James Reynolds for the rape of Mrs. J. W. Noble in Decatur County, Iowa, in August 1887, despite considerable doubt as to his guilt. Mrs. Noble identified Reynolds as her assailant, and a fear of contact between itinerant men and farm wives left alone when their husbands worked in the fields probably motivated the men from the surrounding district who participated in the hanging. In a formula similar to the southern experience in lynchings for rape, newspaper coverage portrayed Mrs. Noble complimentarily, emphasizing the contrast between her feminine virtue and the failed manhood of her "brute" attacker.[107] Interracial same-sex sexual relations could also spur mob killings. A mob of white railworkers shot, bludgeoned, and tarred and feathered an African American itinerant, James Cummings, in Mojave, California, in March 1904, following an allegation that he had raped a white hobo boy.[108]

Interracial rape, always a powerful allegation in postbellum Louisiana, had special force in upcountry districts of that state. White yeomen often lived in parishes with white majorities and had less of a well-defined protocol of racial interaction than did whites from Cotton Belt districts. Upcountry whites especially feared interracial sexual contact and tended to react hysterically after an allegation that a black man had "attempted to criminally assault" a white woman. In predominantly white north central Louisiana, reversing the pattern throughout the rest of the state, lynchers cited rape as a reason for mob murder more often than they did homicide.[109] Relations between black men and white women, although they did not inspire the majority of lynchings in Louisiana, nonetheless dominated the debate over mob violence and the status of African Americans in postbellum Louisiana. In early twentieth-century Louisiana, bourgeois whites would seek to preclude the social disorder of white working-class mobs determined to dramatically reinscribe racial and gender boundaries by instituting laws that legally segregated black men and white women in public space and by remaking the criminal justice system to emphasize efficient, race- and gender-conscious justice.

Wife-murderers, whose crime offended strongly held conceptions of familial roles, also provoked communal anger, for example in the lynching of James Cullen, a carpenter, by a mob of more than five hundred men, women, and children on January 9, 1907, in Charles City, Iowa, for murdering his wife and stepson. Similarly, a mob of thirty from Dunsmuir, California, stepped off a train in nearby Castella on September 20, 1892, seizing J. W. Smyth, a carpenter who had murdered his wife and child in Dunsmuir, from a waiting sheriff and hanged him. Passengers on the next morning's northbound Portland Express witnessed Smyth's corpse hanging from a tree near the Castella station. In the Charles City and Castella lynchings, mobbers cited fears that a father and husband who had murdered his family would elude justice through the "insanity dodge." In an inversion, several hundred near lynchers sought the murderer of R. W. Stubbs in Polk City, Iowa, in April 1882. Stubbs was shot while defending his house against a nighttime burglar. The mob was reportedly infuriated that his death deprived his wife and four children of a paternal provider.[110]

In the South, white yeomen, like white planters, placed a heavy premium on the enforcement of personal and familial honor when it was infringed by verbal insults or crimes committed by whites or blacks. Some notion of masculine honor informed virtually every lynching that occurred in northern Louisiana. Groups of white men or, much less frequently, African American men attempted through mob murder to avenge deviant acts that supposedly damaged societal order and, by extension, their collective honor.[111]

A series of events in the north central hill parish of Catahoula in December 1881 illustrated not only how masculine honor could incline lower-class whites toward mob violence but also how parish elites might oppose this method of settling differences. Two young white cotton farmers, Myce Taylor and Frank Curington, had a longstanding grudge that ended when Curington fatally stabbed Taylor at a store. Local whites feared that Taylor's friends, seeking to exact vengeance for his death, would take Curington and his brother from jail and lynch them before the preliminary examination.[112] The mob hanging did not come off, but judges, ministers, and other prominent whites soon staged a mass meeting in Harrisonburg, the seat of Catahoula Parish. The assembly endorsed a preamble and resolutions condemning rampant criminality, the possibility of mob law, and attorneys who manipulated legal process to allow miscreants "to go unwhipped of justice."[113] Distancing themselves from "mob law, which should be discountenanced by good citizens," and the methods of white yeomen, the professional men also denigrated what seemed to them the most troublesome aspects of due-process law, namely, attorneys who drilled witnesses, filed bills of exceptions (particularly for changes of venue), or sought to sway the opinions of jurors.[114]

In north central Louisiana, mobs killed at least seven people[115] as the result of frustration with the criminal court, with concerns at times revolving around the proper punishment of crime that thwarted communal notions of gender roles and the family. In April 1905, lynchers in Claiborne Parish attacked the jail and killed a white man, Richard Craighead, who had murdered his brother's child and wife. The state supreme court had reversed Craighead's original conviction over the procedure used in handling sworn and unsworn jurors. A correspondent speculated that men from the rural neighborhood where Craighead had perpetrated the crime, frustrated by delays in the rendering of justice, were responsible.[116] In June 1908, again in Claiborne Parish, mobbers shot and killed Bird Cooper, an African American, near where he had allegedly murdered Lettie Bond and her child. Cooper had been acquitted of the homicide the previous fall, and the lynchers were reportedly angered by the failure of the criminal justice system to convict someone for the crime.[117] When the intrinsic inefficiencies of deliberative law combined with the moral imperatives of gender and generation aroused by serious offenses against women and children, mob murder could ensue.

Yet the proponents of lynching hardly held a monopoly on manliness and the prerogatives of masculinity. The due-process advocates who deplored lynching sometimes underlined the cruelty and brutality of an act of mob murder, suggesting that a lynching that pitted overwhelming numbers against a defenseless victim hardly constituted a fair, manly contest.[118] A Bakersfield, California, editor made this point following the lynching of the accused murderers Thomas and William Yoakum in May 1879: "No one of those who acted the part of executioners would probably be pleased to be charged with seizing an unarmed man, manacled and chained to the floor, beating and shooting him to death, and then hanging his dead body to the roof of his dungeon, but the remembrance of the bloody victims of the assassins will come to assert the justice of the act, and it may soften the criticism, though it may not entirely excuse the dreadful retribution."[119]

A San Francisco editor similarly invoked standards of respectable manhood, including decency and fair play, when a Santa Cruz mob, defended by a local newspaper as "'property owners and tax payers, representatives of almost every trade, profession and business interest,'"[120] hanged Francisco Arias and Jose Chamalis, who had allegedly murdered Henry De Forest for money to attend a circus, on May 3, 1877: "'The men may have, under our laws, deserved death. But the mob which hung them had no authority nor right to violate the law and good name of the state by inflicting punishment which takes the character of personal vengeance. If they have sufficient justification[,] why do they sneak out of the responsibility by not only performing the deed in the darkness, but by disappearing afterwards, afraid to take responsibility for their act.'"[121]

In short, lynching was far from an ephemeral phenomenon. The motivation, organization, and practice of mob killing was consistent with the most deeply held beliefs and social identities of the residents of the regions beyond the Alleghenies, where it held sway in the postbellum era. Lynchers and those who opposed their actions were strongly invested in certain understandings of retributive violence as a performance, in differences of social status, culture, and ethnicity, and in differences between men and women and adults and children. But for lynchers one difference mattered more than any other: what they perceived as the difference between the races and how they could best ensure white domination.

3   *Judge Lynch and the Color Line: Mobs and Race*

Whites who collectively murdered African Americans in the South, Midwest, West, and Northeast in the late nineteenth and early twentieth centuries not only made a statement about racial hierarchy but also a statement about law. Law was too capricious, too unpredictable, too formal, too abstract, and too concerned with process and at least the procedures of fairness to regulate the crucial social distinctions of the color line. Racist whites throughout much of the country viewed lynching as the most effective means of responding to instances of African American resistance and interracial criminality. For them, the criminal justice system in its maddening variability could not be entrusted with the sacred responsibility of performatively reenacting white supremacy when it was challenged.

Although whites everywhere at times held this view of the relation between race and law, factors of demography, economics, and culture affected how often and under what circumstances whites lynched blacks. In northern Louisiana's Cotton Belt, planters dominated the polity, kept the criminal justice system weak, and through rampant lynching and corporal punishment reserved for themselves the right to punish what they defined as African American deviancy. In Louisiana's Mississippi Delta parishes and southern Sugarland, planters lynched in moments of racial crisis but more often accommodated the black majority by manipulating the criminal justice system for the purpose of racial control. In New Orleans's urbanizing hinterland, whites unleashed racial pogroms that sought to ensure white dominance amid a shifting socioeconomic landscape. In the Midwest and West after 1900, working-class whites brutally implemented Jim Crow understandings of racialized and gendered space in rural industrial and urban settings with relatively small black populations. But lynching as white supremacy's favored weapon was hardly reserved for African Americans. Sicilians, Chinese, Mexicans, and American Indians also fell prey to Judge Lynch in the postbellum South, West, and Midwest. In the urbanized Northeast, as analyzed in this book's final chapter, lawmakers and prosecutors headed off lynching as they precociously crafted a prolific death penalty into a reliable means of ensuring racialized rough justice.

The Cotton Belt

Whites in the Cotton Belt believed that informal authority and violence, not formal law, could best regulate a severe racial hierarchy inherited, along with an anemic legal system, from slavery. The prevalence of lynching in Louisiana's northwestern Red River Valley,[1] where mobs killed eighty-seven persons, eighty-two of them African Americans, is not especially surprising. The cotton-rich Red River Delta had been distinguished by the cruelty of its antebellum slavery regime. It experienced an especially traumatic, homicidal Reconstruction and Redemption, as whites violently reclaimed authority over freedpeople in political affairs and labor relations. Northwestern Louisiana was also the birthplace of the exodus of disappointed African Americans to Kansas in 1879.[2] The Red River parishes of Bossier and Caddo, with more than 70 percent of their residents African American, comprised a variant of the plantation Cotton Belt identified by historians as the southern region most prone to mob violence.[3] More than two-thirds of the Red River Delta's lynchings occurred in these two parishes.[4] As elsewhere in the cotton South, a uniform devotion to the staple crop of cotton, the labor arrangement of sharecropping, and the rigidity of racial interaction conspired with planters' traditional prerogative of labor control to make lynching a common weapon in the punitive repertoire of planter-class whites.[5]

The Ouachita River Valley,[6] where lynchers murdered sixty-eight blacks, provided a more complicated setting for mob murder. Alluvial cotton plantations along the Ouachita River adjoined hilly oak areas that were also sometimes amenable to cotton cultivation. African American cotton laborers constituted more than half of the population of these parishes. Nearby, longleaf pine hills and pine flatlands largely populated by yeomen whites yielded far less cotton when pulled into the staple crop economy in the 1870s and 1880s. Ouachita Parish, with its notable diversity in "soil type and economy," included a large African American cotton labor force, white planters, and a substantial number of whites who were small landholders. By the early twentieth century, lumber camps supplemented the cotton economy.[7]

Most mob killings in northwestern Louisiana broadcast messages asserting white superiority to an overwhelmingly black labor force, a message that the planter class believed could be conveyed more effectively through deadly collective violence than through the criminal justice system. A number of lynchings followed violent disputes over the terms of labor between white planters and African American tenants or domestic servants.[8] In February 1903, Tim McDade, a Bossier Parish planter, struck an African American farmer, Jim Brown, in an argument over tardiness in getting to work. Brown apparently retaliated by shooting McDade in the arm and an overseer in the leg. A posse captured Brown and hanged him from a tree next to the gin house at McDade Station.[9] These incidents resulted from black workers' contestation of the oppressive conditions and inequitable compensation of cotton labor. A familiar pattern emerged: African American males challenged the authority of white planters and overseers over specific grievances, and a physical confrontation ensued. Rural Red River Delta whites responded to black laborers' physical assault or, in extreme cases, murder of a planter or overseer with a collective killing that offered an explicit lesson to other blacks who might overtly question cotton labor arrangements.[10]

Planters like Tim McDade insisted on their right to physically punish black subordinates who flouted orders. Corporal punishment was an inheritance from slavery and an aspect of planters' expansive conception of their supervisorial role. Few things rankled postbellum African American cotton laborers more than the effort of a planter or overseer to correct through a flogging. Corporal punishment vividly embodied the failure of Reconstruction to dismantle the racially hierarchical nature of cotton labor arrangements and the personal authority of planters. African Americans' resistance to whipping highlighted black notions of autonomy and planters' projection of their power over laborers.[11] These dynamics were at work in October 1896, when an African American farmer in Bossier Parish, Lewis Hamilton, quarrelled with an overseer, who responded by flogging him. Hamilton supposedly retaliated by setting a cotton house on fire. Taking him from law officers, lynchers hanged Hamilton on a road leading to Shreveport. Bossier whites had once again expunged a threat to the cotton labor system with a collective killing.[12]

The relations between black domestic servants and their white employers also drew upon understandings of white privilege that severely undercut the autonomy of African American women who worked in white homes. Black domestics found ways to level conditions by appropriating household items.[13] More rarely, African American servants might find other ways to retaliate against unjust treatment. On July 25, 1903, in a rural area near Shreveport, a small mob lynched Jennie Steers, an African American domestic servant accused of fatally poisoning Lizzie Dolan, the daughter of a Bossier Parish planter. Soon after a posse had captured Steers, a crowd of whites demanded that she confess to the crime. Steers defiantly refused, and the mob soon hanged her from a limb.[14] Eleven years earlier, a private mob in Richland Parish killed Ella, a teenage black domestic who had allegedly poisoned the family that employed her.[15] Black women rarely fell victim to mobs, but in exceptional instances the friction of the domestic service arrangement could lead to the massive retaliation of a lynching.

Postbellum economic relations in northern Louisiana informed episodes of mob violence in other ways. Profoundly inequitable land distribution and an underdeveloped banking and credit system meant that African American and white farmers were often bound to a plantation-merchant system that severely undermined their wages and purchasing power.[16] Widespread poverty and the dearness of consumer goods may have enhanced the attractiveness of property crime for blacks and lower-class whites. The racial and class authority wielded by large landholders and merchants exaggerated the socially transgressive nature of larceny and robbery and enhanced the penalties exacted of perpetrators.

Ten mob murders in northern Louisiana parishes resulted primarily from a property violation; twenty-eight more victims died after being accused of a property crime such as robbery in addition to a more serious charge such as murder.[17] In November 1894, an unnamed African American and a man of Mexican extraction, Charlie Williams, reportedly killed and robbed a merchant, Thomas A. Keys, in his store in Rapides Parish. A mob attacked the jail that held the accused, hanged one of the alleged assailants, and shot the other.[18] Itinerant peddlers, typically German Jewish or French immigrants, were a common feature of rural Louisiana's transitional capitalist landscape. In January 1892 Eli Foster and Horace Dishroon reputedly robbed and murdered a German peddler, Mike Brinkin. A crowd of four hundred broke into the Richland Parish jail, pulled the two African Americans from their cells, and hanged them in the courthouse yard.[19] Both of these collective murders sought to brutally define the sanctity of white property holding amidst the degradation and desperation of a stagnant socioeconomic order.

The response of whites to articulations of black racial consciousness was another significant theme that permeated Cotton Belt Louisiana's encounter with mob violence. The discussion above has already noted the importance of the African American contestation of white authority in many disputes that led to lynchings. In some instances, though, African Americans explicitly challenged the narrowing of black rights and the protocol of racial interaction that began in the early 1890s and continued into the early twentieth century. Between 1890 and 1910, Louisiana state and municipal governments stripped African Americans of their voting rights and revived antimiscegenation laws, backed with harsh penalties. Louisiana lawmakers also ended the traditional legal distinction between light-skinned black Creoles and the darker-complected descendants of English-speaking slaves and imposed racial segregation in numerous public conveyances, including streetcars and trains.[20] African Americans, led by Creoles of Color in New Orleans, fought the onset of Jim Crow and disfranchisement through political lobbying, federal lawsuits, and opinions voiced in the *Crusader,* a newspaper published in New Orleans.[21] Enjoying less political clout and enmeshed in a less fluid set of social relations than African Americans in southern Louisiana, black northern Louisianans found less formal means to subvert Jim Crow policies and the inordinate power wielded by rural elites.

African American defiance of resurgent white supremacist arrangements catalyzed a series of lynchings in the late nineteenth and early twentieth centuries.[22] Two such episodes occurred in Bossier Parish. In June 1901 a mob of two hundred whites hanged Frank Smith and F. D. McLand, alleged accessories to the murder of a white man, John Gray Foster. Bossier Parish whites believed that Smith was the leader of the Church of God, a covert religious organization of African Americans that orchestrated retaliation against white enemies. A newspaper correspondent asserted that several whites in the district had recently been killed and that blacks in the countryside had assisted the escape of African American assailants. The reporter argued that the double mob killing was a "NECESSARY PRECAUTION to preserve the lives of white men in this locality." Reading between the lines of paranoid white hyperbole, we can discern a cooperative apparatus among blacks in northwestern Louisiana that resisted the encroachments of planter-class whites and aided African Americans fleeing from law enforcement agencies.[23] In October 1903, an African American, George Kennedy, fought with a train conductor who on several occasions had refused him entry into the white coach. After Kennedy was found the next day waiting with a pistol near the tracks of the Red River Valley Road, a posse of a hundred captured and hanged him.

Kennedy apparently wanted vengeance for one of the myriad injustices inflicted upon northern Louisiana blacks by Jim Crow and died at the hands of a mob for this affront to the racial order.[24]

The Mississippi Delta and Upcountry

Patterns of extralegal racial violence elsewhere in northern Louisiana differed markedly from those in the lynching-prone Red River Delta and Ouachita River Valley. Racial composition and economic orientation explain much of the variation. African Americans predominated by large proportions in the populations of the Mississippi Delta parishes,[25] where forty-four persons died at the hands of mobs. Whites made up the majority of the residents in the north central and western upcountry areas,[26] where lynchers took sixty-one lives. The rich lands along the Mississippi River yielded the most cotton in northern Louisiana through a racial labor system that only rarely deployed collective violence against African Americans. Vastly outnumbered planters instead sought to achieve racial control through formal legal institutions, particularly the death penalty. The poor soil of the extensive central and western upcountry produced the least cotton in northern Louisiana but considerable class and racial friction among impoverished white and black farmers drawn into the postbellum cotton economy. Upcountry whites who were skeptical of law employed lynching to express their class frustrations and racial fears.[27]

In the relatively unfertile upcountry, white and black farmers were pulled into a cotton monoculture and fought over scarce resources. White yeomen strove to assert their racial superiority without the prerogatives of economic power that planters in Cotton Belt areas possessed. The contest between lower-class blacks and whites took one of its most vivid forms at grist mills, where upcountry African Americans and whites met on nearly equal terms as they delivered grain to be ground into meal. Whites lynched blacks after arguments erupted at grist mills in Lincoln Parish in 1898 and Claiborne Parish in 1911.[28] Whitecappers killed five more African Americans in upcountry areas. In June 1894 in Bienville Parish, for instance, a group of white men kidnapped Mark Jacobs, "an honorable, industrious colored farmer" from his farm field. The whites took Jacobs into the woods, blindfolded him, and inflicted a severe beating that killed him. Public opinion condemned the lynching. Officials arrested six men, and a sheriff's posse pursued additional persons believed to be responsible.[29]

The overwhelming nature of black majorities strongly influenced the contours of racial interaction in Mississippi River Delta parishes. In 1900,

African Americans outnumbered whites by nearly a nine-to-one ratio in the Delta.[30] White planters eliminated African American political autonomy in the late 1870s through mass intimidation and murder and reclaimed extensive powers over black sharecroppers and tenants.[31] After ensuring their domination of Delta society and politics by the early 1880s, the planter class resorted to vigilantism only in circumstances that especially challenged white supremacy. More frequent episodes of mob violence could have threatened the morale of black workers or even the possibility of controlling an enormous African American workforce.[32]

Instead, the planter elite that ran the Mississippi Delta's criminal justice system employed abundant legal executions to punish African American offenders.[33] From 1878 through 1920, more legal executions occurred in the Mississippi Delta than in any other northern Louisiana subregion.[34] Strikingly, Delta parishes that experienced few lynchings possessed overactive gallows. In the most notable example, lynchers murdered one person (a white man) in Tensas Parish; the executioner claimed twelve persons between 1880 and 1920, at least seven of them blacks.[35] The gallows in the Delta, as elsewhere in Louisiana, were a considerable popular spectacle. Officials sought, through this captive audience, to impress upon African Americans the ramifications of serious crimes. Joe Walker, an African American, murdered another African American, Major Gray, in October 1879. Convicted by a black jury on evidence provided by African American witnesses, Walker made a final statement and died on the gallows before a "well-behaved" crowd of more than three thousand in Lake Providence.[36]

Several distinctive trends can be discerned in the rare lynchings that occurred in the Mississippi Delta. Mobs acted after an allegation of homicide more often than any other allegation (55 percent of victims), and large mobs performed a higher percentage of the collective killings (nearly 40 percent) than they did elsewhere in northern Louisiana. Delta whites tended to utilize mob violence to seek to frighten the African American population after blacks had murdered white planters or merchants. Lynchings of multiple victims signaled the vastly outnumbered whites' desire to send a harrowing message about the consequences of interracial homicide. In October 1909, Joe Gilford and Alexander Hill allegedly stole hogs from M. G. Brock, a white farmer, and then stabbed him to death when he said he would arrest them. A mob of a hundred seized the two African Americans from the West Carroll Parish jail and hanged them. The lynching reportedly "terrorized" the parish's black population.[37]

The Mississippi River Delta's most extreme instance of mob violence occurred in April 1894 in Madison Parish, and it also embodied the tendencies toward allegations of homicide and mass mobs. A black laborer, Josh Hopkins, assaulted a white supervisor in an argument over the treatment of mules. When a posse arrived to arrest him, a group of African American men reportedly told them that they "did not propose to be controlled by any white man, etc." The blacks shot into the posse, killing a white plantation manager named Boyce. Whites, believing that a "negro mafia" that had sworn defiance of white authority was responsible, descended on the Madison Parish seat of Tallulah. A mob of seventy-five attacked the jail and killed three black prisoners, Samuel Slaughter, Thomas Claxton, and David Hawkins, suspected as leaders in the African Americans' "protective association." Meanwhile, posses scoured the Delta swampland, looking for more blacks implicated in the killing of Boyce. A band of whites captured four African Americans, Shell Claxton, Tony McCoy, Pomp Claxton, and Scott Harvey, and then a mob of two hundred seized them from deputies and hanged them at the site of the murder.[38] A newspaper correspondent attempted to explain the lynching of the seven African Americans by citing the possibility of organized resistance among blacks. This was a horrifying prospect for planter whites, who ruled the Mississippi Delta despite their slim numbers.[39]

Anti-Sicilian nativism, expressed in a racialist idiom that posited that Sicilians were physiologically and culturally inferior to southern whites and prone to organized criminality, infected the Delta as well as the southern parishes of Louisiana. Nativism inspired lynchers in four parishes between 1891 and 1907; twenty-one Sicilians were killed. In the late nineteenth century, Sicilians migrated to New Orleans, rural southern parishes, and the rural Delta to work in unskilled labor and as entrepreneurs. Several of the disputes leading to lynchings stemmed from the economic competition between Italian plantation laborers and merchants and white Creole and Anglo-American laborers and merchants.[40] In July 1899 in Madison Parish, two Sicilians, Charles and Joe Difatta, quarrelled with a doctor over a goat, exchanging gunfire and gunshot wounds. In three separate attacks, a mob of 175 whites captured and hanged Charles, Joe, and Frank Difatta and two more Sicilians, Joseph Cereno and Sy Deferroch. Economic rivalries played a role in the quintuple lynching, as whites and Sicilians had exchanged accusations over the Sicilians' operation of a store. The Italian government issued a protest over the affair and the slipshod investigation that followed, and the Italian Consul in New Orleans cancelled an investigative trip to Tallulah because he feared that his life would be threatened.[41]

The Sugarland

The Sugarland, a large swath of southern Louisiana distinguished by its ethnic and racial complexity, comprised twelve parishes in the south central portion of the state. In the late nineteenth century a largely new sugar-planter class composed of elite Creole, Anglo-American, and northern elements generally sought to control a large African American labor force through institutions of law rather than lynching. A complementary mercantile class of white Creoles and Anglo-Americans greased the wheels of the sugar plantation economy. Lower-class Cajuns filled the lowest rung in the Sugarland's native white social order. The racial and ethnic mix of the Sugarland was further complicated by descendants of French-speaking "gens de couleur libre" (free persons of color) who maintained increasingly precarious communities of property holders. By the early twentieth century, Creoles of Color lost much of their former status as an intermediate, propertied caste. Gens de couleur libre melded into a larger population of descendants of French-speaking slaves, black Creoles, who labored on sugar plantations with the descendants of English-speaking blacks.[42]

Racial repression and intimidation underlay southern Louisiana's sugar labor system, which differed substantially from the cotton regime prevalent in northern parishes. Many postbellum sugar plantations utilized a gang labor arrangement that paid wages. The gang wage system was less prone to erupt into the individual confrontations between white employers and African American subordinates over the terms and compensation of labor that characterized sharecropping in northwestern Louisiana. Experienced sugar laborers also possessed the lucrative skill that enabled them to properly harvest the sucrose-rich bottom inch of cane, and they were thus more difficult to replace than cotton workers.[43] However, the centralized plantation system of gang labor in the sugar parishes aided "labor riots," periodic large-scale work stoppages and demonstrations demanding higher wages. Sugar planters suppressed wage strikes in St. John, St. Charles, and neighboring parishes in the early 1880s with the assistance of militia dispatched by the governor.[44] By comparison, the decentralized nature of cotton plantations elsewhere in the state discouraged unified protests. Although lynching did not constitute a regular aspect of sugar planters' efforts to keep their workforce in line, they might resort to lethal vigilantism in desperate circumstances. In 1887, after the Knights of Labor achieved substantial success in organizing African American sugar workers, planters from

St. Mary and neighboring parishes orchestrated the murder of at least thirty African Americans.[45]

The political diversity of the Sugarland also varied significantly from the political monoculture of northern Louisiana. The Republican party's tariff position attracted white sugar planters who sought to keep sugar from foreign sources out of the domestic market.[46] As a result, white and black Republicans received significant proportions of the vote and held local political positions into the late nineteenth century. Republican "fusion" tickets with independent Democratic and Populist candidates for statewide offices could sometimes compete with the regular Democratic slate in the sugar parishes. From the Reconstruction period through the mid 1880s, Democrats employed terrorist tactics in some parts of the Sugarland to intimidate African Americans and retake power.[47] Yet the Democrats failed to consolidate one-party dominance and white supremacy in electoral politics. Until 1900, African American males in the sugar parishes retained many of the perquisites of citizenship they had gained in Reconstruction. These included largely unencumbered voting rights, office holding, and jury duty.[48] By 1900, however, a new voter-registration law and state constitution effectively disfranchised blacks statewide.[49]

Lynchers murdered forty-six persons in the Sugarland between 1878 and 1930, far fewer than in the northwestern Cotton Belt. Respective racial compositions do not account for the difference, since African Americans comprised between 50 to 80 percent of persons in most Sugarland parishes and in most northwestern ones in the postbellum era.[50] Exploitative sugar labor arrangements that nonetheless preserved a greater degree of black solidarity against the authority of the white planter class may account for some of the disparity in extralegal violence. A more flexible political system and the survival of African American participation in governmental institutions also may have mitigated naked displays of white power. Crucially, the formal legal system enjoyed greater prestige in southern parishes and earlier had become a well-honed instrument for racial control.[51]

The complicated ethnic and cultural matrix of the southern parishes contrasted markedly with that in northern Louisiana, where the descendants of Anglo-American white southerners and English-speaking slaves contested in the cotton economy. The Sugarland's reconstituted planter class included northerners and white Creoles relatively unschooled in the traditions of Anglo-American slavery and its concomitant race relations. With the special intermediate social status granted to free blacks of color, southern Louisiana's antebellum racial caste system had involved a greater degree of elasticity than elsewhere in the Deep South.[52] While lynching occurred relatively infrequently in the Sugarland, its incidence nonetheless reflected the social, cultural, and legal relations of the sugar economy. Sporadic lynchings punctuated white sugar planters' and merchants' efforts to subdue a black labor force and ensure white supremacy in the Sugarland's social order in the two decades that followed Reconstruction.

Sugar labor arrangements were apparently less prone than those in the Cotton Belt to erupt into violent disputes and eventually into a lynching. Despite this, nearly a fourth of mob killings in the sugar parishes can be traced to tensions between white sugar planters or overseers and the African American laborers they employed. For example, in April 1878 lynchers in a parish outside of New Orleans murdered "a man . . . for attempting to set fire to a sugar house."[53] In October 1892, a posse of whites shot and killed Thomas Courtney, an African American who had allegedly shot and wounded Mr. Moreau, an overseer on the Hundred Mile plantation in Iberville Parish.[54] In lynchings such as these, Sugarland whites responded to challenges to the sugar labor system and, beyond punishing individual African Americans who violated the plantation racial order, sought to cow the collective black labor force into compliance. This aim backfired in West Baton Rouge Parish in 1900, as black laborers would not go back to work on sugar plantations near the area where whites lynched Ned Cobb on June 12.[55] The sugar plantation-merchant system, with its low wages and exploitative prices, also generated animosities. Five Sugarland mob killings involved allegations that African Americans had murdered white clerks while in the act of robbing general stores.[56]

Lynch mobs in the sugar parishes cited homicide far more often than they did an accusation of rape (48 percent to 22 percent of lynching victims). The alleged murder of a white man by a black man sometimes signaled for Sugarland whites a temporary crisis in the maintenance of racial boundaries. The murder of a sugar planter represented perhaps the most direct assault on the sugar labor system. Accordingly, the killing of a planter, James Norman, in West Baton Rouge Parish motivated a small masked mob to hang Norm Cadore in December 1912 in view of the state capitol across the Mississippi River.[57] Challenges to white authority could take other forms as well. In the same parish in October 1900, a mob of around seventy-five hanged Melby Dotson near the railroad junction where he had supposedly shot and killed a white train conductor, Will Jordan.[58]

The massive reprisal of southern Louisiana whites against an African American who flouted the prerogatives of white power can be seen most vividly in a posse's slaying of John Thomas in January 1903. Thomas worked on sugar plantations and as a railroad laborer in the area surrounding Luling, a town populated by freedpeople during Reconstruction. White officials targeted Thomas for alleged involvement in gambling and theft operations. After officials seized guns from his home, Thomas swore out an affidavit at the parish courthouse charging them with robbery. When law officers tried to arrest him on an assault charge, Thomas killed Sheriff Lewis Oury in a gunfight. After a prolonged chase and fight, members of a posse managed to shoot Thomas, who had taken refuge in a drainage ditch. The crowd then dragged his corpse back to his house and, after making a funeral pyre of his possessions, burned it. In his homicidal dispute with Sheriff Oury, Thomas recapitulated the contestation of white authority by African Americans in St. Charles Parish after the Civil War. Lewis Oury served as the parish's public recorder during the latter years of Reconstruction and became the first Democratic sheriff in the "Redeemed" parish in 1884. Thomas's refusal to submit to white officials, their characterization of him as a "bad negro," and the burning of his body and possessions drew significance from the white officials' long struggle with the autonomous black settlement of Luling.[59]

Racial and sexual phobias motivated whites in southern Louisiana, but the fear of African American rapists catalyzed few episodes of collective violence. Of the ten Sugarland mobs that cited a charge of rape, several were small mobs that failed to elicit the participation or overt support of large numbers of local whites. For instance, in 1878 a small mob of relatives and acquaintances of the white sheriff of St. Mary Parish hanged a black man named Moustand from a belfry and then threw his body into the Bayou Teche in Franklin. These lynchers responded to an allegation that Moustand had made sexual advances to a female member of the sheriff's family.[60] Accusations of rape on rare occasions did provoke substantial numbers of whites to join in a lynching. In November 1888 in Ascension Parish, an African American man allegedly raped a white girl "in the [sugar] cane." Several hours after the supposed assailant had been placed in jail, a mob reported at more than a hundred seized him and hanged him. The mob victim's corpse remained suspended outside the jail building until the next day.[61]

Some areas of southern Louisiana were plagued by intense political factionalism that occasionally spilled into mob violence. Rooted in unresolved contests over political and communal leadership from the Reconstruction era, these conflicts pitted conservative whites who wished to impose a strict racial order against moderate whites who were more flexible concerning the status of African Americans. Moderate Sugarland whites sometimes allied with Creoles of Color, who composed a black political and social elite in several locales. This problem was perhaps most acute in Iberia Parish. White Democrats reclaimed political power in the parish in 1884 by killing more than twenty African Americans and arresting prominent white Republicans.[62] Politically motivated resentments and divisions persisted, however. In January 1889, a posse shot Samuel Wakefield, an African American accused of shooting his white supervisor at a manufacturing firm in New Iberia. Wakefield's relatives were black Republicans who had held political offices. Not content with the lynching's assertion of white dominance in the parish, "Regulators" attacked business establishments owned by black Creoles, hanged another African American accused of theft, and flogged several other blacks in the days that followed.[63]

The division in white opinion in the Sugarland over lynching underlines why extralegal violence remained a relatively minor component in the region's approach to crime and punishment. The mixture of Creoles, northerners, and Anglo-Americans in the Sugarland's ruling class and the influence of continental European legal traditions may have encouraged a greater emphasis on and respect for formal law in this region.[64] Politically and ethnically diverse southern Louisiana whites did not agree that mob violence was an appropriate means for enforcing a racially hierarchical society. Instead, many Sugarland whites entrusted the criminal justice system with that critical responsibility. Expressions of frustration with legal mechanisms were rare in Sugarland lynchings.[65] Criminal courts in southern Louisiana enjoyed greater jurisdiction over serious offenses against persons and property, prosecuted more stringently, and received greater popular respect than in northern Louisiana. The criminal justice system's role in the social control of crime was more comprehensive in the Sugarland than in north central and northwestern parishes, where informal white authority often coopted the formal justice system in severely punishing alleged African American offenders. Criminal courts in sugar parishes frequently imposed the death penalty in the late nineteenth century against African Americans convicted of serious crimes, whereas northwestern and north central cotton parishes did so rarely.[66]

The Sugarland's formal legal system sought, through the harsh punishment of black crime, to amplify the subordinate position of African Americans in the region's intricate social order. Despite the ethnic and racial complexity of the sugar parishes, the color line was the clearest demarcation of social status in the region, as black Creoles, Creoles of

Color, and blacks of English-speaking ancestry who met their end on the gallows could attest. The overwhelming majority of persons legally hanged in the Sugarland were African American (88 percent).[67]

An analysis of the postbellum rite of execution in the Sugarland indicates its significance as a means for parish officials to convey the consequences of black deviancy and the prerogatives of white power. In the late nineteenth century, large crowds composed predominately of African Americans gathered to view legal hangings in sugar parishes. Crowds reported at more than two thousand assembled in Iberville Parish in 1879, West Baton Rouge and St. James Parishes in 1880, and Ascension Parish in 1882.[68] After a dramatic procession of the prisoner and officials to the gallows, the condemned often made a long, personal, and occasionally eloquent statement, repenting for their crime and wayward life or professing innocence. Following final prayers offered by a priest or minister, the hangman "adjusted the noose and cowl, tied the feet of the victim, and cut with one blow of his hatchet the rope supporting the trap."[69] It is difficult to interpret the meaning of the rite of execution for black witnesses. Drawn perhaps by curiosity and a sense of racial solidarity or perhaps compelled to attend by whites, African Americans could not fail to miss the intent of white authorities to impress a message of racial control upon them. Battalions of armed guards, sometimes numbering more than fifty, ensured "order" at legal executions. White officials may have feared that a restive black crowd might interrupt the performance of "justice." The gallows militia also signified the superior firepower that whites enjoyed in parishes with large black majorities.

Sugarland executions remained highly public events even after the state legislature reformed the death penalty statute in 1884 by stipulating that executions must be performed in an enclosed area with only fifteen witnesses. Defying the statute, in 1896 Iberia Parish officials hanged William Patterson, an African American convicted of murdering a black woman, "in full sight of some 2,000 people, negro men and women from all parts of the parish thronging the courthouse yard."[70] The emphasis that white southern Louisianans placed on the communal supervision and racial symbolism of retributive justice—the goals of rough justice, which were usually achieved in the southern parishes without lynching—persisted in practice despite the reform of the state's death penalty law.

New Orleans's Hinterland

The growth of New Orleans in the late nineteenth century sparked in-migration to areas on its periphery. This altered older economic relations and destabilized social arrangements by mixing blacks and whites unfamiliar with customary patterns of race relations. In this expanding urban hinterland, whites rejected formal legal institutions in favor of collective killing that would dramatically assert white superiority. In Jefferson Parish, an urbanizing Bayou backwater lying just beyond New Orleans, lynching violence that enforced racial prerogatives became a characteristic feature of the last years of the nineteenth century. The eastern Florida Parishes, a piney-woods subregion north of New Orleans that experienced rapid industrialization and in-migration after Reconstruction, also witnessed elevated rates of lynching comparable to those in Jefferson Parish and northern Louisiana. In the eastern Florida Parishes, a period of drastic socioeconomic transformation catalyzed political factionalism that fractured legal authority. In this vacuum, plainfolk whites unfamiliar with Cotton and Sugar Belt systems of racial control exercised their wrath on African Americans.

In September 1896, a white woman living on a Mississippi River houseboat characterized race relations on the outskirts of New Orleans in a letter to a Massachusetts relative: "Jefferson Parish of which Gretna is the county seat seems to have a great antipathy to the nigger in general and are daily shooting and lynching them: without apparent cause."[71] This evaluation of racial attitudes and violence in the mixed suburban/ plantation district adjoining the Crescent City was not hyperbolic. A small group of whites styling themselves as "Regulators" killed Jack Tillman, a black lumber laborer accused of arguing with white men, at Harvey's Canal in March 1892.[72] Mobs killed eleven more persons, nine of them African Americans, in the parish by the end of 1897.

The example of Jefferson Parish suggests how mob murder could become endemic in a particular locale. The parish adjoins New Orleans at the city's western boundary north of the Mississippi River but also lies below it south of the river, stretching to the Gulf of Mexico. Like much of the Bayou in the late nineteenth century, Jefferson entailed extensive wetlands that supported sugar plantations and extractive enterprises such as moss gathering.[73] The lynchings in the 1890s all occurred in the immediate environs of New Orleans, the majority directly across the river: in the parish seat of Gretna, along the series of canals that radiated from the river, or on a riverside plantation facing the city's outlying neighborhoods. Only three mobs cited serious crimes such as rape or homicide. Six groups of lynchers in the parish killed African Americans for minor offenses such as being a "dangerous character," miscegenation, the physical assault of a boy, and the violation of a quarantine.[74] Whites living along the Mississippi River outside of New Orleans came to accept and expect collective killings whenever and however a rigidly construed racial order was challenged. Only small proportions of the white population participated in the violence, and the interests of elite planters, property owners, and officials were most often served. Political disputes between black community leaders and white Democrats strongly influenced several of the collective killings.

Perhaps the most egregious episode of the 1890s cycle of violence in Jefferson Parish occurred in September 1893. Roselius Julian, an African American moss gatherer and barber, murdered a planter and magistrate, Victor Estopinal, in Estopinal's plantation courtroom "above" Carrollton. Julian, who had been arrested on a wife-beating allegation, lived and worked on Estopinal's plantation. The planter-magistrate had "figured prominently in wresting the parish from Republican rule." Whites threatened Julian after he backed an African American candidate for the judgeship, which Estopinal won. But the planter interceded for Julian and became the prominent black barber's patron. After the murder of Estopinal, posses scoured nearby swamps for Julian, but they could not find him. Seeking to avenge the judge's death, a mob that included elite whites hanged three of Julian's brothers and severely beat his mother and several of his relatives. New Orleans newspapers denounced the lynching, since there was little evidence for the brothers' guilt. Even the race-baiting *Daily States*, edited by "Major" Henry J. Hearsey, who satisfied a rural white readership in the Red River Delta with frequent white supremacist editorials that countenanced lynching, found it wrong that Julian's brothers were lynched for merely being his brothers.[75]

The Jefferson lynching spree took place in dialogue with an emergent understanding of legal order and race relations in the Crescent City. Denouncing rampant "lawlessness" and the alleged malfeasance of the criminal justice system, particularly the jury system, New Orleans's American entrepreneurial elite had endorsed and participated in the March 1891 lynching of eleven Sicilians acquitted in the alleged mafiosi-linked murder of the police chief, David Hennessy.[76] Earlier, quasi-legal agencies staffed by white elites and styling themselves as "vigilante committees" had emerged several times in the 1880s, seeking to assist purportedly incompetent law enforcement and criminal courts in fighting crime in the city.[77] But the nearby Jefferson lynchings provoked dismay from city opinion-makers. Sympathizing with the Jefferson white populace's anxiety about "lawlessness," New Orleans editors decried the racial lynching syndrome as an embarrassing and unreliable anachronism. A police force that employed brutally excessive violence against African Americans and municipal laws codifying racial segregation may have seemed more dependable devices for racial regulation than lynching.[78] However, race riots that targeted the entire "colored" population in the battle for political control in Reconstruction in 1866 and following the mass shooting of whites by an African American, Robert Charles, who lashed out lethally against racial humiliation, in 1900 became the characteristic form of collective violence in New Orleans and displayed the limits of the Crescent City's orderly and cosmopolitan urbanity.[79]

North of New Orleans and Lake Ponchartrain, the Florida Parishes filled out the complex sociocultural geography of southern Louisiana.[80] Beginning with Reconstruction, the eastern Florida Parishes of Livingston, St. Helena, Washington, St. Tammany, and Tangipahoa experienced rapid economic transformation and persistent social conflict. Piney-woods yeoman farmers resisted the reimposition of planter-class political control. Northern and native speculators fought over burgeoning railroad, timber, truck-farming, and manufacturing interests. Midwestern and Sicilian immigrants also flooded into the region.[81] In the late nineteenth century, African Americans composed one-fourth of the residents of the eastern Florida Parishes. Racial tensions added yet another volatile element to the turmoil resulting from the contestation of ethnic, cultural, political, and commercial differences.[82] Piney-woods folkways that emphasized personal honor and independence encouraged extralegal solutions, such as feuding and whitecapping, to disputes between individuals and within communities. Severe political factionalism undermined the administration of criminal justice by parish officeholders. All of these factors conspired, in the words of an author of a recent study of the Florida Parishes, to produce "some of the highest rural murder rates in the nation."[83]

The eastern Florida parishes suffered the highest rate of lynching in southern Louisiana. Lynchers murdered forty-five persons, at least forty-one of them black, from 1879 through 1919. Private mobs committed more than a third of the collective killings, and mobs cited homicide charges in 44 percent of the cases.[84]

Tangipahoa Parish was the site of especially pronounced in-migration of northerners and Sicilians, rapid commercial and industrial development along the Illinois Central Railroad, and crippling political factionalism. "Bloody Tangipahoa" tallied twenty-two African American victims of mob violence, the most of any parish in southern Louisiana. Lynchings in the piney woods reflected the racial antipathies of the industrializing upcountry. Upcountry whites were unfamiliar with the systems of racial control long established in Louisiana's Sugar and Cotton Belts. Piney-woods whites responded fiercely to temporary crises in local race relations, such as an accusation that an African American had murdered a white person. A chaotic political situation meant that regional elites could not or would not intervene to prevent the worst excesses of racially motivated violence.[85]

Beyond their frequency, mob killings in Tangipahoa and other eastern piney-woods parishes often possessed an especially brutal quality. Plainfolk whites who were unfamiliar with blacks occasionally attempted to expel or symbolically annihilate, through ferocious acts of destruction, their African American competitors in a nascent industrial economy. In January 1897, a mob of two hundred whites attacked the Tangipahoa Parish jail in Amite and seized Gustave Williams, a black man accused of murdering his wife. The lynchers also seized John Johnson and Archie Joiner, African Americans who had allegedly killed five members of a white family. The crowd hanged Williams in front of a black church. The mobbers then traveled eight miles through a severe rainstorm to the rural homestead where Johnson and Joiner had supposedly murdered the Cotton family. A debate ensued over whether the two African Americans should be burned to death or shot and hanged. Some mob members constructed funeral pyres, but several in the crowd argued that hanging and shooting were more "civilized." The latter views prevailed and, after interrogations, protests of innocence, and opportunities for prayers, the lynchers hanged Johnson and Joiner and mutilated their bodies in a mass orgy of bullets.[86]

The collective killing undermined the credibility of the "Courthouse faction," led by Judge Robert Reid, who had obtained confessions from and sought to protect the lynched men. The mob execution highlighted the protracted feud between the Courthouse faction, businessmen who employed African American labor and supported the Democratic party, and "Branch men," who illegally distributed whiskey through "blind tigers," wished to exclude blacks, and backed the Populist-Republican ticket. From 1896 through 1899, Branch men mounted a series of assassinations of Courthouse partisans and, in whitecapping campaigns, systematically terrorized employers of black labor and African American workers. Governor Murphy J. Foster failed to intervene forcefully to stop the violence, which paralyzed the criminal justice system in Tangipahoa Parish.[87]

In tandem with the prevalence of extralegal violence, the eastern Florida Parishes experienced a style of criminal justice exceptional in Louisiana. Deep-seated economic, political, and social divisions undercut law enforcement and the courts. Despite the ubiquity of homicide, legal executions were rare. Parish authorities hanged approximately seven men in the five piney-woods parishes between 1878 and 1910, easily the lowest rate of gallows activity in the state. A lack of consensus among a diverse white population precluded parish officials from utilizing a mechanism often used to enforce the social and racial control of crime in the Sugarland and in the Mississippi Delta Parishes.[88]

The West and Midwest

The boundaries of Dixie did not confine or define racial lynching, even if the social and legal legacies of slavery made it much more prevalent there. Beyond the South, whites similarly used collective violence to assert racial control in a more rapid and harsh way than formal legal institutions could. African Americans became the victims of lynching violence everywhere in the country, but members of other racially marginalized groups, such as Mexican Americans, Native Americans, and Chinese, also felt the lethal force resulting from postbellum whites' insistence upon racial hierarchy and suspicion of the efficacy of law.

Mexican and Native Americans, peoples who had long lived in the lands that became the American West, were the victims of racially motivated lynch mobs in the nineteenth century. Widespread collective violence against Mexicans assisted the cultural and social conquest of southwestern borderlands by the Americans in the 1840s and 1850s. The historians William D. Carrigan and Clive Webb observe that the widespread lynching of Mexicans in Texas and California predated the postbellum waves of lynchings of African Americans in the South. Lynchings of Mexican Americans also accompanied conflict over the borderlands in the 1870s and 1910s. Arraying an impressive amount of evidence, Carrigan and Webb estimate that 571 persons of Mexican descent were lynched in the United States, most of them in the Southwest, between 1848 and 1928. Allegations of property crime ("banditry") and homicide loomed large, and sexual allegations were less prominent in the accusations that whites made against Mexican lynching victims compared to those made against African American lynching victims in the South. Carrigan and Webb argue that diplomatic pressure from Mexico helped eventually to stem the lynching of Mexicans.[89]

From 1875 through 1947, white mobs killed at least fifteen Mexican Americans in California, with two-thirds of those lynchings occurring before 1880. A third of the Mexicans were accused of horse theft. In Bakersfield on December 22, 1877, for example, one hundred men overpowered the jailer and undersheriff and seized and hanged Anthony Maron, Francisco Ensinas, Miguel Elias, Fermin Eldeo, and Bessena Ruiz. Mexican Americans in the locality of Bakersfield protested that the five alleged "bandits" had been lynched because of anti-Mexican prejudice, an assertion that a Bakersfield editor belittled: "'Some of the most indifferent of the Mexican population are endeavoring to convey the impression that the act was aimed at them as a class. They are mistaken. It would have made no difference had the highwaymen been Americans. . . . There is no room for the assumption that they aimed at a class. They found the men guilty, and there [*sic*] condemnation was for crimes, and not for nationality.'"[90]

Whites killed two-thirds of the Mexican American lynching victims in California after allegations that they had committed homicide. On April 7, 1893, for instance, a mob of between one hundred and 750 seized Jesus Fuen from the jail at San Bernardino and hanged him. Fuen, a ranch hand, had fatally stabbed his mistress, Francisca Flores, and an elderly white man, William Goldkoffer.[91] The *Los Angeles Times* reported that hundreds of men, women, and children avidly viewed the corpse of "the dead greaser";[92] some participants in the "hanging bee" served as jurors in the coroner's inquest that followed. A San Bernardino editor argued that lynch law resulted from the people's belief that "the murderer must hang" and that Fresno, where no hangings of murderers had occurred in recent years, might learn from San Bernardino's "cheap and effective remedy."[93] The preference that white Californians had for rough justice for Mexican Americans was also evident in the same county in July 1878, when an armed mob seized Rufugio Boca from his preliminary examination in Riverside and hanged him from a tree outside the courthouse. Boca was accused of murdering William Palmerston and injuring Palmerston's wife after the white couple had denied his requests for food.[94]

By the late nineteenth century, Indian fighting by state-sponsored militia and the U.S. army had subdued Native Americans and confined them to reservations theoretically separated from a hostile white populace. Yet American Indians periodically died at the hands of postbellum white lynchers.[95] Indian hating sometimes conspired lethally with Native Americans' awkward legal status as participants in sovereign aboriginal legal cultures, as wards of the federal government, and as alleged criminals confronting white Americans' profound suspicion of formal legal process. For instance, "prominent whites" removed a fifteen-year-old Colville Indian, Steven, from the jail at Conconully in north central Washington in January 1891 and hanged him for his alleged role in the murder of a "well-known freighter," Samuel Smith Cole. Tensions in Indian-white relations and jurisdictional problems in local criminal justice administration over Indian and white populations influenced the mob killing of Steven.[96]

The popular association of Native American male and white female sexuality translated into collective murder in southwestern Iowa in June 1889, when white farmers from the rural district surrounding Bedford hanged "an Indian tramp named Olaf."[97] The mob's Native American victim was charged with raping Mrs. Frank Glassman, "the wife of a well to do farmer."[98] "Olaf" supposedly approached the Glassman farmstead when Mrs. Glassman was home alone. She reportedly screamed, and "Olaf" pursued her as she ran across a cornfield; she claimed that he raped her. Frank Glassman arrived and tried to shoot "Olaf," who was taken to Bedford by male neighbors. A mob of seventy-five men, mostly undisguised, broke into the jail with a sledgehammer, took "Olaf" out, and twice hanged him in the courthouse yard before a crowd estimated at five hundred.[99] The murder by a mass mob in Taylor County in 1889 stressed the significance of white midwesterners' sexualized perception of Native Americans. Although the federal government had banished most Indians from Iowa before statehood, a myriad of cultural sources identified indigenous men as racially inferior and a libidinous threat to white women.[100]

The lynchings of Mexicans and Native Americans in the postbellum era were the legacy of the racial ideologies formed during white Americans' conquest of the West. In contrast, the lynching of Chinese and African Americans in the postbellum West reflected the salience of white solidarity and the power of conceptions of racial order amid the fluid social landscape of what the historian Carlos Schwantes has termed the "wageworkers' frontier," that is, the camps and company towns associated with the railroad and extractive industries such as logging and mining.[101]

On July 9, 1901, at a lumber camp thirty-five miles east of Bakersfield, California, a Chinese cook at a boarding house, Yung Fook, slashed Mrs. G. C. Kenney across the face with a knife. Fook had apparently been angered by an order delivered by Mrs. Kenney, the wife of the sawmill's foreman; locals and the press claimed he was "insane" from opium. Learning of the assault, millhands, led by G. C. Kenney, rushed Fook as he slashed at several of them. One of the millhands rendered Fook unconscious with a blow to the head. Then the lumbermen secured a rope, placed it around his neck, took him to a nearby oak tree, and hanged him from it until he was dead. A coroner's jury, made up of "eight persons who are not lumber mill employees," questioned approximately sixteen mill workers about the affair, but they all claimed "to know absolutely nothing." The local and state press reported the details of the case but avoided editorial comment. Some of the loggers later said they regretted the mob killing, given that Mrs. Kenney's wounds were not serious and that Fook "was insane at the time of the commission of his violent acts." The

Chinese man's physical assault of a white woman catalyzed the mob killing by drawing on a deep reservoir of working-class white sinophobia and fear of miscegenation, a racial ideology that had emerged amid labor and political competition in California in the mid- to late nineteenth century.[102] The lynching of Yung Fook in Kern County in 1901 had been anticipated by the collective killing of two Chinese, both accused of murder, in California in the preceding fourteen years.[103]

Western lynchings were sometimes performed by groups of working-class white men suddenly aroused by news of a crime that seemed to offend wageworkers' sense of social order. Racial, ethnic, and gender ideologies had particular effect in transient settings where mobile, exploited workers often did not know each other well. Laborers such as miners, loggers, and railroad men relied instead on informal, hastily constructed reputations predicated upon personal friendship and on the reflexive comfort of racial and ethnic solidarities amid temporary social crisis. Working-class white men might respond with nearly spontaneous lethal violence to alleged violations of sexual and gender etiquette, especially those tinged with racial and ethnic overtones. Lynchings of this kind evoked little support from the broader citizenry and usually elicited condemnation or no comment from the petty entrepreneurial men who edited hinterland newspapers.

On December 9, 1918, Joel Woodson, an African American janitor at a Union Pacific railroad social club in Green River, Wyoming, sought to order breakfast from a white waitress. When she stated that they were out of the item he had ordered, he called her a "liar," and she threw several salt shakers at him. Edward Miller, a white switchman, grabbed Woodson and ejected him from the diner. Shortly afterward, Woodson returned with a gun and shot Miller dead. A Union Pacific police officer captured Woodson and took him to the county jail. Soon a mob of several hundred whites gathered, seized Woodson from the jail, dragged him to the railroad depot, and hanged him from a light pole. Woodson's heated encounter with the waitress, which violated white Wyomingites' notion of the deference required from African American men in their encounters with white women, had set off a confrontation with Miller, a reportedly "popular" switchman from Missouri. Mobbers knocked Woodson unconscious as they dragged him to the depot and hanged him, publicly displaying his corpse for four hours until the county coroner finally arrived from Rock Springs to cut it down. Green River whites then expelled the African American residents of the town, many of whom traveled to Ogden, Utah, without the chance to gather their possessions. The class and racial consciousness of white rail employees responding to the murder of a white co-worker played an integral role in the Green River mob killing.[104]

The collective murder of Joel Woodson in Green River in 1918 had been preceded by the mob killings of three African Americans in Wyoming, each accused of raping white women, in the previous fourteen years. Allegations that African American men had committed offenses against white women had special force in Wyoming's towns and cities. In September 1904, Joseph Martin, an African American imprisoned in Laramie, had allegedly attacked a white woman, Delia Krause, with a razor in the basement of the Albany County courthouse after she refused his advances. Martin was serving a jail sentence after a conviction for writing an "obscene letter" to another white woman, and he had allegedly written a "similar putrid" letter to Krause. A Laramie police judge declared Martin a "sexual degerate [*sic*] . . . [who] was dangerous to the community at large." Masked lynchers dragged Martin from the jail and hanged him from a nearby telegraph pole as a crowd of two to three hundred persons, including women and children, watched.[105]

Eight years later, the governor of Wyoming, Joseph Carey, forgot the Laramie lynching when he replied in a letter to the antilynching advocate Ida B. Wells-Barnett that a "negro had never been hanged or burned at the stake in Wyoming" prior to the mob killing of Frank Wigfall in Rawlins in 1912. Soon after his release from a fourteen-year sentence in the penitentiary for rape, Wigfall had allegedly assaulted Esther Higgins, an eighty-one-year-old white woman known for her charity work with penitentiary inmates. A deputy sheriff secretly transferred Wigfall from the Carbon County jail to the state penitentiary after a mob of around sixty persons gathered and threatened to attack the jail and lynch him. The next morning, penitentiary inmates out of their cells on work details locked a lone guard in a cell, took his keys, and hanged Wigfall from the cellhouse ceiling. Governor Carey expressed the views of many white residents of Rawlins when he argued in his letter to Wells-Barnett that the lynching was understandable because "[t]he Negro committed an awful outrage on an old woman who had really been his benefactress." The collective white demonization of the African American male sexual aggressor provoked and explained this unusual lynching by penitentiary inmates.[106]

As we have seen, working-class whites actually performed most of the early twentieth-century western racial violence.[107] Yet middle-class whites, enamored with a "progressive" impulse to cleanse the social disorder allegedly rampant in towns and cities, also contributed a great deal to a marked deterioration in race relations across the West that coincided with the turn of the century.[108] The Wyoming state legislature's enactment of an antimiscegenation law in 1913 represented the "de jure" effort of bourgeois whites to redraw the lines between the races.[109] The antimiscegenation law was merely the statutory pinnacle of white middle-class efforts to purify racially ambiguous areas of urban life. Virtually all of Wyoming's towns and cities had notorious areas where whites, Mexicans, and blacks mixed in saloons, bordellos, and drug dens. Crimes committed in these neighborhoods, especially ones allegedly perpetrated by African Americans, received hysterical newspaper coverage.[110]

Working-class and middle-class white Wyomingites became increasingly concerned in the early twentieth century with limiting African Americans' access to public amenities. By 1905, the majority of Wyoming's African American population was concentrated not in rural settlement but in towns and cities such as Cheyenne, Sheridan, Rock Springs, Green River, Casper, and Laramie. In these small African American communities, men predominated by a five-to-three ratio, and most blacks worked as porters, domestic servants, and in other kinds of unskilled labor. A white fear of the social mixing and the perceived latent sexuality of African American men and white women in urban spaces fueled the trend toward de facto Jim Crow practice in public accommodations. Black Wyomingites protested the infringement of their rights, revealing class divisions that were sublimated by a shared racial consciousness within the state's African American community.[111]

Wyoming's blacks articulated their grievance at the discriminatory treatment they received in attempting to eat in restaurants and rent rooms in hotels. Russel Taylor, a black Presbyterian minister and author, shared his experience in a letter to a Cheyenne newspaper after the 1918 Green River lynching. On the basis of his own experience, Taylor believed that the lynching victim, Joel Woodson, may have been justified in disbelieving the white waitress, who did not wish to serve an African American man, and that there may have been more to his encounter with the white switchman than was revealed in the newspapers. Taylor stated that he had been consistently denied admission to the finer restaurants and hotels in Cheyenne and other Wyoming towns. Proprietors instantly served white patrons, but he had to settle for places that were "of little credit to a minister." In a Chinese restaurant in Cheyenne, the staff served Taylor but also "boxed" him, that is, concealed him from white customers. Taylor pleaded with white Wyomingites "of conscience" to live up to Wyoming's motto as the "equal rights state."[112]

Russel Taylor sought a degree of social respectability in public accommodations that white Wyomingites denied him because of race. He re-

sponded by voicing a shared sense of African American community grievance. He distanced himself from Joel Woodson's "procedure" in Green
River but stressed that he understood the lynched black janitor's aggra-
vation. Similarly, the Reverend Nathaniel Hawthorne Jeltz, pastor of the
A.M.E. Church in Cheyenne, derided Wade Hamilton, who was hanged
and shot by a small mob in a mining suburb of Rock Springs, Wyoming,
in December 1917 for allegedly breaking into the homes of three wom-
en and attempting to assault them, as a "degraded negro—he must have
been a bad sort." But Jeltz also castigated the "race hate" motivating the
lynching of Hamilton, a "member of my race." The pastor argued that a
United States fighting for democracy abroad in World War I must ensure
that justice be served at home.[113]

Mobs of whites also pursued African Americans in the Midwest in
the early twentieth century. On October 30, 1900, law officers in Albia,
Iowa, arrested Edward Booker, an African American, and charged him
with raping Sarah Hovel, a white widow. Fearing that a gathering mob
would attempt to lynch Booker, Sheriff John Doner set out with the prisoner for Ottumwa. The sheriff eventually traveled forty miles to Fort
Madison, where he placed Booker in the state penitentiary for safekeeping. Nearly a month later, on November 24, a detail of the Iowa National Guard protected Booker as he was brought back to Albia for a preliminary hearing. The soldiers escorted the defendant to the courthouse as
a large crowd shouted, "Lynch the nigger brute!" and "String him up!"
Booker's attorney quickly obtained a change of venue to Wapello County, and rumors circulated that several thousand Albia miners would soon
visit Ottumwa and attempt to lynch him there. Although this never
happened, the near lynching of Edward Booker in Albia set a precedent.[114]
In the first decade of the twentieth century, twelve Iowa mobs sought to
kill fourteen African American men, but their efforts were thwarted by
poor planning, effective and determined law enforcement, and sheer
chance.[115] By contrast, in the midwestern states of Missouri, Illinois,
Ohio, Indiana, Minnesota, and Nebraska, as historians have recently
documented, whites succeeded in collectively murdering the African
Americans they pursued.[116]

Participating in general trends in the experience of African Americans in the postbellum Midwest, Iowa's small black population historically concentrated in counties along the Mississippi River and adjoining
the slave state of Missouri, and black migration to the southeastern portion of the state briefly spiraled upward with emancipation in the 1860s.
By the 1880s, African American settlement focused on cities such as
Keokuk, Ottumwa, Des Moines, Council Bluffs, and Sioux City, where

the river and railroad industries offered unskilled employment.[117] In the 1880s and 1890s, mining companies imported African American strike-breakers from Missouri, Virginia, and other southern states, and other blacks also migrated to take mining jobs.[118] Iowa's African Americans organized in the hope of influencing state Republican party politics and securing greater patronage positions. White politicians actively campaigned in black communities in cities such as Des Moines and Ottumwa. Some black professionals maintained close albeit paternalistic social ties with upper-class whites. The quality of interactions between whites and blacks grew markedly worse in the early twentieth century, however, as the older paternalistic relationships eroded. Blacks and whites increasingly lived in racially segregated neighborhoods in Iowa's towns and cities, the political structure neglected African American concerns, and Iowa newspapers relegated coverage of blacks to the crime pages.[119]

Whites sought to lynch blacks in southern Iowa mining counties like Monroe and Appanoose. Mobs gathered in agricultural counties in southeastern Iowa, such as Henry and Louisa, near areas of African American settlement following emancipation. And lynchers pursued blacks in Council Bluffs, Muscatine, Ottumwa, and Des Moines. In these urban centers, African Americans labored in the meager, usually unskilled manufacturing (such as meatpacking) and domestic service jobs that were available to them. In other words, during the early twentieth-century racial lynch-mob syndrome, white mobs sought blacks wherever blacks lived in Iowa.[120]

White Iowans who participated in racially motivated mobs acted out of a commitment to a white supremacist vision that morally coded and prioritized the punishment of certain kinds of crimes. All Iowa mobs charged their intended black victims with harming a white person, and eight cases involved an allegation that an African American man had raped or somehow offended a white woman. Mobs of several hundred persons collected after allegations that black men had violated the unwritten rules of behavior separating African American men and white women in Albia, Valley Junction, Council Bluffs, Des Moines, and Ottumwa.[121]

As the actions of western and midwestern lynch mobs underscored, race was the greatest inspiration for Judge Lynch across postbellum America. In the South, including Louisiana, lynching preserved after emancipation whites' prerogative to define and punish African American deviancy and resistance, a prerogative that many southern whites, including northern Louisianans, simply would not leave to the formal criminal justice system. Thousands of African Americans across the

South,[122] including several hundred in Louisiana, lost their lives to the melding of white supremacy and rough justice. Inspired with the idea that ritualized violence could best serve the purpose of white mastery, whites also killed African Americans in the West, Midwest, and Northeast. Whites similarly collectively murdered Chinese, Native Americans, Mexicans, and Sicilians in their attempt to perpetuate the racial hierarchy of a "white man's country" in ways that it seemed law could not. Only in the first decades of the twentieth century, with the remaking of the death penalty across the country, would law come to seem to them an amenable partner to white supremacy, a notion that whites in places as different as New York State and the Mississippi Delta and Sugarland of Louisiana had already precociously adopted.

4 Rough Justice and the Revolt against Due Process: Lynching as Cultural Conflict

Lynching across the postbellum United States underscored the difference between the criminal justice values held by many rural and working-class people, who sought harsh retribution closely supervised by the community, and those possessed by many middle-class people, who stressed the role of the state as neutral guarantor of justice, the observance of the forms of law, fairness, decorum, and humanitarian considerations. In the West and Midwest lynchers, their defenders, and their adversaries, due-process advocates, talked constantly about their understanding of law. In the South, rough-justice values undergirded the local administration of criminal justice and the tendency of Cotton Belt whites to disregard the institutions of formal law amid interracial conflict. Punitive, localized, white supremacist justice enjoyed a white consensus in the South, but white southerners attempted to defend lynching from northern criticism by asserting, spuriously, that the law was not a reliable instrument for the punishment of the rape of white women by black men.

The West

The revolt against due-process reform broke out everywhere across the vast and diverse West. Extensive vigilantism in the earliest periods of white settlement in the 1850s and 1860s left an important legacy that suggested that harsh, rapid, and communal punishment was the most effective way to respond to criminality in the region. Amid the economic development and social and cultural elaboration of the coastal and interior Wests of Washington, California, and Wyoming in the late nineteenth century, many westerners remembered collective violence as a salutary aspect of their region's past and revived lynching as a means to protest the changing nature of criminal justice. Other westerners feared that lynching violence would only retard the region's growth and advancement into "civilization," a progress that only the observation of due-process law could ensure.

In the early hours of April 11, 1891, a mob of forty masked men arrived by boats at Oysterville, an oyster-harvesting town along the coast of southwest Washington. The mob, after seizing a guard, entered the jail and fired into the cells that held John Rose and John Edwards, killing them. The band of forty then departed in their boats into Shoalwater Bay. Rose, a hotel proprietor and land speculator, and Edwards, a cook in Rose's hotel, had been convicted of killing two homesteading Danish immigrants, Jens Frederichsen and his wife Neilsine, after a land dispute and burying their bodies in a cowpath and pigpen. Their conviction in Pacific County and sentence to hang the previous November had been reversed by the Washington State Supreme Court, which had ordered a new trial on the grounds that the evidence that convicted the men was "the uncorroborated testimony of an accomplice" and that prejudiced jurors had been allowed to stand. The key witness, John Rose's son George, had disappeared from the Montesano jail where he had been taken for safekeeping; rumors circulated that he had been killed. The lawyers for the men, aware of murmurs of "discontent" by the Frederichsens' friends at the legal system's delay, had requested their removal for safekeeping, and their transfer to Chehalis was imminent.[1]

Exactly two weeks after the Oysterville lynching, a masked mob of more than fifty soldiers stationed at the fort near Walla Walla sliced the town's telephone lines and forced their way into the county jail, dragging out the "tin-horn gambler" A. J. Hunt, whom they dispatched in a mass shooting with revolvers and carbines. Hunt, born in Illinois but a resident of Walla Walla since the 1850s, had enraged the fort by mortally shooting Private E. Miller in a saloon after Miller had objected to Hunt's declaration that "[a]ll the soldiers of the First cavalry were s—s of b——s." Fearing further retaliation after the lynching by soldiers who resented the town's saloon proprietors and police, the sheriff deputized and armed one hundred men to patrol Walla Walla's streets; the fort's commanding officer forbade the soldiers from leaving its grounds. In a telegram to his secretary of war, Redfield H. Proctor, President Benjamin Harrison termed the affair "very discreditable to army discipline" and demanded a court of inquiry and a rapid trial. The inspector general, Lt. Col. S. S. Sumner, soon arrived, swore there would not be a "whitewash," and promised to assist the county prosecutor. After a county grand jury indicted seven soldiers, Sheriff McFarland arrested them without incident, although he had prepared with two thousand rounds of ammunition.[2]

Pacific northwesterners compared the two Washington lynchings and saw little likeness, if the views of the editors of the region's newspapers may serve as an index. Some condemned the Oysterville affair, but many offered praise or apology. Most deplored the Walla Walla affair, but even this excoriation suggested by contrast what were and were not acceptable grounds for lynching in the region. The *Astoria (Ore.) Bulletin* argued that "'[a]t Oysterville the mob performed a solemn duty in which the law had failed. At Walla Walla the mob refused to give the law a chance, and by their hasty action disgraced the fair name of Walla Walla and of the state of Washington.'"[3] Similarly, the *Portland Oregonian* asserted that "'[t]he Walla Walla lynching is akin to the Sealand [Oysterville] affair, though it had none of the features which explained, if they did not justify that. Both are the fruit of weak, halting and inefficient administration of justice in the state of Washington, which permitted the murderers of the Frederichsens to escape legal punishment.'"[4] The *Oregonian* posited that the maladministration of capital cases, with the Oregon State Supreme Court a kindred culprit, bred a regional contagion of mob violence: "'The bloody tragedy which followed the act of the supreme court of Washington helped to establish in the public mind throughout the state that familiarity with the idea of public violence which makes it easy to practice.'"[5] The *Seattle Post-Intelligencer* unfavorably compared the Walla Walla mob execution with the one a month earlier in New Orleans, where eleven Sicilians accused of complicity in the murder of the police chief were taken out of jail and shot and hanged by a huge mob: "There had been no failure of justice. There had been no acquittal of the prisoner. He had been promptly arrested and imprisoned, and there was not the slightest reason to doubt that he would be rigorously prosecuted and properly punished."[6]

The Oysterville lynching evoked a mixed reaction that unveiled the Pacific Northwest's cultural conflict over criminal justice. For some, the mob's defiance of the state supreme court's safeguarding of the rights of the defendants resonated deeply with a preference for efficient capital punishment and a suspicion of the deliberative and seemingly haphazard nature of legal process. A *Seattle Post-Intelligencer* headline declared, "Pacific County Men Overrule the Supreme Court," and the correspondent reported that "[w]hile the taking off of these men was awful in the extreme, yet nearly all feel that it was justice. They have paid the penalty for their butchering of a defenseless woman and an honest man with their lives."[7] For others, the lynching's murderous disavowal of law signaled a dangerous descent into social anarchy that would discourage economic development. A. C. A. Perkes, the editor of the neighboring *South Bend Journal,* had praised the state supreme court's decision as legally and morally correct and vehemently warned against lynching amid rampant rumors that it was impending: "Men of Pacific County, the highest Court of Justice created by the glorious Constitution has told you THAT YOU WERE WRONG in condemning John R. Rose upon the evidence you found against him; and that nothing but blind prejudice made you do it! . . . Do you think you can right it by committing another wrong, and by defying the highest tribunal you have placed over yourselves. Perish the thought! For the fair name and fame of our county, desist, or your own children will learn to revile you!"[8]

Underlining the benefits of due process, Perkes cited the opinion of a South Bend merchant that a lynching would "militate against the prosperity of the Harbor" and would discourage immigration to it.[9] After the lynching, Perkes denied aspersions by "the people of Oysterville" that his stance was inspired by ties to the South Bend land corporation in which the lynched John Rose had invested. But he intimated that his elevated social class influenced his perspective on the affair and that cultural distinctions explained differences in opinion in the coastland community: "No doubt there were men in the Oysterville mob who conscientiously thought they were doing right and serving the ends of justice. But this belief did not make them right, or lessen the enormity of their crime. It simply shows that they were very ignorant and most seriously misguided. . . . When right and wrong are so fearfully confounded[,] the more enlightened and law-abiding portion of the community to whom such truths are clear, is morally bound to vehemently uphold the right and condemn the wrong."[10]

A Portland letter writer to the *Oregonian,* J. E. M., also responded with alarm to that paper's "quasi approval" of the Oysterville lynching and denunciation of the Washington State Supreme Court's decision and underscored the pecuniary benefits of due process. The writer amended a seminal line from the Declaration of Independence, displaying the association stalwarts of due process made between the observance of law and the flow of capital: "'The law gives every man a right to a fair trial.

It is the shield of every good citizen in his right to life, liberty and *prosperity.'*"[11]

As in Oysterville, the vagaries of due-process law played a role in the January 8, 1898, hanging of Chadwick "Blackey" Marshall, wearing only "a woolen outer and an under shirt," from a courthouse window by a masked mob of less than fifty in Colfax, Washington. The trial of Marshall and an alleged accomplice, Robert "Dakota Slim" McDonald, for the robbery and murder of Orville Hayden in Farmington, had been delayed when Judge McDonald sustained the objection of defense lawyers that the prosecution had unlawfully failed to hold preliminary hearings for the men before filing a bill of information against them. The prosecution appealed this ruling to the state supreme court. Under the window from which Hayden's body hanged, lynchers affixed a piece of paper that read, "'NOTICE JUDGE' 'don't overrule the supreme court anymore' 'people of Whitman County.'"[12]

"Dakota Slim" McDonald escaped death by feigning it after lynchers shot at him in his cell. A grand jury examined thirty-five witnesses but did not "fix the guilt of the above mentioned lynching on any party, or parties whomsoever." The grand jury did censure a jail guard, William Cantonwine, for his "reprehensible" failure to raise an alarm after the mob's arrival.[13] The *Colfax Commoner* denounced the lynching, asserting its commitment to due-process safeguards: "While it may be true, as many seem to think, that the court committed error in his ruling as to the necessity of a preliminary examination, yet that would not justify the hanging of a man who had been given no opportunity to prove the innocence which he asserted in his last awful moments."[14]

Unlike the mob killings in Oysterville and Colfax, the lynching by soldiers at Walla Walla in 1891 elicited unanimous condemnation because it could not be easily construed as a protest against the vagaries of due process. It seemed a deliberate defiance of civilian legal institutions, and it threw into harsh relief the characteristic tensions between civilian populations and the military, a symbiotic if restive relationship in many locales in the nineteenth-century West. To northwesterners, the troops at Walla Walla had confused their distinctive role in the polity, betraying their assigned role as "the last resort of those who execute and uphold the law" by appointing themselves "the judge and jury."[15]

However, the general disapproval of the soldier-lynchers at Walla Walla coexisted with an understanding that mob law might be the appropriate recourse for citizens of the Northwest under certain circumstances. These notions were tellingly juxtaposed in Judge Upton's grandiloquent charge to the Walla Walla County grand jury that was called to investigate the lynching and find indictments against its perpetrators. Upton spoke in solemn tones of the grandeur of law and the sanctity of due process, A. J. Hunt's rights, and the outrage of their violation by the soldiers: "It is nothing to point out that the victim was a gambler, accused of crime. The saint and the sinner, the rich and poor, the soldier and civilian, the vilest criminal, the meanest vagrant, are as fully entitled to the protection of the law as the priest at the altar. When protection is denied, the chief support of our liberties is undermined. The highest duty which citizens owe to the state is to do all in their power to see that the law is fully and impartially administered, and the greatest misfortune that can befall a community is to be forced to lose faith in the integrity and capacity of those charged with the execution of the laws."[16]

Yet in his next sentence Upton continued: "Then it is that vigilance committees seem to have excuse for existing. That the people of this county are not in that melancholy plight is shown by the patience, hope and confidence with which they wait your action." Furthermore, Upton began his charge by citing the desire to avoid the necessity of the activation of the vigilance committee's quasi-legal cousin, the committee of safety: "The time seems to have come when only the action of a determined, active, fearless grand jury will avoid the necessity of a large, less desirable and more expensive organization, the committee of safety, that last resort of a civilized community against organized lawlessness."[17] Upton understood the power of appeals to traditions of popular sovereignty in ensuring "justice" and crime control in the minds of his farmer and businessmen grand jurors. He framed the grand jury's work as a noble alternative consistent with but preferable to quasi- and extralegal rough-justice precedents.

In comparing the Walla Walla soldier-lynchers unfavorably to "vigilance committees," Upton referenced the precedent of the region's earlier collective violence. Some earlier lynchings in the Northwest had little to do with an absence or distance of law enforcement, as the popular understanding of western lynching holds, but much to do with the contest for order and respectability in novel communities. On January 22, 1870, for example, some "citizens of Muck Prairie" in Pierce County, Washington, formed a vigilance committee and pursued and shot dead B. Gibson and Charles McDonald. Gibson and McDonald had ordered F. A. Clarke and Charles Wren to vacate Wren's property, a barn and farmhouse that Clarke rented from Wren, who in turn had been driven off the property by "the people of this county" in 1864. After several arrests for "molesting" Clarke and his "hired man" and threatening to drive out their livestock, Gibson built a log house on the property and posted a notice declaring himself the owner of it. Twenty men styled by an Olympia newspaper as "the people" destroyed Gibson's house and signed a notice asking him to "leave the property alone." Gibson and McDonald allegedly rode around the countryside threatening to kill those who had signed the notice and anyone "that entered the lane leading to the house" and to forcibly resist arrest by the sheriff.[18]

The local press only with some hesitation sought to justify this lynching, which followed a complicated contest of wills over long-disputed property. After first asking, "Are the acts of a vigilance committee justifiable?" the *Olympia Transcript* answered cautiously, "While we cannot so fully endorse lynch law these men had placed themselves outside of all law by their threats and acts." The Olympia editor further explained: "It was, as you see, self-preservation[;] either Gibson or McDonald must die or these twenty men and God knows how many more, as McDonald and Gibson had made threats that they would have twenty rough and desperate men in Seattle, who would come to their assistance, and who would also take claims here."[19]

The settlers on the prairie draining the western slope of Mt. Rainier did not argue that they acted in the *absence* of law enforcement, but rather that existing law enforcement could not provide a sufficiently harsh *style* of criminal justice necessary to ensure the protection of local settlers. Gibson had been arrested and appeared before a justice of the peace numerous times, and he had vowed to resist arrest by the sheriff. The Pierce County vigilantes argued, drawing heavily on popular sovereignty, that when the law "is overpowered and rendered futile some remedy for the people's rights must be maintained."[20]

Some earlier Northwest lynchings anticipated the characteristics of later episodes of collective violence, which often involved an enraged communal response to an aggravated homicide. This was the case in southern Puget Sound in January 1863, when J. M. Bates, in his late twenties and from Vermont, shot Andrew Byrd, a county commissioner born in Ohio who had been living in Pierce County since 1853. Bates, whose mental competence was questioned by some in the community, had been told that Byrd had stolen one of his cows. Bates lay in wait at the post office for Byrd and shot him twice. After Byrd died, Steilacoom rapidly filled with men; an eyewitness recalled that "as soon as his death became known the town was full of men, and it seemed that those living at a distance had got there as if by magic." The mob of a hundred, "embracing the most worthy and responsible men of the county," attacked the jail with a sledgehammer, axe, crowbar, and a piece of timber, held the sheriff, and broke into the cell. The mobbers took out Bates, who whispered his desires for the distribution of his property and his burial, Reverend Sloan said a prayer, and the lynchers hanged Bates from a pole attached to a barn.[21] The *Puget Sound Herald* expressed the moral economy of the Steilacoom mob responding to a heinous crime with an emphasis on the deterrent effect of harsh and rapid retribution grounded in communal prerogatives: "'As he had given his victim no warning of his hellish purpose, so a speedy retribution was deemed most in accordance with justice. . . . This, the verdict of the people has been executed. Let this fearful loss of a good and generous friend and useful member of a community and the just awful punishment of his murderer, be a lesson in the future to those who contemplate the commission of crime.'"[22]

Thirty years later, an old settler who had participated in the lynching, William D. Vaughan, memorialized the mob murder of Bates as a salutary contribution to the Pacific Northwest's social and cultural progress. Vaughan argued that a particular phase in the development of northwestern society, represented by the lynching of Bates, had been succeeded by a more prosperous and settled one: "Such punished [*sic*] is rarely meted out to anyone in these days, and we all look at the prosperity of this grand country with pride."[23]

In most places in the postbellum West, law enforcement and courts were in place when lynching occurred, so absent or distant law enforcement could not have caused the violence.[24] Rather, lynching represented a protest against alterations in the way in which criminal justice was administered. An exception to this pattern occurred in Alaska. Two lynchings occurred there in the late 1890s as a result of the great distance of criminal justice institutions—several hundred miles away in Sitka—from remote gold camps. In one of the incidents, miners collectively hanged Martin Severts after an informal trial on October 26, 1899, in Lituya Bay off the Gulf of Alaska. Severts had murdered a fellow member of a small party of gold placer miners and had attempted to murder the others; the miners may have feared further violence from him.[25] Residents in Valdez also informally tried and hanged Millard Fillmore Tanner.in Valdez on January 2, 1898, the day after he shot to death two companions.[26] Yet no other lynchings apparently occurred in Alaska. The lateness of Alaska's frontier, which occurred as due-process sentiments had begun to prevail in their cultural conflict with the rough-justice perspective across the West, may account for its dearth of mob killings.

However, the late nineteenth-century rural revolt against the reform of criminal justice had become a significant social movement down the Pacific Slope in California.[27] In the early hours of July 24, 1892, for instance, a mob of around forty men broke into the Shasta County jail in

Redding with a "sledge, drills, and powder" and took out and hanged John and Charles Ruggles, brothers accused of murdering a Wells-Fargo messenger when they robbed a stagecoach.[28] The press cited several factors that activated mobbers. These included "the attentions lavished by certain women of Redding upon the malefactors" in jail visits and news of John Ruggles's legal defense strategy, which would purportedly claim that the murder victim, Buck Montgomery, was a collaborator in a robbery plot gone awry. Moral outrage at the plan for a courtroom assault on the murdered man's character apparently spurred the lynchers into action.[29]

Beyond these specific circumstances, apologists for the lynching composed a broad critique of the criminal justice system that linked anger at a heinous crime, concerns over enforcement of the death penalty and the punishment of murderers, and the uncertainty and expense of due-process law. To this, some editors wedded a righteous invocation of popular sovereignty in support of the lynchers' usurpation of the function of juries and legal executioners. The apologia for the lynching of the Ruggles brothers was succinctly expressed in a summative headline from the *Redding Weekly Republican Free Press*: "CHANGE OF VENUE! RUGGLESES RAISED RIGHT ROYALLY. An Example to Stage-robbers and Murderers—Fearful of the Law's Delays and Inefficiency the Citizens Usurp Its Authority—Montgomery Avenged—Expensive Trials Saved—Sentimental Sentimentality Rebuked."[30] The editor of the *Yreka Journal*, writing in an adjoining county, also approved of the lynching, citing the rationale of fiscal conservatism as well as crime control.[31]

But several California newspapers dissented from the general commentary in favor of the Redding lynchers' actions. The *Sacramento Record Union* argued, for instance, that there had not been a great delay in the trials of the Ruggleses, nor was there much chance that justice would not have been served. Thus there was no excuse for the preference for "mob rule" over "law." The Sacramento editor excoriated the Shasta County sheriff for neglect of duty in not adequately protecting the jail.[32]

The constellation of opinion in favor of the mob execution of the Ruggles brothers in Redding was hardly unique in California. A San Francisco editor similarly explained the multiple lynching of Lawrence H. Johnson, William Null, Luis Moreno, and Garland Stemler, all accused of murder, by a mob of 250 in Yreka in August 1895. Johnson was accused of murdering his wife; Null was accused of killing an acquaintance in a property dispute; and Moreno, a Mexican, and Stemler were sawmill hands charged with committing a double homicide while robbing a saloon near the Oregon line.[33] The *Examiner*'s editor argued that the mob killing constituted the populace's rejection of efforts by the state supreme court to guarantee due-process rights for capital defendants.

> The men of Siskiyou broke into jail and hanged the accused because they did not believe that the State would do the work if they neglected it . . . it is hardly possible that the death penalty would have been inflicted in any one of the four cases. . . . Almost the whole fabric of technical obstacles to the conviction and hanging of murderers is the result of lawmaking by the appellate court. . . . [T]he Supreme Court is steadily making new laws on the subject, and every new law that it announces whittles away something of the right of the people to punish murderers. In the last two years the Supreme Court has upset a large part of the criminal procedure heretofore followed in the State, and has steadily increased the difficulties of the people in punishing criminals. An instance of recent judicial lawmaking is the ruling that a citizen who has read the testimony at an inquest or preliminary examination cannot be a juror—a ruling directly opposed in principle to the statute on which it is founded.[34]

One California editor made the intention of lynchers to lodge the performance of criminal justice in communal prerogatives especially explicit after a mob of twenty seized Jose Antonio Ygarra from his preliminary examination for the murder of William Granjean and hanged him near Hopland in December 1875: "The people in the vicinity of Senel, in Mendocino County are truly determined to have the law executed under their own supervision."[35]

To the east, in the Rocky Mountains and High Plains, Wyomingites similarly turned to lynching to express a vision of highly punitive, communally based justice in the late nineteenth and early twentieth centuries.[36] A lynching in Cheyenne in 1883 was a product of the increasingly complicated sociocultural development of the territory's metropolis. Cheyenne's population numbered more than thirty-five hundred in 1883, and the town was growing rapidly into a center for territorial government, the U.S. military, and the Union Pacific railroad. Cheyenne also hosted mercantile establishments serving a High Plains hinterland and was a playground for the cattle baron aristocracy and the laborers they employed herding stock on the range.[37] In September, Henry Mosier, a freighter, attacked his wagon companions with an axe near Fort Russell with the intention of robbing them and then shot and killed one of them, John H. Wensel. A large crowd greeted a train that brought Mosier to Cheyenne on September 17 after his capture. By late that evening a group of nearly five hundred gathered near the jail. A witness stated that the crowd "represented nearly all grades of society." The mob, mostly masked, entered the jail and seized Mosier. Speeches of the highest government officials in Cheyenne—the territorial secretary, E. S. N. Morgan, the territorial justice, J. W. Fisher, and the mayor of Cheyenne, Joseph M. Carey—stressing the importance of mercy and justice failed to dissuade the lynchers. Mosier died after several botched attempts to hang him.[38]

The lynching of Mosier unveiled class and cultural strains in the increasingly complicated social landscape of Cheyenne. Working-class and middle-class persons combined in an act of collective murder that openly defied the counsel of the most influential persons in the town and territory, who had stressed the virtues of due-process law and humanitarian considerations. A "contributor" to the *Cheyenne Leader* condemned the lynching but then provided an elaborate rationale for it and a multitiered class analysis of opinions concerning the event. The *Leader* denounced the tendency toward passionate vengeance among working-class "scum." But the newspaper admitted that "the middle class" also supported lynching, viewing it as a means to prevent crime and to resolve occasional problems in the administration of justice. The Cheyenne opinion writer identified a third, more elevated social class, presumably the educated elite, "who think that the technicalities of the law and the perverseness of jurors are at fault for insufficiently punishing crime." The writer admonished the "best citizens" to replace ignorant, lower-class jurors and thus effect a reform of the criminal justice system.[39]

Although many Wyomingites subscribed to the rough-justice viewpoint on criminal law and lynching, a portion of residents in Cheyenne and the territory strenuously disagreed, stressing the importance of legal procedures and arguing that the record of the courts had been thoroughly distorted. A letter writer to a Cheyenne newspaper accordingly asserted after the lynching of Mosier that the proposition that "justice failed here" was absurd and cited a district criminal court record of plentiful indictments, convictions, and penitentiary sentences.[40] The 1883 Laramie County district court record reminds us that lynchers and their supporters responded not to an absence of law or the "lax" administration of criminal justice that they so often mentioned. Rather, apologists for lynching in Wyoming sought to supplant the deliberative nature of due-process law and a territorial criminal justice system that rarely utilized the death penalty. Rough-justice enthusiasts, who promoted harsh and public punishments for those who committed homicide, faced off against judges, lawyers, territorial officeholders, and a smattering of newspaper editors, who were committed to the due-process ideological orientation by the early 1880s.[41]

A mixture of northeastern influences and peculiarly western attitudes shaped Wyoming's criminal justice system. Northeastern and midwestern immigrants, who became the territory's judiciary, lawyers, and political officeholders, contributed philosophies and practices mimicking established conventions in the East, most notably the inclosure of the gallows from public view from the inception of the territory in 1869.[42] Even after statehood in 1890, though, a distinctly western sensibility influenced legal praxis. Some district judges, such as C. W. Bramel in Natrona County, advocated a crime-control strategy that privileged communal opinion, blurred distinctions between legal and extralegal measures, and ignored due-process safeguards.[43] Law enforcement officials such as county sheriffs and county attorneys often blinked at vigilantism, especially in retaliation for property violations. Moreover, administrators of the death penalty acted out of real concern for the potential alternative of mob justice. Lynchers argued, in the words of a petitioner urging the beneficial effect that would be produced by the legal execution of seventeen-year-old Charles Miller in 1892, "that the courts were unable to visit proper penalties for capital crimes or were careless in the discharge of their duties."[44] Petitioners who wrote to the governor in favor of executions frequently articulated the rural perspective emphasizing rough justice. For example, A. S. Peabody, a retailer in Laramie, urged the execution of George Black in 1890: "Life is much too cheap here, convictions are secured with difficulty and society needs better protection." Peabody also criticized locals who petitioned in favor of commutation to a life sentence for Black as "activated by a false sentiment or a lack of moral courage."[45]

Rough-justice partisans often argued that homicide was spiraling out of control, encouraged by negligent criminal courts. A study of court records for Laramie County (the most populous county in Wyoming, with Cheyenne as its seat) undermines this characterization, as well as notions of an exceptionally violent late nineteenth-century West. From 1890 through 1894, coroner's juries found homicides in five deaths they investigated. The district court prosecuted five cases of homicide, securing convictions in three, acquitting one, and withdrawing charges against twelve persons implicated in the Johnson County War.[46] By comparison, the southwestern county of Sweetwater, home of several mining communities, saw a slightly higher rate of homicide from 1891 through 1894. The criminal court there prosecuted four homicides, convicting two and acquitting two.[47] In the combined seven first-degree murder prosecutions in the two counties, one resulted in a death sentence and legal execution, one in a twenty-year prison term, two in manslaughter convictions and lesser prison terms, two in acquittals, and one in withdrawal of prosecution. From this record, it appears that the murder rate in these Wyoming jurisdictions was not especially high and that criminal courts were not especially lax in the handling of murder prosecutions. Nonetheless, the style with which officials administered capital cases sometimes differed substantially from the wishes of the rural populace.[48]

Crime-control partisans in Wyoming particularly scorned the appellate process, arguing that the state supreme court commonly reversed convictions and granted new trials to murderers and granted stays of execution to those who had received death sentences. Following a spate of lynchings in 1902 and 1903, the attorney general, J. A. Van Orsdel, agreed that the law should be amended to hasten the appeals process in death penalty cases but noted that this was the responsibility of the legislature, not the scapegoated judiciary. Reviewing the courts' recent record, Van Orsdel also pointed out that popular perceptions of reversals in homicide cases were erroneous.

> [J]uries and the trial courts have not been lax in the performance of their duties. In other words, convictions of murderers has been the popular thing in Wyoming for sometime past. There has been no disposition shown on the part of the Supreme Court to reverse any of these convictions. The Supreme Court of Wyoming has never reversed a capital case since statehood, and only one during the territorial period. I doubt whether there is a state in the Union that will show as large a percentage of criminal cases affirmed by its Supreme Court, as is shown by the Wyoming records. Every lawyer knows that in the older states, judgments are reversed upon a single error, while our supreme court, apparently believing that reversals are dangerous when they can be avoided, has gone to great lengths and sustained the judgments of the trial courts, in many instances pointing out numerous errors, but finding a way in the furtherance of justice, to affirm the case.[49]

Wyoming governors also uniformly rejected pleas for clemency in death penalty cases, in one instance deriding humanitarian appeals from clergy and reform-minded individuals as "mere sentimentalism."[50] Yet, as the Laramie and Sweetwater County figures help to illustrate, Wyoming courts rarely applied the death penalty on a homicide conviction, favoring instead lesser penalties such as a substantial prison term. This meant that legal executions were infrequent, and many years sometimes elapsed between spurts of gallows activity. The Territory and State of Wyoming executed ten men between 1869 and 1911, all on homicide convictions. Long dry spells on the gallows twice coincided with spasms of lynching for homicide. The gallows was inactive from 1875 through 1883; lynchers killed four men on homicide charges between 1879 and

1884. The gallows was also dormant from 1895 through 1902; mobbers assassinated four persons accused of murder in 1902 and 1903.[51]

Although rarely applied, the institution of the death penalty attracted a popular following and communalistic ritual, which suggests the transitional nature of legal systems in Wyoming in the late nineteenth and early twentieth centuries. The territorial statute specified that executions must occur within a county jail or within an inclosure that "shall be higher than the gallows, and so constructed as to exclude the view of persons outside thereof." The law limited witnesses to "the sheriff and his assistants," a clergyman acting as spiritual advisor, six individuals chosen by the prisoner, and twelve persons selected by the sheriff. Wyomingites routinely violated these stipulations, demonstrating their commitment to collective supervision of the execution rite despite the statutory concealment of the ceremony.[52] During the hanging of Charles Miller in 1892, twenty people watched from the top of a building overlooking the scaffold. Sixty witnesses viewed the execution from within the stockade that served as an inclosure. Additionally, "several hundred orderly people" gathered around the courthouse.[53] Late nineteenth-century executions occurred at midday, possibly to accommodate the large numbers of people attracted from the surrounding area. Crowds of "stock and ranchmen from Ft. Laramie" gathered in Cheyenne in November 1874 for the hanging of the "Sioux half-breed" Toussaint Kensler, and "[h]undreds of people, led by a morbid curiosity, visited the jail" the day before county officials hanged George Black in Laramie in February 1890.[54] As described in chapter 2, Wyomingites further spurned the bourgeois attempt to sanitize legal executions by taking mementoes from the corpses of hanged men and by expressing enthusiasm for other practices that degraded a dead prisoner's body. Many Wyoming residents thus failed to inculcate reformist notions of a sterilized, physically segregated, and allegedly more humane death penalty prevalent in eastern states in the postbellum period.[55]

By the late 1890s, cattle barons in Wyoming increasingly employed expert assassins instead of lynch mobs to exterminate their enemies and redirected their focus from stock thieves to sheepworkers who competed for grazing rights on the range. Simultaneously, responding to tensions resulting from the adjudication of aggravated murder cases, rural and small-town Wyomingites reinvented lynching as a response to homicide. This early twentieth-century social movement recapitulated many motifs evident in the early 1880s: a regionalist articulation of retributive justice that rejected bourgeois reforms of the death penalty and criminal procedure. The vision of punitive social control seemed especially compelling to a rural working class of cowboys, sheepworkers, and farmers and to a small-town elite of entrepreneurs, ranchers, and editors. In March 1902, a masked mob of cowboys, ranchers, and sheepworkers hanged Charles Woodard in Casper. Woodard had murdered the sheriff of Natrona County, W. C. Ricker.[56] On May 27, 1903, a mob of thirty cowboys and "ranch hands" took W. C. Clifton from the county jail at Newcastle and hanged him from a railroad bridge. Clifton had murdered Mr. and Mrs. J. W. Lynch, who owned a ranch in Weston County, reportedly because Mrs. Lynch had rejected his "improper proposal."[57] Less than two months later, a mob of approximately thirty "[r]anchmen and cowboys from the surrounding country" shot James Gorman and J. P. Walters to death in their jail cells in Basin in north central Wyoming, and their bullets also killed the deputy county clerk, C. E. Price. Gorman had murdered his brother and hidden the corpse as the result of an affair he was having with his brother's wife. J. P. Walters had murdered a widow, Agness Hoover, who had spurned his marriage proposal.[58]

The Wyoming mobs in 1902 and 1903 shared a perspective on legal systems with many rural and small-town residents that stressed the necessity of harsh punishment of especially offensive crimes, in this case the murder of a law officer and homicides that defied sexual and gender norms. In the mob murders in Newcastle and Casper, lynchers explicitly expressed their perception of the relationship between their performances of mob violence and the functioning of the criminal justice system. The lynchers in Newcastle attached a sign to W. C. Clifton's corpse protesting that the law was "too slow."[59] A lyncher in Casper pinned a card to Charles Woodard's shirt that read: "NOTICE. 'Process of law is a trifle slow, So this is the way we have to go, Murderers and thieves beware!' PEOPLES VERDICT."[60]

Wyoming's district judge, C. W. Bramel, embodied well the rough-justice philosophy, which prioritized the punishment of accused criminals over legal process. Bramel presided over Woodard's murder trial and guaranteed, in his words, "[to] the people of Casper . . . a speedy trial, withal a fair and impartial hearing, and under this promise they kept their hands off the prisoner and allowed the law to take its course." This verbal agreement between a judge and potential lynchers resulted in the denial of Woodard's motion for a change of venue and the completion of a trial, conviction, and sentencing to death within less than a week.[61] The delay in Woodard's execution as the state supreme court prepared to hear his appeal permitted the lynch mob to invoke popular sovereignty, Bramel argued: "Woodard was given a fair trial, as well as speedy, and the finding of the jury was accepted as the voice of the court. Woodard's blood was demanded, but nothing short of his execution would do them. They were wronged in the wanton murder of an officer in whom they had placed their trust, and the Biblical 'eye for an eye' was to them as Holy Writ. The voice of the people is indeed the voice of God, in this as in other things that go to make up the sum of life, and the people cannot be fooled."[62]

Complaints that the deliberative nature of the administration of capital punishment thwarted the satisfaction of "justice" pervaded the early twentieth-century cycle of mob murder. The Wyoming Supreme Court had granted a stay of execution to James Gorman, as it had Charles Woodard, and the press cited "the delays in law" in explaining the lynching of Gorman.[63] The tensions between legal process and the state's administration of the death penalty and the demands of rural and small-town Wyomingites for rough justice thus underlay the turn-of-the-century surge in lynching. Hamstrung by limits on gubernatorial powers and the popularity of crime-control positions among county officials and the rural electorate, Governor Fenimore Chatterton could do little but admonish county officeholders to be more aggressive in heading off mobs or chide them for their complacency after a mob killing. The governor believed that mob justice sullied Wyoming's reputation in the East and might hurt badly needed migration to the state.[64]

The Midwest

In mid June 1883, following three lynchings in Iowa in less than a week, Governor Buren Sherman discussed the problem of lynch mobs with his attorney general, Smith McPherson. Sherman argued that there was little he could do to prevent lynching, except perhaps to send a circular to the district judges, as Governor Crittenden of Missouri had done recently, suggesting a more rigid application of the laws. But the governor dismissed the idea as a poor one, since the district judges would reject such an instruction as an "impertinence," an "encroachment on their authority and dignity." McPherson responded with a curious story, related to him by a district judge in southern Iowa. The populace of Adams County, whose district court Judge McGill presided over, was thoroughly aroused when the attorney for an alleged murderer filed a motion for a change of venue. The judge instructed the sheriff to arm the prisoner with two pistols, and there was no disturbance at the jail that night. The next day "the whole countryside" came to court, prepared to lynch the defendant if the judge granted the change of venue. When the motion came up, Judge McGill admonished the crowd that a mob killing could result in a civil suit brought against the lynchers in a distant county. At this, the "wealthier men" in the audience departed and the rest of the assembled listened calmly as the court approved the motion.[65]

Judge McGill's story reflects several important themes in midwesterners' reception of law in the late nineteenth century. Iowans were extremely litigious and made extensive use of civil law,[66] but they possessed an ambivalent view of the criminal law and especially of due-process mechanisms. Iowans accepted the authority of law officers and the criminal courts but sometimes rebelled against that authority with lynchings. Iowans most often accepted the role of the criminal justice system in punishing violators of social norms, but they voiced a litany of complaints about the supposed weaknesses of the criminal justice apparatus. These complaints had their roots in the nature of due-process law, the adversarial system, and in the limitations of the county-level criminal justice apparatus. State government, as reflected in Governor Sherman's comment, envisioned only a minor role for itself in criminal law enforcement.

Like any legislative enactment, the Iowa statutory code in the late nineteenth century reflected an idealized view of the role of law in shaping and regulating human behavior. Statutes applying to individuals charged with serious crimes against persons embodied legislators' conception of the criminal court's social-control function. The Iowa code limited the application of capital punishment to first-degree murder. State law granted a jury the discretion to determine whether a first-degree murder conviction merited the gallows or life imprisonment, although if the defendant pleaded guilty to the charge, a judge decided. Statutory requirements for the punishment of lesser crimes against persons were marked by flexibility and judicial discretion. The 1897 code specified a penitentiary term of not less than ten years for second-degree murder. The prerogative of the district court was especially expansive in rapes and in other sexual cases. The 1885 and 1897 codes indicated only that a prison term for rape should be "life or any term of years."[67]

As demonstrated in Sherman's reluctance to instruct the district judges, criminal justice in nineteenth-century Iowa was largely a local affair. Characteristics such as limited financial resources, a populace's penchant for fiscal conservatism, and a high degree of communal supervision over legal proceedings were common throughout the state, as in much of the rural United States. Southern Iowa counties more fully embodied these concerns, however. A survey of county court expenses in different regions in 1904 illustrates that rural southwestern and south central counties ranged from budget extremes of prodigal (Appanoose

County spent $9,249) to stingy (Adams County allotted $1,889). Northern counties paid more uniformly and moderately for justice: most ex-
pended three to four thousand dollars. The striking variability of district
court expenditures in southern Iowa may have reflected the volatility of
legal affairs there.[68]

District judges in southern Iowa weathered the challenge of popular
frustration with due-process law more frequently than their bench breth-
ren in northern counties. Three examples from the southern portion of
the state occurred in the early to mid 1880s. Judge McGill dispersed a
lynch mob in Adams County and then granted a change of venue. Judge
Loofbourow feared he might be physically attacked after a change-of-
venue ruling and fled Audubon County in 1885, where a lynching soon
ensued. Judge McHenry drew withering press criticism for his alleged
leniency toward "several of the coldest blooded murderers" after an acquittal on a self-defense plea in an 1885 Madison County murder trial.
Editorial critics alluded to McHenry's background as a criminal lawyer
in disparaging his crime-control credentials and contrasted him unfavorably with the hard-nosed Judge Johnson of Marion County.[69] Well-attend-
ed court sessions and comprehensive small-town newspaper coverage of
"court business" ensured that district court activities attracted a wide
audience and that the vagaries of legal process would provoke an animated
reception. District court judges, the local symbols of judicial authority,
with considerable discretionary powers (and powers even more extensive
in the popular mind), were natural magnets for public respect and vitriol.

Expressions of frustration with the mechanics of due-process law,
especially with the opportunities available to skilled defense lawyers, the
change of venue, and the jury system, were commonplace in Iowa newspapers. The change of venue especially offended the localistic emphasis
on the community's supervision of criminal justice institutions. The
lynchings of Pleasant Anderson in Wapello County in December 1884 and
C. B. Jellerson, J. A. Smyth, and J. J. Wilson in Audubon County in February 1885 occurred after judges had granted changes of venue. Further,
in several mob executions, apologists cited the strain of the prosecution
of an alleged murderer on the county coffers, with the possibilities of an
acquittal, a guilty verdict reversed on appeal, or even the frustration of a
conviction that lacked a death sentence and resulted instead in a life
sentence and perhaps an eventual pardon.[70] The *Anita Times* expressed
a common sentiment in favor of fiscal conservatism following the June
1883 lynching of John Anderson and Frank Brown, deploring the regional criminal courts for which "[c]ounties are taxed heavily to pay for the
trial of criminals that are seldom convicted." The Anita editorialist ar-

gued that by contrast, "Lynch Law does its work speedily, surely and without cost to the country."[71]

These pervasive complaints from the rough-justice camp, characteristically hyperbolic, internally inconsistent, and accompanied by dubious statistics, underlined a widespread desire for criminal justice reform, a concern shared even by ardent defenders of due-process law. Embracing the English system for its reputedly "swift and sure justice," Iowa's literati scored the incompetence and leniency of juries.[72] The popular press also attacked technicalities that were deplored as intrinsic to the adversarial system of contentious procedure.[73] Rough-justice advocates linked all of these defects in a general excoriation of Iowa's criminal justice system for its supposed failure to enforce the death penalty. Indeed, tirades over due-process law and the adversarial system swept across the United States in the late nineteenth century.[74] Yet Iowa rhetoricians responded to regional circumstances and drew upon local examples to make their arguments, and the debate seemed loudest in southern Iowa.

An 1885 letter writer from Jasper County expressed the rough-justice critique of the administration of criminal justice. A. K. Campbell sought a "radical reform [of] our courts . . . for the protection of society and the credit of our courts." He derided the district juries as "stupid," easily misled by lawyers continually filing motions. The Newton correspondent praised lynching, by comparison, as "a new court" noteworthy for its "promptness and economy in dealing with crime." In this utopian vision of a legal system conforming to communal requirements for punitive justice, a revamped administration of criminal law would merge the rapidity and thoroughness of the lynch court with the "forms" and "safeguards of law."[75]

When Iowa literati attempted to explain the anomaly of lynching in the state, they found a simple explanation in the allegedly lax enforcement of the death penalty law. The criminal justice system would not execute murderers, they said, and therefore mobs usurped the punitive power of the criminal court and took the lives of those guilty of homicide.[76] An editorial in the *Iowa State Register* expressed a common argument following lynchings in Cass and Madison Counties in 1883: "Human life has been cheapened in Iowa, and nearly as much by lenient courts as by murderous men, until the people feel that by Judge Lynch alone may its value and security be enhanced and murder discouraged. For twenty years not a murderer has been hanged in Iowa!"[77]

A close examination of the cases of the six men who were executed in Iowa between 1887 and 1910 discloses the intimate relationship between lynching violence and legal authority in the popular understanding of the punishment of capital crimes. Lynch mobs thrice sought one of the men convicted of first-degree murder, an African American named John Junkin. The final attempted lynching occurred after Junkin was sentenced to death at Centerville on June 1, 1909, as officers only with difficulty kept him from a mob and put him on a special train to the penitentiary in Fort Madison.[78] The threat of lynching informed the trials and subsequent appeals of candidates for the gallows in more subtle ways, too. Authorities feared that several of them would be lynched. Officers removed J. K. Cumberland, eventually executed in 1895, from Harlan to Council Bluffs for safekeeping, and Cumberland wrote up a secret confession that cleared his wife in the event that the couple was "mobbed." In a petition to the governor for commutation, Cumberland claimed that he pleaded guilty because his lawyer had told him he would be lynched if he did not.[79] Petitioners argued that the governor should not commute the sentences of prisoners on death row because this might encourage lynch mobs. A seed dealer from Adams County, the home of the seventeen-year-old "boy murderer" James Dooley, executed in 1894, warned Governor Frank Jackson that if Dooley were not legally executed, the next murder in the southern Iowa county would provoke a tragic response: "I don't think the people will wait or allow the courts to decide or have anything to do with it."[80]

The state only executed a small number of the individuals convicted of first-degree murder. Most typically, Iowa's fin-de-siècle criminal justice system punished the most serious crimes against persons with a sentence of life imprisonment. The great majority of lifers had been convicted of first-degree murder, distantly followed by second-degree murder and rape. A few others suffered life imprisonment for manslaughter and obstructing railroad tracks.[81] Iowa's lifers included several individuals sought by mobs before conviction in district court, including Albert Parnitzke, who was nearly lynched for murder in Van Buren County in July 1891, and A. D. Storms, who was nearly lynched for murder in Burlington in February 1898.[82] Other lifers avoided a death sentence after reviews by appellate courts and commutations by the governor. Several of these escaped both a mob and an initial death sentence, including George Weems and John Hamill, who were nearly lynched in Des Moines in 1894.[83]

As the use of the sentence of life imprisonment suggests, Iowans were ambivalent about the death penalty. The state legislature had abolished capital punishment in 1872 but restored the gallows in 1878 after a spirited debate in which supporters of restoration cited recent lynchings and well-publicized murders. But humanitarian sentiment against the death penalty remained strong in religious and political circles. Numerous people wrote to governors seeking clemency for death-row candidates, citing extenuating circumstances in their cases, the sanctity of life, and the importance of mercy in religious traditions.[84] State legislators also periodically reintroduced bills that would abolish capital punishment.[85]

Jury selection in murder trials in Iowa incorporated the cultural division in the Midwest over the death penalty and notions of retributive justice. Prosecution and defense lawyers carefully queried prospective jurors concerning their religious affiliations and asked follow-up questions such as, "If you are selected as a juryman to try this case will you try it on your conscience as a Christian man?"[86] Iowa literati singled out the reluctance of juries to apply the death penalty as the primary reason why few were executed. Rough-justice partisans also argued that juries were hesitant to impose a sentence of life imprisonment.[87] Undoubtedly this histrionic analysis contained some truth. Sentiment in favor of retributive justice ebbed and flowed throughout the period, with important regional differences within the state, as southern Iowans articulated a stronger crime-control stance. But aside from the rare homicides that Iowans perceived as exceptionally aggravated and charged with social meaning, jurors most often declined to apply the ultimate penalty.[88]

Wisconsinites evinced an even greater ambivalence and division over the morality of the death penalty, reflecting substantial Yankee roots and a robust middle class with strong humanitarian reformist impulses. But five lynchings that occurred in the last two decades of the nineteenth century compelled Wisconsinites to reexamine the status of crime and punishment and social order in the upper Midwest. Their conversation revolved around the implications of the state's abolition of the death penalty in 1853. The impetus for abolition in the northeastern United States had stemmed from concern over the effects of public executions on the masses that avidly viewed them. The movement eventually reached the growing Midwest, where anti–death penalty forces achieved their legislative aims in Michigan (1846) and Wisconsin. Several thousand had watched the public hanging of John McCaffary in Kenosha, Wisconsin, in 1851, leading a Madison editor to bemoan "[m]urder before the people, with the horrors removed by the respectability of those engaged in its execution." Christopher Latham Sholes, an assemblyman who published the *Kenosha Telegraph*, led the legislative campaign for abolition with a farmer and legislator from Waukesha County, Marvin Bovee.[89]

Those postbellum Wisconsinites who advocated rough justice argued that a criminal justice system that offered life imprisonment as its greatest penalty could not sufficiently deter murderers or protect communities. They also expressed a profound suspicion of the deliberative and unpredictable nature of due-process law, particularly of the insanity plea, which some well-publicized Gilded Age murders and trials had made suspect. Proponents of due process countered that the forms of law offered the greatest protection to individuals and society in the Badger State.

Following the mass mob killing of the alleged murderer Andrew Grandstaff in October 1884, the *Vernon County Censor* quoted another Wisconsin editor who believed the lynching illustrated the need for the restoration of capital punishment.

> "The laws of Wisconsin are such that if this infamous specimen of the race is found the worst thing that can happen to him is imprisonment for life, where he is sure of plenty to eat, enough to wear and constant employment. Is this a suitable punishment for a man who kills four innocent people, two of them mere children? . . . Let us hope that the next legislature will be made up of men who care more for justice than they do for sentimental nonsense, and they will lose no time in getting a bill through providing for the restoration of the death penalty. Grandstaff is the tenth murderer who has been lynched in Wisconsin during the last twenty years. It is time that the miserable wretches did not deserve to live, but they ought to have died in a lawful way. Restore the death penalty."[90]

In 1881 Charles Guiteau, a disappointed Republican office seeker who apparently suffered from profound mental illness, assassinated President James Garfield in Washington, D.C. Guiteau's legal defense of insanity failed to convince a jury, and he was eventually legally executed. Yet his trial received immense publicity as the prosecution and defense summoned experts in the infant field of psychiatric medicine. As a result of the Guiteau trial many Americans, particularly rural ones, became convinced of the dangers of the "insanity dodge."[91]

In October 1884, the *La Crosse Morning Chronicle* argued that the hanging by a mass mob of Nathaniel Mitchell, a riverman with a history of unstable personal behavior who had shot to death Frank Burton, a businessman and political leader, as thousands thronged the streets of La Crosse for an election-night parade, resulted from the deleterious effect of the insanity plea upon criminal justice in Wisconsin: "Yet every man who was engaged in last night's business will know to day [sic] that he helped hang a maniac. The wicked law of the state that set Bennett [a man accused of murder in Wausau who had avoided prison by pleading insane] free will be the excuse and much may justly be charged to it."[92]

A debate over the merits of rough justice versus due-process law also erupted in northwestern Wisconsin in July 1881 following the lynching of Edward Williams, alias Maxwell, in Durand after he and his brother shot and killed two law officers.[93] This public conversation was especially divided and bitter, reflecting the community of Durand's stalwart defense of its act of collective killing as well as the extensive support for due process in the upper Midwest. A Durand editor derided the critics of the lynching as "'[s]ickly sentimentalists'" and mocked "'the morbid anxiety of the sentimental whiners,'" such as the editor of the *Eau Claire News,* who had stated that it was "cowardly" of the mob to hang Williams while he was still handcuffed.[94] However, the editor of the *Dunn County News* saw the affair very differently, as he cited the majesty of law denigrated in the collective killing of Ed Williams: "'As a matter of fact, the men engaged in this affair, trampled upon all law and that action culminated in the highest crime known to the law. It is impossible to justify their conduct by any rule of right and justice.'"[95] In nearby Eau Galle, a writer noted a "'diversity of opinion'" in that town but also a fear that the lynching indicated a cultural degeneration: "'the general sentiment down this way is—that a more brutal affair never happened anywhere, and that it is a reflection upon the morality and civilization of Northwestern Wisconsin.'"[96]

The South

The battle between rough justice and due process drew less ink on the South's editorial pages than in the West and Midwest because few white southerners in the late nineteenth century dissented from a white consensus that favored harsh punishment rooted in white supremacist, communal prerogatives. Sometimes, though, southern editors felt it necessary to defend those preferences against criticism leveled by northern due-process advocates. Southern editors argued incessantly, for instance, that the criminal justice system did not afford sufficiently rapid and harsh punishment for rape allegedly committed by African American men upon white women and that lynchers thus felt compelled to act to protect white communities.[97] For example, the *New Orleans Times-Democrat* opined in 1887, "There have been lynchings in the South for crimes against women, but they have occurred because public sentiment in these districts did not think the law went far enough or was immediate enough for the offense; and because it aimed to teach a lesson as a warning to all those who might feel inclined to insult or attack women alone or unprotected. . . . The South has chosen to regard the protection of woman as of the supremest importance. Hence, its code on this point is severe; its unwritten lynch laws are more so."[98]

As antilynching advocates at the time and a number of historians since have pointed out, this argument was disingenuous, since only a minority of southern lynchings followed allegations of rape.[99] Moreover, white juries would not have been reluctant to convict an African American defendant of rape, which was a capital crime in Louisiana.[100]

In practice, the white consensus for rough justice was enacted in local legal systems in the South in a variety of ways. In Cotton Belt areas such as northern Louisiana, the planter class reserved for itself the police powers associated with disciplining an African American labor force. Therefore criminal justice agencies languished in the Cotton Belt in favor of lethal collective violence administered by rural whites. In other areas of the South—for instance, those with overwhelming black majorities, such as Louisiana's Mississippi Delta, or those lacking the traditions of the Anglo-American cotton regime, as in southern Louisiana—rough justice was implemented through a highly informal style of criminal justice that was consistent with the preferences of white communal opinion and racial hierarchy.

Lower-class French folkways and communal ties in St. Landry Parish in southwestern Louisiana shaped its style of criminal justice, which emphasized leniency for white offenders and harsh punishment for blacks. The style of criminal justice in St. Landry Parish emphasized the informality of legal institutions and may have lessened any impulse to collective violence.[101] For instance, a lawyer in St. Landry admitted in a 1905 letter to a friend that Cajun whites had railroaded a black defendant accused of shooting into a white man's house. The lawyer believed the charge was manufactured to consolidate political alliances.[102] Although the case of Helaire Carrière, executed in 1917 for murdering the sheriff of St. Landry Parish, Marion Swords, is hardly typical, it suggests some interesting things about courtroom procedure and the way in which legal safeguards could be disregarded in favor of communal opinion. Carrière, a Cajun, escaped from the jail at Jennings where he was imprisoned for killing an African American. In some reflection of Cajun racial ideology, Carrière argued that he only shot the sheriff because the sheriff's posse that pursued him included "negroes." In the voir dire examination of potential jurors, the judge consistently overruled defense objections that a juror could not serve impartially because they already had strong opinions concerning the defendant's guilt. The judge argued in at least three instances that he knew these men of Cajun descent would make "impartial jurors" because he had known them personally for twenty years. The judge rejected a motion for a change of venue, heard in the presence of the impanelled jury, despite the murdered sheriff's prominence and threats made to lynch Carrière. A close reading of the transcript of the trial reveals the prevalence of the forms over the substance of justice, the significance of personal relationships in the Cajun community in the administration of the courtroom, and a predetermination of the result of the trial based upon community opinion.[103]

In contrast with the southwestern Louisiana courtroom, in the Red River Delta and the Ouachita River Valley mob violence was a critical mechanism through which planter-class whites exercised the social control of African Americans accused of crimes against whites in the late nineteenth and early twentieth centuries. In the three leading lynching parishes in the state, Bossier, Ouachita, and Caddo,[104] elites disabled the formal administration of criminal justice in plantation districts and replaced its statutory authority with informal police powers. Northern Cotton Belt whites measured the appropriate degree of punishment by the calculus of where an alleged crime or act of resistance fit into a highly racialized moral geography. White planters accumulated extraordinary coercive power in their regulation of an African American workforce. In consequence, the criminal court seldom adjudicated interracial crimes and sparingly punished perpetrators of intraracial offenses.[105]

A careful reading of coroner's inquests filed in Ouachita Parish is suggestive. In September 1879 and March 1885, rural whites made citizens' arrests of African Americans. In the first, George Williams had reputedly made threats against the son of one of the whites who arrested him; in the second, Moses Johnson, in the words of E. Whitley, who participated in the arrest, "got into a gambling scrape, Committed a Crime of so grave a nature, as I thought to justify any law abiding Citizen to arrest and convey him to Prison." Neither Williams nor Johnson made it to jail. Mobbers seized Williams from a constable, who was guarding him overnight after an appearance before a magistrate, and hanged him. Johnson's life ended mysteriously in the Ouachita River, with a rope tied around his neck. Coroner's inquests failed to identify parties responsible for the deaths, much less recommend that the parish's criminal court pursue charges. The coroner's evidence and the circumstances of several additional lynchings indicate that Ouachita Parish's criminal justice system effectively delegated responsibility for the sanction of African American deviance to white property holders.[106]

An examination of the district court minute book for Ouachita Parish between 1890 and 1900 is revealing. Through the minute book, one can follow all prosecutions from indictment or bill of information through the final disposition of a case. Remarkably, parish authorities failed to charge a single person with rape or any kind of related sexual assault charge in the decade of the 1890s. But mobs cited rape in lynchings of blacks in Ouachita in 1889, 1896, and 1897.[107] The absence of rape prosecutions in Ouachita surely does not reflect a paucity of rapes in that parish. Rather, legal authorities in north central Louisiana may have neglected to prosecute sexual assault because they expected an extralegal response when whites accused African Americans of that crime. Officials perhaps anticipated some sort of informal sanctioning when individuals were accused of intraracial rape. In September 1896, for example, whites in a country district of Ouachita Parish reportedly urged blacks to lynch an African American, Jones McCauley, accused of raping two black children, and they did, as the whites watched.[108] By contrast, in southern and central Louisiana prosecutions of rape were not uncommon, and lynchings following rape allegations were rare. In St. Landry Parish, authorities charged three persons with rape in 1890 and 1891, although none of the charges resulted in a conviction. Grand juries in Natchitoches Parish in central Louisiana in the 1880s and 1890s indicted several men for rape. But neither parish experienced a mob killing for rape.[109]

The disposition of homicide charges in Ouachita Parish, with its approximately eighteen thousand residents, is similarly curious. During the 1890s, the Ouachita Parish criminal district court sentenced one person, a white wife-murderer named Pat Paine, to death.[110] Prosecutors and grand jurors charged thirty-one additional men with murder. Four of these received life sentences in the penitentiary; the rest were given reduced charges and sentences, had charges dropped, underwent prosecutions that resulted in mistrials, or were acquitted.[111]

The limited activity of Ouachita Parish's criminal court can best be understood in tandem with the rampant mob killings that occurred in the region. In northern Cotton Belt parishes like Ouachita, informal collective violence prevailed against African Americans when they were accused of offenses against whites. As we have seen, whites who murdered blacks often avoided trial completely. Whites accused in intraracial deaths could plead self-defense and escape with much lighter sentences or convince a jury to acquit.[112]

The unlikelihood that criminal courts in Cotton Belt parishes would stringently prosecute blacks who committed serious crimes against blacks helps to explain why mobs of African Americans occasionally murdered blacks. Equally, the cultural practice of collective killing held such sway in isolated portions of the Red River Delta and the Ouachita

River Valley that rural blacks may have found lynching a natural solution for especially aggravated intraracial homicides and rapes. Five percent of all lynching victims in northern Louisiana died at the hands of black or racially mixed mobs.[113]

The circumstances surrounding two lynchings performed by black mobs shed some light on this phenomenon. In November 1901 Frank Thomas, an African American living on "the Herndon place" in Bossier Parish, shot and killed Welburn, a fourteen-year-old African American, in an argument over a debt of thirty cents. A posse of two hundred blacks in the rural plantation district quickly assembled and apprehended Thomas. A deputy sheriff began to convey Thomas to Shreveport, but a mob of two hundred African Americans and six whites reportedly overpowered the law officer and hanged Thomas from a nearby tree.[114] Two years later, a black cotton laborer, Joseph Craddock, who had been recently hired on the A. J. Smith plantation, fatally assaulted three black men with an axe. Craddock reportedly confessed when confronted by a witness and said that he had done it "just for fun." A mob of up to three hundred, comprised almost entirely of African Americans, seized Craddock from a posse and hanged him.[115] Both of the black-on-black homicides qualified as heinous, whether because of the age of the victim, the lack of provocation, or the method of killing. In the second case, Craddock was new to the area and had few social ties with African Americans living on the Smith plantation. Moreover, these incidents were part of a spate of nine separate lynching events that occurred in Bossier Parish between April 1900 and November 1903. Thus African Americans living in areas where lynching proliferated and where criminal justice systems existed to serve the legal interests of whites sometimes found in lynching a solution to the dilemma of jurisprudence posed by crime within the black community.[116]

Another variable in the dynamic between the criminal justice system and lynching in Louisiana involved the response to the physical segregation of the execution rite. As in the Midwest and West, legal executions were immensely popular events in the nineteenth-century South, sometimes drawing several thousand from the surrounding countryside to a county or parish seat to observe an elaborate and dramatic ritual of public justice. Performed on a scaffold outside the county or parish jail, executions might involve an opportunity for the convicted to make a final statement or confession, receive baptism, and then be blindfolded and hanged by the sheriff and deputies.[117] However, in 1884 the Louisiana legislature passed and Governor Samuel McEnery signed into law an act that stipulated that executions throughout the state must occur in an enclosed area with no more than fifteen witnesses.[118]

Accounts of executions in the 1890s indicate that the law limiting public access to legal hangings was frequently ignored or flouted by local authorities and by the crowds that still flocked to parish jails on execution day. A newspaper reporter chronicled the October 1897 execution of Pat Paine, a white man, in Monroe: "Paine's execution was private, as near as could be, but there were hundreds who took advantage of the surrounding houses and tree tops to witness the hanging, some of the men coming from the extreme limits of the parish, as well as others from the adjoining parishes."[119]

By the early twentieth century, state authorities more vigorously enforced the private nature of executions. In 1910, state officials even centralized legal hangings so that all were performed within the walls of the state penitentiary in Baton Rouge. By the end of the decade, state legislators returned the enforcement of the death penalty to the parishes, resuming the local administration of capital punishment.[120] Yet the late nineteenth-century privatization of the execution rite may have enhanced the expressive power of lynching. In north central and northwestern Louisiana, many whites preferred the grisly public punishment administered by lynch mobs to the newly sanitized and concealed gallows.

Rural Louisianans' insistence that executions remain public even after the law said otherwise embodied the cultural conflict between rough justice and due process that swept the South, Midwest, and West in the last decades of the nineteenth century. As due-process reform had emanated from the Northeast, however, so did the means by which rough justice and due process would be reconciled: the remaking of capital punishment.

5   Judge Lynch's Demise:
Legal and Cultural Change and the Decline of Mobs

Lynching declined across the country with the coalescence of middle classes, which advocated for due-process law and worked to reshape the death penalty. Lynching had been precluded in the Northeast by the antebellum formation of a middle class that disavowed public executions and ritualistic collective violence, investing its faith eventually in a prolific and technocratic death penalty. Yankees helped to populate the Midwest and the West in the mid- to late nineteenth centuries. They brought reformist notions of criminal justice to those regions and fought with many rural and working-class persons, including some from the South, who sought to preserve the values of rough justice through public executions and lynchings. In the late nineteenth and early twentieth centuries, in a quest for social order and the panoply of "modernity" that would ensure economic development, midwestern and western states revamped criminal justice institutions and regularized the death penalty, ending the embarrassing fin-de-siècle revolt against due process. But the process of cultural and legal change took longer in the South, where whites had responded to the social leveling of emancipation and urbanization by reinventing the instrumentalist, lethal understanding of white popular sovereignty that had always undergirded slavery and that defended it in its moments of crisis. Eventually, by the end of the first third of the twentieth century, the integrative forces of the market led a growing southern white middle class to disavow lynching. White southerners fashioned instead a legal order that eschewed the social chaos and unseemliness of lynching but nonetheless perpetuated its symbolic functions of ritualistic lethal retribution and the enactment of white supremacy in the punishment of crime.

Collective Violence and the Death Penalty in the Northeast

Ethnocultural and developmental factors contributed to northeasterners' preference for crime-control measures that fell short of extralegal killing. Yankees from New England migrated west into New York State in the late eighteenth and early nineteenth centuries, carrying with them commercial and political values and a Puritan religious tradition that emphasized regularity, probity, and communal governance as they populated counties from the Hudson Valley to Lake Erie. Rapid capitalist expansion propelled by New York City's central role as a port and financial center and the construction of the Erie Canal meant extensive industrialization and urban growth in New York, Rochester, and Buffalo. A large middle class, interested in a stable economic and social order safeguarded by due-process law, simultaneously emerged. The rural "burnt-over district" of upstate New York favored religious enthusiasm and experimentation in the first half of the nineteenth century in Protestant revivalism and in radical sects like the Mormons and Millerites (Seventh-Day Adventists) that foreswore traditional doctrines and social arrangements. Slavery had been an important component of colonial New York's mercantile economy, but individual manumissions and a gradual emancipation statute in 1799 ended the institution in the egalitarian era of the revolution and early republic.[1]

Middle-class reform impulses that stressed the reformation of the human and social condition, including the campaigns seeking the abolition of slavery, the improved treatment of prisoners and the mentally ill, and the end of the death penalty, also flourished in this social and cultural ferment. Religious liberals (Unitarians and Universalists), opposed by conservative Protestants (Congregationalists), failed to convince the New York state legislature to abolish the death penalty in 1841. But reform elements did compel the antebellum refashioning of the New York gallows into a private, carefully controlled affair. Perhaps most importantly, middle-class reformers, with their stress on humanitarianism and legal and institutional solutions to social problems, molded the cultural and political climate in New York in such a way that lynching could never enjoy substantial popular and political support, as it did in other regions of the United States.[2]

Collective violence propelled by racial, ethnic, and class animosities was, however, a familiar phenomenon in the cities of the Northeast in the nineteenth and early twentieth centuries. This urban mayhem differed significantly from lynching. Rioters in New York City, Philadelphia, Boston, Providence, and elsewhere selected wider victims than the lynch mobs that pursued individuals accused of particular crimes (although many lynchings did of course broadcast messages of racial and class intimidation). Urban rioters targeted entire groups, such as African Americans or Irish Catholics, in large-scale enactments of racial, ethnic, class, and political grievance. Urban northeastern mobs sometimes murdered their victims, as in the New York City Draft Riots in 1863, when Irish laborers hanged African Americans. But the lethal response of militia also accounted for casualties in urban rioting, as in the Orange Riots in New York City in 1871, when authorities fired upon Irish Catholic crowds protesting the Irish Protestant Orangemen's parade, killing sixty.[3]

Group violence against property and persons was thus familiar to urban northeasterners. But the peculiar configuration of lynching—narrowly targeted collective killing often motivated by criminal justice concerns—was rare in the Northeast. New York's criminal justice system offered an alternative to the punitive vision embraced by lynchers and their defenders in other regions. Reform impulses profoundly reshaped New York's death row, recasting law enforcement agencies and legal executions as quintessentially "modern" instruments for the reinforcement of the social and racial control of crime.[4]

Between 1891, when electrocutions were inaugurated in the prison at Sing Sing, and 1946, 517 persons died in New York State's centralized and "scientific" electric chair.[5] Analyzing data compiled in a meticulous register by the wardens at Sing Sing through 1933, a portrait of the state's death penalty emerges. Of the 357 persons electrocuted from the late nineteenth century through the early years of the Great Depression, all but two were male. At least one-fourth, and probably more, of those executed had allegedly killed women, suggesting the severe social-control sanction that the murder of a female provoked. The cauldron of Gotham's intense urbanization fired the wires of the overactive electric chair at Sing Sing: three-fourths of those electrocuted had been sentenced from the metropolitan area surrounding New York City.[6]

In many respects, Sing Sing's death row was an index of social disadvantage in the nation's largest metropolis. More than half of those electrocuted were Roman Catholic, most were in their early to mid twenties, and the great majority of inmates cited labor in unskilled, skilled, and service occupations when queried about their personal history upon admittance. But two ethnic and racial groups in particular swarmed the ranks of the condemned: Italians and blacks, in numbers that outstripped their contributions to the region's population. Between 1891 and 1933, authorities executed seventy-one men who had been born in Italy, 20 percent of the electric chair's yield. If second-generation Italians were included, the tally of Italian Americans would be higher. In the same years, authorities electrocuted sixty blacks, 17 percent of the total, most of whom had been born in southern or northeastern states, but some of whom were immigrants from the Caribbean.[7]

In the minds of downstate New York police, prosecutors, judges, and juries, Italian and African American defendants represented the gravest threats to social order amid extraordinary urban growth and successive waves of migration. No doubt a factor in the preponderance of Italian and black death row inmates was the difficulty the urban criminal justice system faced in dealing with immigrants from southern Europe and the American South, who brought with them traditions in which disputes were often settled informally and violently. Yet critical understandings of ethnic and racial difference also shaped the dire circumstances of Sicilians or African Americans accused of murder. A generalized fear of black violence, violent Italian crime, and the corrupt influence of "mafiosi" organizations gripped New York and other northeastern cities in the late nineteenth century. Through the mid-twentieth century, law enforcement, newspaper editorials, and political rhetoric periodically focused on the problem of Italian crime, particularly criminal organizations, and on the alleged criminal propensities of African Americans.[8]

In this atmosphere, however, the electrocution of Italians and blacks aided a wider goal, that of cleansing the urban environment of what middle-class whites perceived as one of its most dangerous elements, the tendency of Italians and blacks to erupt into homicidal violence. Antonio Salemne, a twenty-six-year-old laborer, was convicted of killing a woman with a razor in Rochester and was executed in September 1915. Emilio Semione, a thirty-eight-year-old laborer, was convicted of killing an Italian man with a blackjack in Buffalo and was executed in December 1923. Michael Fradiano, a fifty-year-old laborer, was convicted after the shooting death of a policeman in the Bronx and was executed in April 1923. Alberigo Mastrota, a thirty-two-year-old shoemaker, was convicted of killing a man with an iron shoe in Queens and was electrocuted in June 1924. David DeMaio, a thirty-four-year-old auto mechanic, was convicted of killing two trolley employees in a holdup in Westchester County and died in the electric chair in August 1926. It is unlikely that any of these murders involved a sophisticated mafiosi criminal operation. But New Yorkers' concern with Italian violence and the sheer number of Italians charged with murder made Sing Sing the location where southern European folkways met the ostensibly abstract principles of American justice. Similarly, Henry Brown, a twenty-three-year-old black laborer from Alabama, was convicted of killing a man with a club in the Bronx and was executed in January 1923. Ernest Mimms, a twenty-nine-year-old black chauffeur from South Carolina, was convicted in the shooting death of a police officer in the Bronx and was executed in February 1926. And George Budd Williams, a twenty-seven-year-old black seaman born in the West Indies, was sentenced from New York City after a conviction for killing a man and executed in January 1927. Brown, Mimms, and Williams confronted the racial fears evoked in white New Yorkers by the migration of southern blacks, Caribbean blacks, and the development of Harlem as an African American enclave in the late 1910s and 1920s.[9]

Death row inmates also encountered a novel technocratic culture that emerged around capital punishment in the Empire State. Executions were physically segregated in 1835 and were removed from the counties and centralized in the electric chair in the state prison at Sing Sing in 1891. With these developments, authorities sought to create, through the application of scientific techniques and principles, a sterilized and efficient death penalty that reconciled the popular clamor for retributive justice with the virtues of modernity.[10]

In an unusually celebrated and prolonged New York City case that invoked a fear of the lethal capacity of gambler and gangster culture and anxiety over police corruption, five men—the East Side gangsters Harry "Gyp the Blood" Horowitz, "Lefty Louis" Rosenberg, "Whitey Lewis" Jacob Seidenshner, "Dago Frank" Corofisi, and the police detective Frank Becker—died in the electric chair for the July 1912 murder of the gambler Herman Rosenthal.[11]

A *New York Tribune* writer dissected the cultural currents at work in the death ritual when the three Jewish gangsters and their Italian comrade were electrocuted at sunrise on April 13, 1914. The correspondent, Arthur Ruhl, underlining the tragic aspects of the affair, attributed the ritual to "a society which has not yet found the way to bridge the ghastly contrast between its modern sensibilities and mediaeval modes of punishment." Ruhl detailed the depraved urban environment that ostensibly produced the murderers and expressed the middle-class argument that the electrocution served the interests of "the people" as retribution against "hired assassins" and unlawful law officers. This view was not shared by working-class East Siders, who protested the execution. Ruhl also depicted the relentless attention of journalists eager to broadcast all aspects of the execution to consumers. Finally, he sketched the peculiar technocracy of the New York electric chair witnessed by a rapt audience of doctors, journalists, and curious citizens.

A wooden screen rose behind the chair, concealing the switchboard, and standing behind this screen, peering now at his electrical apparatus, now at the chair, was a studious looking elderly man with spectacles. He was the executioner, although he might well have been some rather near-sighted, preoccupied librarian. He turned a switch, testing the current, and lamps glowed brilliantly above and beneath the chair. Then two of the assistants dipped the cap and the electrodes in the pail of water. . . . The warden, pale himself now, turned to men sitting on the benches. "This man may make a statement," he said. "If he does you are to say nothing and ask him no questions."

The steady murmur of prayers and the shuffle of feet on stone came nearer. Two tall broad-shouldered keepers in blue and brass buttons, marching side by side, with a rather quaint air of doing what they could to lend the dignity of a procession, came through the door. Then, with his confessor, came "Dago Frank." . . . His head rolled weakly from side to side as his hands were strapped to the arms of the chair, the belt wrapped 'round his middle, and the cap and the straps across eyes and chin. . . . He was sitting thus, murmuring in a dazed fashion, his confessor, standing a little to the side in front of him, repeating the words before him, when the old gentleman standing beside the screen made a motion with his hand. The boy's words were cut short, his body stiffened and rose as far as the straps would permit it. . . . The current was turned off and the body, a trifle paler, if anything, where the forehead and mouth showed, sank down a little in the chair.

. . . Free from his long ordeal, at least as far as consciousness is concerned, the current was nevertheless turned on twice more. Each time the huddled shape rose stiffly, and on the second and third times there was a sizzling of hair or flesh beneath the cap and the odor spread through the room.

Then the boy's shirt was pulled open, the doctors applied their stethoscopes, turned back his eyelids and a tall, melancholy, youngish man, who has this duty frequently, turned to the spectators and said in a dull voice: "I pronounce this man dead." At the same instant two men in white uniforms appeared at the door at the left of the screen leading to the autopsy room. The cap and straps were removed and the Italian's limp head fell forward. . . .

The room was cleared; another group of spectators were admitted;

again the cap was dipped in the water; the door opened and the shuffling of feet and droning of prayers began again.[12]

The smoothness of the multiple electrocution was not accidental. The condemned were given narcotics before being led to the chair (supposedly to assist the flow of electricity), and the order of death was arranged to proceed from the weakest temperament to the strongest. In fact, Jacob Seidenshner's turn was accelerated from fourth to second after he started to loudly proclaim his innocence. Similar procedures were followed in other New York executions, which differed in one significant respect: they received far less press attention. Most electrocutions at Sing Sing in the early twentieth century elicited scant newspaper coverage, seldom meriting more than several paragraphs. This was true even in the upstate cities and towns where a minority of murders occurred and where, presumably, murders were not as anonymous as they sometimes seemed in New York City. As a result of the frequency with which the currents of the electric chair flowed, capital punishment in New York State became routinized, a regular and unexceptional exercise in state retribution. The routinization of the death penalty through carefully controlled proceedings, the application of science, and tedious repetition achieved a far-reaching transformation of the death rite. Removed from its communal origins, New York's death penalty achieved the aura of regularity and control that due-process advocates admired but that also satisfied rough-justice enthusiasts with its relentless retribution for homicide, especially among ethnic- and racial-minority offenders.[13]

The northeastern trends in which the death penalty was physically segregated from the public, removed from the counties and its local basis, technocratized, and routinized through the electric chair and gas chamber were replicated in the Midwest, West, and South, as lynching declined and then ceased in the early twentieth century. But rough-justice impulses had never soared in New England and the mid Atlantic as they had in the Midwest, West, and South. Instead, northeastern authorities channeled popular demands for harsh retributive justice, especially against ethnic and racial minorities in urban areas, into concealed, controlled, and frequent capital punishment. A large and highly influential middle class had shaped a death penalty unlikely to arouse popular passions yet able to satisfy popular demands for retribution and racial and ethnic control. The late nineteenth-century cultural war over due-process law that raged in other regions through lynching was thus stillborn in the Northeast. Bourgeois northeasterners instead remade the death penalty in accordance with their ideological preferences for regularity, privacy, efficiency, and ethnic and racial hierarchy.

The End of Lynching in the Midwest

In the lower Midwest, Yankee and Butternut traditions competed for supremacy in popular understandings of criminal justice, yet reformist notions of law emanating from the Northeast increasingly won out, in tandem with the elaboration of a sophisticated agricultural capitalism. The more ethnically diverse and urbanized upper Midwest had seen only sporadic lynchings; acceptance of centralized state authority and aggressive law enforcement to avert mob violence had come easily there by the late nineteenth century. Midwestern lynchers did occasionally still take lives, however, in circumstances of early twentieth-century racial and antiradical hysteria, for instance, in Collinsville, Illinois, in 1917, in Duluth, Minnesota, in 1920, and in Marion, Indiana, in 1930.[14]

Iowa's governors centralized law enforcement authority in the executive office beginning in the late nineteenth century, replacing an archaic and increasingly inadequate system that had privileged local authority. Many local officials wrote to the governor in the late nineteenth and early twentieth centuries pleading the poverty of county budgets and begging for funds that would aid the efforts of county law enforcement to apprehend criminals that their communities especially feared. In petitions to the governor for rewards for the arrest and conviction of murderers, county attorneys often referred to the indignation in a locality following a particular homicide. County officeholders cited the inability of the sheriff to make headway in investigating and prosecuting a case without the incentive of funds provided to private individuals, including self-styled detectives, by the governor's office. These petitions, which placed county officials in the position of supplicants for the governor's discretionary funds, indicated the frequent inadequacy of county resources in serious criminal cases.[15] Hardly a novel element in criminal justice administration, executive rewards in Iowa were a remnant of the makeshift law enforcement efforts during the period of settlement, consistent with the nineteenth-century "self-help" approach to fighting crime.[16] By the last decades of the century, traditional self-help, quasi-legal organizations formed by rural landholders to fight property crime, often termed "Anti–Horse Thief Associations," had faded into sentimental clubs for old settlers. Like their close extralegal relation, the vigilante committee, the Anti–Horse Thief Association lost its purpose after the development of a sophisticated agrarian capitalism, which reconfigured transportation networks and the means of production.[17]

In the 1890s the legislature expanded the governor's authority to offer rewards in serious criminal cases, from exclusively in arsons and homicides to any felony punishable by ten years or more in the penitentiary.[18] Commentators increasingly pressed for a greater role for the executive office in coordinating the capture of criminals, especially in light of the risks and disorder inherent in the impressment of communal posses. Following a spate of lynchings, the *Dubuque Times* noted in 1883 that "[t]he state, instead of employing the shrewdest detective talent and organizing a force that would make certain the capture of even these bold highwaymen, permits sheriff's posses to hunt the desperate devils and to be shot down by them as fast as they are overtaken. Private individuals are compelled to take steps for securing the protection already guaranteed to them by the state, and to make the attempt in what must necessarily be an inefficient way. . . . It is a shame and an outrage that in a country with a perfect network of railroads and telegraph lines these brutes are still uncaptured for want of proper state assistance in the chase."[19]

A sophisticated state agency that could facilitate crime-fighting efforts would not exist for several more decades in Iowa. Nonetheless, the state executive gradually accumulated more power in the criminal justice system. In the early twentieth century, the progressive Republican governor Albert B. Cummins initiated a series of penal reforms that reduced some of the discretionary authority of the district judges, including the introduction of indeterminate prison sentences administered by a board of parole.[20]

Crucially, the response of state and local governments to lynching changed dramatically by the end of the nineteenth century. Reticence characterized the attitude of governors when mob killings occurred in the 1880s. Although enabled by statute to send militia to prevent mobs from storming jails, state executives aggressively used militia only when requested by railroad and mining companies to put down labor disturbances.[21] When asked in the 1880s to take measures to offset lynching, state officials argued that the authority lay with district judges and county sheriffs.[22] The approach of state and local governments shifted in the 1890s, as county officials and governors ordered troops to protect prisoners from mobs. Local and state officials began to worry about the bad publicity lynchings attracted; governors had an increasing consciousness of their own powers over law enforcement matters. Iowa law gave local officials the ability to call out troops within their county if circumstances warranted, with post facto supervision by the governor. If additional forces were necessary, the governor could dispatch them from other counties. Militia protected jails in Des Moines in June 1891, in Council Bluffs in January 1893, in Taylor County in September 1893, and in Albia in November 1900.[23]

As Iowa officials assigned militia to defend jails, mobs were consistently thwarted in their objectives. Energetic and effective law enforcement, including the enlistment of police reinforcements from neighboring municipalities and the secret removal of prisoners to safety, similarly signaled the heightened efforts of officials to prevent lynching.[24] The concentration of supervision over criminal justice in the state executive branch and the new reluctance of county and municipal officials to cooperate with lynch mobs undermined the recourse to collective violence in serious criminal cases by the early twentieth century.

In 1894 the Iowa legislature largely divorced the administration of the death penalty from its local basis in the county of conviction by centralizing the gallows at the state penitentiary in Ft. Madison.[25] In practice, Iowa executions now adhered to a familiar, spare ritual in which guards led in the condemned man, who had spent his last moments with a spiritual advisor. The prisoner had an opportunity to make a final statement, and he was then blindfolded and hanged. Attendants quickly took the corpse away as spectators departed.[26] In comparison to antebellum procedures and contemporaneous lynchings, this mode of operation was antiseptic, formalized, and unlikely to provoke scenes of public disorder.[27]

In a letter written in 1911, the former governor William Larrabee asserted that the legal hangings administered while he was in office (1886–90) undercut lynching in Iowa. Larrabee noted that two executions occurred during his administration, whereas previously "there had not been a legal execution for 22 years, but . . . there had been several lynchings." Larrabee argued, "After the two executions referred to, I think it was about 18 years before there was another lynching and only this one in all this time. They were numerous before."[28] Lynchings in Iowa had in fact become rare in the last decade of the nineteenth century and then ceased entirely in the early 1900s, as legal executions became more frequent. The gallows was dormant between 1865 and 1887, and lynchers killed thirty-three men during those years, the majority on homicide charges.[29] The state reinaugurated the death penalty in 1887 and legally hanged six men through 1910. Lynchings slowed considerably, as five mob executions occurred between 1888 and 1895 and only one afterwards, in Charles City in 1907.[30] In the 1920s, state officials radically sped up the rate of execution, hanging eight men from 1922 through 1925 and another eight convicted murderers from 1931 through 1938. At the same time, lynching disappeared from Iowa's social-control repertoire.[31]

In the upper Midwest, where lynchers had never held great sway, the June 1, 1888, lynching of Andrew Grandstaff by a mob of a thousand in Viroqua, Wisconsin, after the murder of an elderly farm couple and their grandchildren, anticipated the forces that would end lynching in Wisconsin. Substantial evidence suggests that Vernon County officials aggressively sought to thwart the mob's intentions. Although they may have feared that they could not carry Grandstaff to La Crosse for safekeeping through an angry and growing crowd, law officers determinedly fought and argued with the mob. Moreover, the county's officials unsuccessfully sought assistance from Governor Jeremiah Rusk. As the crowd grew, officers telegraphed the governor requesting that he dispatch militia to guard the jail. Rusk reportedly refused, replying that "he had full faith in the conduct of the citizens of Vernon county." As this faith proved sadly misplaced, officers telegraphed him again in the evening as the mob remained outside the jail. This time, Rusk replied that it was too late for trains to take the "nearest company of national guards" to Viroqua and that help would have to wait until morning. He reportedly suggested that the sheriff swear in as many special deputies as possible to protect the jail. But this naïve recommendation was clearly impossible, the *Milwaukee Sentinel*'s correspondent wrote, because "[e]very man within a radius of twenty miles and more . . . was in sympathy with the fast multiplying mob."[32]

The aggressive action of law enforcement to outwit lynchers helped to end the practice in Wisconsin in the succeeding decade. For instance, in May 1893, rumors abounded in Eau Claire of the impending attempt to lynch William Dukelow, who had been convicted of raping a four-year-old, Agnes McSheffery. After the judge pronounced a sentence of thirty years in prison following a guilty plea, law officers hurriedly transported Dukelow by hack to outside the city limits, where they placed him on a train to Waupun. The girl's father and others denounced the authorities' quick action, but it may have saved Dukelow's life.[33] Thus a shift from a preference by midwesterners for criminal justice exacted locally to an acceptance of the efficacy of justice administered by centralized state authorities, along with the increasingly aggressive actions taken by law officers to avert mob violence, ended lynching along the Middle Border.

Lynching's Demise in the West

The waning of lynching in the West was similar to the erosion of the practice in the Midwest. Fear of the social disorder catalyzed by serious crime, public executions, and lynchings provoked legal changes by the early twentieth century. Officials centralized and regularized the death penalty, ensuring that it would be administered in private and in a carefully controlled manner. Westerners accepted these alterations, which accompanied the industrialization of parts of the vast and diverse region as well as its increasing integration into a national mass culture. Yet powerful, sentimentalized memories of an "Old West" in which collective violence had supposedly enforced popular mandates for social order and justice against rampant criminal elements remained. This collective regional memory of rough justice sustained occasional lynchings against African Americans, Mexicans, particularly heinous criminals, and political radicals through the World War II era.[34]

The legal execution of the celebrated gunfighter Tom Horn in Cheyenne, Wyoming, in November 1903 triggered a sea change in the administration of capital punishment and in Wyomingites' understanding of the punishment of homicide. On October 24, 1902, a jury found Horn guilty of murdering Willie Nickell, the fifteen-year-old son of a sheepworker targeted by cattle ranchers in Laramie County. A judge sentenced Horn to hang on January 9, but the state supreme court issued a stay of execution to review his conviction. In October 1903 the supreme court affirmed the district court's verdict and scheduled Horn's execution for November 30. Governor Fenimore Chatterton rejected numerous petitions insisting on Horn's innocence and refused to intervene to block the death penalty.[35]

In the months leading up to the legal execution of Horn, a crisis arose in Cheyenne. State and county authorities deployed militia out of fear that Horn's influential friends among the cattle operators might try to forcibly free him or that a working-class mob aroused by Horn's crimes against the range proletariat and the legal delays in his case might lynch him.[36] Editorialists in Wyoming's newspapers melded a pseudopopulist critique of the state's legal systems with a crime-control perspective in their support for the erstwhile cattle detective's death sentence. These writers argued that the execution was necessary because it would prove that even a man supported by wealthy capitalists and defended by talented lawyers could die on the gallows. According to this rationale, the legal hanging of Horn would restore confidence in the fairness of the criminal justice system, defend communities by deterring homicide, and implicitly discourage lynching.[37]

The execution of Horn would be the last legal hanging in Wyoming to attract a festive, popular following. Horn died on an elaborate water-trap gallows just after eleven in the morning before more than thirty witnesses. Outside the Laramie County jail, a large crowd, watched carefully by militia, released a "half-hearted shout" after learning of Horn's death.[38] Following the execution, the *Laramie Republican* exulted that "'the people of Wyoming have risen above the methods of the anarchist'" and that "'[h]ereafter in Wyoming the occupation of the assassin who kills for hire will be gone.'"[39] But the demise of Tom Horn signaled more than the passing of the age of the incorporation gunfighters.

The state government of Wyoming responded to the turmoil surrounding Horn's execution and the early twentieth-century lynching spree by thoroughly revamping the institution of the death penalty.[40] The legislature rewrote the capital punishment statute, centralizing the gallows from the counties to the state penitentiary. The new law specified that visits to the condemned would be strictly limited and that the warden and his deputies must perform executions within the penitentiary "before the hour of sunrise." These reforms eliminated the popular elements that had persisted in the administration of the gallows in late nineteenth-century Wyoming. Legislators banished the communalistic carnival of execution day by removing the local interest of the sheriff and county officials, preventing any possibility that a fascinated public might peer down upon an inadequate enclosure outside a county jail, prohibiting death-watch visits by curious strangers, and eliminating midday crowds.[41] Editors linked the impetus for the revised death penalty statute specifically to the prevention of lynching. The *Wyoming Tribune* argued, "Aside from preventing lynchings, escapes and jail deliveries of criminals sentenced to die, by removing them to the state prison it will eliminate from the community the nervous strain which for days precedes an execution and the depression of feeling among many people for days after it occurs." The *Tribune* cited Cheyenne's recent "unpleasant experience" with the legal hanging of Tom Horn.[42] The *Cheyenne Leader* similarly believed that with the new statute, "the heretofore dangerous factor of an inflamed local sentiment with the possibility of a lynching will be disposed of."[43]

In the next two decades, Wyomingites assimilated the novel conception of the death penalty as a state-sponsored rite of retributive justice concealed from public view and divorced from ceremonial local interest. This cultural transformation occurred at least in part because the state sped up the pace of execution in the 1910s. Private, technocratic, and comparatively efficient capital punishment replaced accessible but rare legal hangings, satisfying the exponents of retributive justice. The state took the lives of five prisoners from May 1912 through October 1916.[44]

Joseph M. Carey, governor from 1910 to 1914, exemplified the fusion of nineteenth-century rough-justice principles with the new state machinery of death. Carey had been a force in Wyoming politics for four decades. As mayor of Cheyenne he pleaded with the mob that lynched Henry Mosier in 1883, was selected by the legislature as a U.S. senator in 1890, and, long after a fallout with the Republican machine of F. E. Warren, was elected governor as a Democrat on a "Progressive" platform.[45] Carey reviewed the convictions of Joseph Seng in 1912 and Warren Jenkins in 1913 and adamantly refused to intervene before they were hanged in sparse early-morning ceremonies overseen by a few officials, a spiritual advisor, and several acquaintances of the prisoners. To those who petitioned for mercy, Carey bluntly asserted that criminal courts had proven the guilt of the two men. To Joseph Seng's mother, Carey wrote: "He [Seng] murdered his victim and gave him no chance whatever for his life . . . at this time I do not see any excuse whatever for executive clemency in his case."[46]

Carey's stress on retributive justice for murderers and his impatience with humanitarian sentiment that opposed the death penalty recalls the disdain of nineteenth-century Wyomingites for "mere sentimentalism." Yet the punitive apparatus that he oversaw in death penalty cases differed substantially from that of nineteenth-century governors, as did the acquiescence of Wyomingites to the new mode of capital punishment.

The execution of Wilmer Palmer in 1916, a year in which Wyoming executed three men, the most in its history, represented the convergence of industrializing and urbanizing trends in the New West, the renovation of the death penalty, and the transfiguration of the popular understanding of the punishment of homicide. Palmer, a cook at a boarding house in the burgeoning oil district outside Casper, had recently arrived from Nebraska with his wife, Jessie, a waitress. After Wilmer Palmer murdered Jessie Palmer, reportedly out of jealousy at the attention she was receiving in the nearly all-male environment of the oil fields, oil hands in the Salt Creek camp began forming a lynch mob before Palmer was secreted by automobile to Casper. Palmer received inconsistent assistance from his attorneys as his case made its way through the criminal justice system, and the state pardons board denied his appeal of a death sentence. Palmer died on the gallows at the penitentiary in Rawlins at 3:22 A.M., attended by a spiritual advisor, the prison warden, and several other witnesses.[47]

Employment opportunities in the rapidly growing oil fields drew Wilmer and Jessie Palmer to east central Wyoming, and the social conditions of proto-industrializing Natrona County may have contributed to the act of homicide and to the near lynching. But industrializing and urbanizing trends also ran counter to the rural cultural complex that endorsed lynching and had bolstered extensive communal participation in legal executions. Thirteen years earlier, residents of Casper and outlying areas had lynched Charles Woodard. Between 1905 and 1915, Natrona County's population, spurred by oil development, doubled from less than twenty-five hundred to more than five thousand.[48] The contrast between the celebrated lynching of Charles Woodard and the staid, concealed legal hanging of Wilmer Palmer denoted the abandonment of the collective element in the punishment of murderers and the acceptance of the formalization of the death rite by Wyomingites. Only the demands of racial hierarchy would briefly preserve the tradition of mob murder in the Equality State, as was analyzed in chapter 3.[49]

Lynching attenuated in the Pacific Northwest as it had in the Rocky Mountain and High Plains West. Mob violence faded in the region in the early years of the twentieth century as due-process sentiments became more influential, mob killings became too incongruous with the Northwest's development and ambitions, and working-class and rural northwesterners increasingly placed their confidence in a technocratic and bureaucratic death penalty instead of customary retributive justice rituals of public executions and lynchings. A thousand had watched the legal execution of the convicted murderer Jack Leonard on March 25, 1898, at Colfax in southeastern Washington, fifteen of them bearing invitations to the execution platform, three hundred from the courthouse yard surrounding the scaffold, and the remaining hundreds from a "snow-clad hill" with a view of "the instrument of death."[50] Significantly, statutory reform in the early twentieth century eradicated the highly popular and localistic elements that had surrounded legal executions from Washington's inception as a territory. Executions were removed from the counties and centralized behind four walls and before limited witnesses at the penitentiary in Walla Walla. Legislators sought to prohibit even the vicarious experience of an execution. A 1909 law went so far as to forbid the publication of "any detailed account of the execution of any person convicted of crime."[51] The pace of executions also accelerated in these years. Nineteen persons met their end on the Evergreen State's gallows between 1873 and 1898, twenty-three from 1900 through 1911, and forty-six between 1921 and 1947.[52]

Interestingly, the mob hanging of William Hamilton, a "well-to-do" young rancher, for the alleged rape and murder of a twelve-year-old, Mabel Richards, in Asotin in southeastern Washington in August 1903 provoked little editorial comment, unlike earlier Northwest lynchings. A masked mob of around a hundred easily seized Hamilton from jail and then debated whether to torture and burn him. Settling on more moderate means, the masked lynchers hanged Hamilton from an electric guy wire with his head enshrouded in a black hood as a crowd of a thousand raptly observed from more than a city block away.[53] The *Asotin County Sentinel* reported the cheers that erupted upon Hamilton's expiration, from a crowd "happy in knowing that the slayer of an innocent child could no more run at large, and that the murder of little Mabel Richards had, so far as public sentiment was concerned, been speedily avenged without the aid of court or jury."[54] No attempt at further defending or explaining the lynching or jousting among editors with contrary opinions ensued. In Asotin, the act seemed self-explanatory. Elsewhere in the Northwest, the mob killing of Hamilton may have seemed an atavistic anomaly that hardly required the hand-wringing reexamination of northwestern society that earlier mob murders had elicited. No longer did the practice resonate with ambivalent and changing regional perspectives on law, crime, and punishment. The Northwest's tradition of lynching briefly reemerged, however, in Centralia, Washington, when the divisive aftermath of World War I pitted the labor radicalism of the Wobblies against the hyperpatriotic Legionnaires amid a polarized logging economy. On November 11, 1919, a small mob took Wesley Everest, a Wobbly, from jail, hanged him from a bridge over the Chehalis River, and possibly castrated him. The lynching occurred after a shootout in which four Legionnaires died in Centralia.[55]

California experienced legal and cultural changes analogous to those in the interior West and the Northwest in the late nineteenth and early twentieth centuries. Characteristically in the vanguard of social and cultural ferment as the West's largest state in population and territory, California's encounter with capital punishment reform in some ways resembled that in the Northeast. California saw many more legal executions than other western states, and it revamped its death penalty earlier. In line with reformist notions of how capital punishment might be modernized for social good, legislators in Sacramento centralized legal executions from the counties to state prisons in 1891; the law took effect with the hanging of José Gabriel at San Quentin on March 3, 1893. In 1937, state officials replaced the gallows with the gas chamber. Between 1866 and 1892, 89 executions occurred in California; from 1893 through 1947 officials executed 376 persons, 245 of these between 1920 and 1947.[56]

Yet mob violence persisted in the Golden State, as the symbolic and retributive allures of lynching violence incongruously bridged "Old West" mythology with the social-control dilemmas of urbanization. In December 1920 three members of the Howard Street Gang in San Francisco fled to Santa Rosa to escape arrest for assaulting young women and then shot and killed two San Francisco detectives and the Sonoma County sheriff who sought to arrest them. Early on the morning of December 10, a mob estimated at sixty easily obtained jail keys from the sheriff's office and took George Boyd, Terrence Fitts, and Charles Valento out to a cemetery and hanged them from a tree. Rumors circulated that San Francisco police officers and Sonoma County deputies had performed the lynching.[57] The *San Francisco Chronicle* denounced the collective killing as a "reversion to barbarism," but the *Oakland Tribune* attributed it to a lack of "confidence" in "the regularly constituted machinery of justice," and the *Santa Rosa Republican* declared that "the people of Santa Rosa and Sonoma County are satisfied with the outcome" of the "act of lawlessness." Governor William D. Stephens excoriated the lynching but did not offer a reward for the capture of the perpetrators. His denunciation recast the perennial rough-justice critique of the inadequate administration of criminal justice with the perceived menace of urban criminality: "No matter how good the standing of the citizens who participated, theirs was mob rule, and defiance of the law; and even if they were convinced that their act was one of substantial justice, the example they set undermines respect for law, and weakens the administration of justice. If the police are remiss in permitting lawless gangs to exist in our cities, if the courts fail in their duty, if the administration of our criminal statutes is ineffective, then let us remedy such conditions. . . . They set a dangerous example and I hope that the people of our State will recognize this fact so that this unhappy incidence will tend to make lynch-law all the more impossible in California."[58]

Thirteen years later, in 1933, another California governor, James Rolph Jr., was less equivocal in defending his failure to dispatch the National Guard to protect two accused kidnappers and murderers, John M. Holmes and Thomas H. Thurmond, from a mass mob in San Jose. The press likened the crowd of fifteen thousand assembled in St. James Park, across the street from the Santa Clara County jail, to "'a Roman holiday'" in which spectators danced and mothers encouraged children to watch the "'mob inflict its sadistic wrath.'" Holmes and Thurmond allegedly kidnapped, demanded a ransom for, and murdered Brooke Hart, the twenty-two-year-old son of an affluent San Jose merchant. They allegedly threw Hart off the San Mateo Bridge and were traced through a telephone call to the victim's father.[59] The recovery of Hart's body on November 26 catalyzed the public rage that culminated in the mob's assault on the jail that evening. The crime occurred amid a wave of well-publicized

Depression-era kidnappings and murders. Rolph described the lynching as a deterrent to a high-profile offense: "'I would not permit innocent men and children to be killed in the troubles which might have ensued should troops be sent to the San Jose jail. . . . I stand for law and order, of course, and as regrettable as was this lynching, I believe that it was a fine lesson to the whole nation. There will be less kidnapping in the country now.'"[60]

Editorials in California and elsewhere condemned the governor (the *New York Times* deriding him as "Governor Lynch") and the San Jose mob execution, but state and county authorities did not pursue an investigation. Beyond the urban Bay Area, the remote region surrounding Mt. Shasta near the Oregon border, which had been prone to lynching in the late nineteenth century, claimed two final victims, both hanged in Siskiyou County: the white alleged murderer of a small-town police chief in August 1935 and an African American butcher and alleged cattle rustler in January 1947. The California attorney general found the explanation for the "uncontrollable unrest" of the 1935 lynching near Yreka in the recent postponement of the execution of a convicted murderer in the state and the "apathy of the Supreme Court of the United States."[61] California state officials consistently sought to rationalize the odd persistence of mob violence in the Golden State, finding an explanation in the travails of urban life, modern crime, and a rough-justice heritage.

The Decline of Southern Lynching

Lynching was most deeply rooted in the South, as white southerners in the postbellum era discovered in mob violence the mechanism for enforcing the racial order that emancipation and the growth of towns and cities disrupted. Originating in the elastic police powers and popular sovereignty that the white citizenry had originally assumed in the slave patrol, lynching violence complemented and supplanted anemic legal agencies in vivid demonstration that challenges to white supremacy would be met with lethal force. In the late nineteenth century, as African American leaders such as Ida B. Wells agitated against lynching, a small minority of white southerners protested the arbitrary, cruel, and unlawful nature of mob killings. However, in the early twentieth century, as urban growth and capitalist development intensified and created a significant southern middle class, white elites recognized in lynching a threat to social order and the flow of capital. In Louisiana after 1900, white elites castigated lynching and sought to erect a new legal order that would replace communal retribution with efficient, regularized, and racialized legal executions, that is, what some have termed "legal lynchings."

Shortly before midnight on December 31, 1886, a young district judge in north central Louisiana, Andrew Augustus Gunby, sat down to compose his thoughts on the achievements and failures of the previous twelve months. Waxing eloquent, Gunby explained the joys of his first year of marriage and the birth of his daughter. In penitential tones, the diarist chided tendencies toward indulgence and overexpenditure and a failure to progress in his personal studies and writing. Gunby reserved his deepest regret, however, for his defeat in the canvass for the Democratic nomination for Congress from Louisiana's Fifth District. After stating his confidence in his superior political talents, Gunby lamented: "My defeat was unquestionably due to the opposition of Ouachita Parish and this opposition was founded solely on my course in condemning the lynching of a negro man in Feb. 1886."[62]

The affair that culminated in the mob hanging of George Robinson had its roots in a confrontation on the streets of Monroe seven months earlier. Two upper-class white youths insulted a black woman with whom Robinson was traveling home from an evening out. In an ensuing fight, Robinson struck one of the young whites and was shot in the hand. Charged with assault with intent to murder, Robinson paid a fine and left Monroe. When he returned in December, the white youths and two acquaintances sought vengeance by visiting his house and demanding entrance so that they could flog him. When he tried to escape, Robinson was shot by Milliard F. Parker. One of the other whites, named Fullam, also attempted to shoot him, but the bullet instead hit Parker, and the wound proved fatal. Robinson fled, but authorities jailed him in Monroe after his capture in Mississippi. Rumors of lynching soon circulated, and a mob of more than a hundred broke into jail, paraded Robinson through town, and hanged him. Hundreds viewed the corpse in the hours that followed.[63]

Andrew Augustus Gunby, a friend of Milliard F. Parker, bitterly attacked the lynching in a public speech the next day in Monroe. Gunby argued that Robinson was not legally guilty of the crime, that the lynching undercut law and order, and that the act of mob violence was an injustice that profoundly damaged the community's social fabric. Gunby believed that after mob participants learned of his speech, they combined with a number of influential whites and politicians to derail his congressional nomination at the canvass in Ruston. He insisted that his opponents, many of them friends and acquaintances, had misunderstood his position: "I am sure that some of them never doubted my fealty to the Democratic Party or my unswerving devotion to the supremacy of the White race in the South. They knew and acknowledged in their hearts that I am and always have been as true a Southern man as any of them. . . . I admit I am sorry I was defeated—but I am not sorry that I condemned Mob Law—I am not sorry that I upheld Law and Order—for I am sure my course was moral and right and must remain so for all time to come."[64]

Gunby's denunciation of mob murder was not singular. A cultural chasm developed among northern Louisiana whites concerning the propriety of lynching. Detectable in Gunby's principled defense of law and order in the mid 1880s, the cleavage separated middle-class urban whites from the working-class and rural whites who advocated rough justice. Like Gunby and all white Louisianans, bourgeois northern Louisianans stressed the inviolability of white supremacy and the impossibility of "social equality" (that is, the social mixing of blacks and whites, with its heavily sexual connotations). Yet in the throes of northern Louisiana's urbanization and industrialization, elite urbanites feared the convulsive disorder of lynch mobs and promoted the efficacy of a streamlined legal process, especially state-sponsored capital punishment, as the remedy when African Americans were accused of crimes against whites. The business-class urbanites' position marked a radical transformation of the traditional conception of white cotton planters' prerogative, which had included the extralegal corporal punishment—and, by extension, lynching—of African American laborers that resisted white authority. Novel urban and industrial arrangements provoked racial and sexual anxieties among working-class whites and lynching sprees in Monroe and Shreveport. Bourgeois whites, influenced by outside criticism and financial pressures, responded with a scathing critique of mob violence that lay the seeds for the decline in popular support for and the incidence of mob killings in northern Louisiana in the early twentieth century. Middle-class advocates of legal process responded to lynchings and the threat they posed to public order and the flow of capital by reshaping capital punishment into a comparatively efficient, allegedly "modern," and thoroughly racial mechanism of retributive justice.

Economic and social changes thoroughly reconfigured northern Louisiana in the years after 1900. The mercantile center of north central Louisiana, the Ouachita Parish seat of Monroe, doubled in size to ten thousand in the first decade of the century.[65] Caddo Parish experienced considerable transformation in the first decade of the twentieth century as oil was discovered in the northern part of the parish, and Shreveport doubled in size to nearly thirty thousand.[66]

The urbanization and industrialization of northern Louisiana had contradictory results. The conglomeration of rural African Americans and country whites in developing urban and industrial spaces provoked substantial tensions, especially racial-sexual ones, which were sometimes channeled into large working-class white mobs. Yet northern Louisiana's towns and cities also formed middle classes of businessmen and lawyers who found the procedures of due-process law, stripped of the substance of deliberative justice, a more amenable guarantor of social order and profits. This urban bourgeoisie challenged the rough-justice perspective of working-class whites and rural white landholders by denouncing lynching. Their increasingly vocal opposition to mob violence undercut the legitimacy that lynching had enjoyed in northern Louisiana in the late nineteenth century.[67]

An entrenched culture of mob killings accompanied the growth of Monroe and Shreveport in the 1890s and early 1900s. Mobs murdered nine African Americans in Monroe between 1906 and 1914, four on rape or sexual charges, three by mass mobs.[68] Lynchers killed twenty-one blacks in Caddo Parish from 1900 through 1923, eight on rape or sexual charges, seven by large mobs.[69] Many of these incidents occurred in rural areas west of Shreveport, where an intransigent planter elite enmeshed itself after the turn of the century in a cycle of collective retaliation against African Americans. But four of the lynchings took place in Shreveport, all on rape or sexual allegations. Enormous mobs of working-class whites, provoked by accusations that black men had raped young white women, performed two of the collective killings in Shreveport.[70] Small mobs of less than ten murdered Leslie Leggett, accused of becoming intimate with an Italian girl, in 1923 and Thomas Miles, for writing letters to a white woman, in 1912. Monroe mobbers also pulled George Holden off a train and shot him dead in April 1919 for writing "an insulting note" to a white woman. The lethal response of city whites to the peculiar accusation that black men had authored letters to white women may have represented the uneasy adaptation of rural blacks and whites to urban life and its necessarily reordered arrangement of race and gender relations. Black migrants from Cotton Belt districts and white migrants from upcountry areas were unaccustomed to dealing with each other. This may have posed a special challenge during the intricacies of everyday interaction, particularly the ubiquitous anonymous encounters in cities.[71]

The urbanizing landscape of northern Louisiana also nurtured cultural forces that eroded support for mob violence. In February 1906, Governor Newton Blanchard intervened in Shreveport to prevent the lynching of Charles Coleman, an African American accused of murdering a white teenager, Margaret Lear. A Natchitoches editor characterized the situation in Louisiana's second largest city as a prolonged "contest" pitting "those who felt that swift and terrible punishment ought to be dealt out to the brute . . . [against] the press, the pulpit and a large part of the substantial citizens of the place united in a demand for the maintenance of law, and a compliance with its solemn forms."[72]

Deploying militia around the parish courthouse, Blanchard watched approvingly as the parish district court tried Coleman in four hours and the jury returned a verdict in three minutes. After impatiently waiting a week between conviction and execution, which was required under Louisiana law, officials hanged Coleman in the confines of the parish jail. Having supervised what amounted to a legal lynching, Blanchard declared that the majesty of the law had triumphed over the mob spirit in Shreveport.[73]

The Charles Coleman affair was only the most dramatic incident in Newton Blanchard's campaign against mob violence. During his tenure as governor from 1904 through 1908, Blanchard occasionally spoke out in condemnation of specific lynchings, personally admonished grand jurors and local law enforcement to punish mobbers, and sent militia to protect jails where prisoners were threatened.[74] Late nineteenth-century Louisiana governors had ignored the phenomenon of lynching, even as it exploded in the 1890s. But Blanchard's aggressive stance was at least partially a product of political calculation and image building, and it was not especially effective. In northern Louisiana alone, twenty-six mob killings occurred during his term in office, and the pace of mob violence increased in 1907 and 1908.[75] Furthermore, the governor neglected to support far-reaching legislation that would have penalized localities that inflicted mob executions or law enforcement in parishes where lynchings occurred.[76] Blanchard's critique of mob killing did annoy sectors of Louisiana society, white planters, the yeomanry, and the urban working class, who still viewed lynching as an acceptable solution to supposed problems of racial control. The influential governor's opinion marked a significant abandonment of the noninterventionist approach that local and state leaders had taken in the past. It also assisted the crystallization of urban middle-class opinion against lynching in Louisiana.[77]

The ideological evolution of the conservative Democrat Blanchard illuminates the process of cultural change in northern Louisiana. Born into the cotton-planter elite in the Red River Delta parish of Rapides in 1849, Blanchard began his professional career in Shreveport as an attorney for the railroads in the early 1870s. The highly successful corporation lawyer became chairman of the Democratic party in Caddo Parish during Redemption, and the federal government indicted him for his role in a fear campaign against black Republicans in 1878. In the next two decades, Blanchard's ties to the reactionary Bourbons who controlled the state Democratic party secured for him positions as a U.S. congressman and senator and on the state supreme court. Blanchard's term as governor saw efforts at "progressive" reform within the substantial constraints of the racist and one-party political culture of fin-de-siècle Louisiana. These initiatives included increased funding for public education (for whites), the institution of the white primary, the curbing of the governor's extraordinary appointive powers, and a modest revamping of the extremely inequitable property tax system.[78]

Blanchard pledged in his 1905 inaugural address to doggedly fight lynching, and thus the potential for a mob killing in his hometown of Shreveport took on symbolic importance. This consideration sparked the governor's direct role in forestalling the impending lynching of Charles Coleman.[79] In later speeches, Blanchard argued that mob violence damaged Louisiana's reputation, discouraged immigration, and retarded the state's growth. According to this rationale, lynching interfered with the gospel of economic and social progress promulgated by the Pelican State's business leaders.[80]

In the Charles Coleman affair, the governor rhetorically linked the prevalence of mob activity to the slow and deliberate pace of due-process law and asserted that the rapid trial and execution of Coleman was a worthy example for courts throughout the state. Expanding on this theme, Blanchard argued in a message to the state legislature that criminal courts throughout the state should expedite the administration of justice in aggravated cases where popular sentiment was aroused. This would destroy the conventional justification for lynching, which insisted that it was the only way to ensure swift and certain punishment for terrible offenses: "If, in cases of certain crimes, preference be given over all other business of the courts; if special sessions of the Grand Jury be held; if, in case of indictment, trial be had quickly, and, in case of conviction, a speedy execution of the sentence follow, the mob spirit will subside."[81]

In early twentieth-century Louisiana, the crimes that whites perceived as the most heinous were almost always those allegedly perpetrated by African American men. The Bourbon chief executive believed that in such instances streamlined legal process, observant of the forms but not of the substance of justice, should replace lynching. This would benefit "[e]very interest of the state," especially financial interests. Reared in the planter gentry, which had dominated Louisiana's Bourbon democracy in the late nineteenth century, Blanchard now expressed the urban bourgeois sensibility he had assimilated through his participation in Shreveport's business class and his familiarity with the state's leading economic players. Planter prerogatives transposed into capitalists' need for a social climate conducive to immigration and investment. Jim Crow, disfranchisement, and quick capital punishment bereft of legal safeguards could better ensure white supremacy, public order, and prosperity.[82]

Blanchard retired to his law firm in Shreveport after the end of his gubernatorial term, but his instrumental role in discouraging mob violence continued.[83] In late 1914, mobs in rural Caddo Parish murdered five blacks, provoking vociferous condemnation from the former governor and Shreveport's middle-class leaders and an energetic, if fruitless, investigation by state officials. On December 2, a posse of white farmers hanged Jobie Lewis and Elijah Durden, African Americans accused of murdering and robbing Charles Hicks, a white merchant. On December 11, a mob of fifty whites seized Charles Washington and Beard Henderson from a deputy sheriff and shot and killed them for the murder and robbery of Cyrus Hotchkin, a white man. The next day a mob of two hundred stormed the unsecured Shreveport jail, pulled Watkins Lewis from his cell, and carried him to the remote site where he had supposedly aided the murder of Charles Hicks. Lewis refused to confess his guilt when hanged over a fire and died after he was overcome by the smoke and heat.[84]

Middle-class opinion coalesced against the spate of mob executions. The *Shreveport Times* condemned the lynchings, scoring the "motley rabble" who performed the collective killings but also attacking parish officials who had failed to aggressively intervene and may have tacitly cooperated with the mob.[85] The Shreveport Chamber of Commerce and the Caddo Bar Association passed resolutions denouncing the mob murders and offered their support and assistance in a full investigation. The Chamber of Commerce pressed for legislation permitting governors to remove sheriffs who neglected their duty to prevent lynchings. Blanchard orchestrated the bar resolutions, stating, "nothing is so calculated to keep investors from the state as these cowardly lynchings." The former governor feared that the reputation of his "up-to-date and prosperous" parish would once again be besmirched as "Bloody Caddo," as it had been in Reconstruction and Redemption.[86]

Governor Luther Hall sent his attorney general, Ruffin Pleasant, to Shreveport to investigate the mob assassinations. Pleasant mounted a public examination of one hundred witnesses, virtually all of whom responded evasively. Even sheriff's deputies refused to reveal details, citing supposed threats made against their lives. Yet testimony from some observers uncovered the failure of deputies to take appropriate action to circumvent the mobs, the attendance of working-class Shreveport residents (including a manicurist and a junk dealer) at the mob execution of

Watkins Lewis, and a critical gap between urban-bourgeois views of legal process and those of rural whites. The sheriff, J. P. Flournoy, blamed prolynching sentiment among the "country people" who killed the five African Americans on the fact that "young lawyers" typically removed them from juries, believing that rural whites were more prejudiced against blacks. Sheriff Flournoy dismissed allegations that his deputies had neglected to adequately protect black prisoners, stating, "'I can take ten deputies and hold off any ordinary mob except in cases of criminal assault on women or children.'" In contrast, in one sample of middle-class opinion, the Louisiana Prison Reform Association termed the Caddo Parish lynchings a regression into the "'barbarism of the dark ages.'" The aftermath of the December 1914 lynchings underlined a significant cleavage aligning the Caddo Parish sheriff's office and white planters, who condoned or endorsed lynching, against Shreveport businessmen and lawyers, who vowed to stamp out what they perceived as a nefarious and atavistic practice.[87]

Following the 1914 controversy and the pronounced class and cultural strains it revealed, mobs killed only two more African Americans in Caddo Parish, the last in 1923. Lynching briefly surged again in the era of the First World War—there were eight mob killings in northern parishes in 1918 and eight more in 1919—as wartime tensions and reawakened questions concerning the meaning of black citizenship inspired another round of mob killing. But the practice of mob murder, so endemic in localized areas of northern Louisiana, was in inexorable decline by the 1910s. Mobs killed an average of 6.4 lynching victims a year in the first decade of the twentieth century, but this slipped to 3.9 per year in the 1910s, and one per year in the 1920s.[88] Simultaneously, the pace of legal executions across the region increased, suggesting that white northern Louisianans were perhaps unconsciously heeding the advice proffered by Newton Blanchard and assorted editorialists: to replace lynching with rapid convictions and legal hangings of African Americans.[89] The efforts of antilynching advocates such as Ida B. Wells and organizations such as the National Association for the Advancement of Colored People (NAACP) and the Association of Southern Women for the Prevention of Lynching (ASWPL), the unwanted publicity accorded by a rapidly nationalizing culture, and the burst of migration of African Americans to northern cities during World War I also played crucial roles in the demise of lynching.[90]

However, mob murder in postbellum northern Louisiana had traditionally served the purposes of local elites, whose authority now waned as a burgeoning urban middle class sought to set retrograde Louisiana on

the path toward economic and industrial development. White landholders in the Red River Delta and Ouachita River Valley had found lynching to be the solution when African Americans challenged their dominance of labor arrangements. Vastly outnumbered Mississippi Delta
whites turned to collective homicide during unusual moments when
black laborers seemed to overtly question white supremacy. Upcountry
whites found in extralegal killing an occasional outlet for economic and
sexual anxieties. In the first decades of the twentieth century, an emerg-
ing urban bourgeoisie wary of public disorder and threats to the accumu-
lation of capital pressed for systematic legal methods for the sustenance
of white supremacy. The regularity of Jim Crow, disfranchisement,
"efficient" convictions, and state-sponsored executions supplanted the
informal and extralegal police powers and violence through which white
northern Louisianans had formerly enforced the social control of African
Americans.[91]

EPILOGUE

The story of the evolution of lynching and criminal justice in the United States is in many ways a tragic one. This book chronicles Americans' predilection for violent and often cruel solutions to what they viewed as the social problem of crime. It depicts white Americans' obsession with the physical maintenance of racial hierarchy, a tendency without regional boundaries nor limited to the targeting of a single racial or ethnic group. It also describes the roots of the contemporary institution of capital punishment. The arbitrary and racist application of the death penalty today is not surprising when we learn that the modern death penalty originated in a compromise between proponents of rough justice and middle-class advocates of due process. Rough-justice enthusiasts, who were committed to the symbolic reinforcement of white supremacy through collective punishment, had never accepted the value of abstract principles of justice. Most middle-class supporters of legal process also subscribed to a racially hierarchical vision of American society. Many bourgeois whites abandoned their commitment to neutral legal process, beyond adherence to the forms of law, when criminal cases involved ethnic- or racial-minority defendants.

Lynching was more deeply entrenched in the South than elsewhere, and it persisted longer there. But as in the Northeast, Midwest, and West, one perspective on law and criminal justice—stressing the performance by the community of physical retribution on the serious offender—gave way to another, which emphasized the economic and moral efficacy of having the state exact regularized and sanitized punishment. That the Northeast made this transition easily by the mid-nineteenth century, the Midwest made it with a little difficulty by the late nineteenth century, the West made it with some difficulty by the early twentieth century, and the South made it with much difficulty by World War II highlights the cultural and legal legacy of slavery as well as the relationship of the country's regions to the middle-class cultural formation wrought by capitalist transformation.

The African American novelist Richard Wright, a Mississippi-born and -raised migrant to Chicago, captured well the tragic and extraordinarily consequential remaking of rough justice in the United States in the first half of the twentieth century. In his 1940 novel *Native Son*, Wright depicts Bigger Thomas, a young African American murderer created by the squalor, inhumanity, and hopelessness of the racially segregated northern metropolis. Bigger is accused of murdering and raping a young white woman, Mary Dalton. After a manhunt by Chicago police through the black South Side, Bigger engages in a rooftop shootout with police and is wounded and captured. As a mass mob of Chicago whites stands outside the courthouse shouting "Lynch 'im!" the prosecuting attorney, Buckley, argues that Bigger must be sentenced to death to protect white women from black male criminals but also to uphold "sacred law" and its "holy" role as guarantor of social order.[1] Bigger Thomas is rapidly convicted and sentenced to death; the governor of Illinois refuses to intervene to block the execution.

By 1940, the transition in legal systems was largely accomplished throughout the country. Rough justice was enacted no longer through lynching but through legal executions that combined legal forms, symbolically charged and arbitrary retributive justice, and white supremacy and through racially motivated, lethally excessive urban policing. Having lived as an African American in both the rural South and the urban North, Wright captured well the social experience and rhetoric of this transition. By the last third of the twentieth century, urban African Americans rebelled against the new legal order. Allegations of police brutality sparked extensive riots in Watts in south central Los Angeles in 1965, Newark in 1966, and Detroit in 1967.[2] At the end of the twentieth century, the acquittal of four white police officers accused of beating the African American motorist Rodney King in April 1992 precipitated large-scale riots in Los Angeles and smaller-scale riots throughout North America.[3] In Cincinnati in April 2001, the police shooting of Timothy Thomas, the fifteenth African American male killed by Cincinnati police since 1995, provoked several days of rioting by African Americans and renewed debate over police brutality.[4]

The other inheritance of rough justice, capital punishment, has also come under scrutiny. After a hiatus in the 1970s, when the U.S. Supreme Court declared it unconstitutional but then reversed itself, the death penalty gathered steam through the 1980s and 1990s, as states executed more and more of the inmates on their death rows. In January 2000, the discovery of a series of errors in capital convictions in Illinois led Governor George Ryan to place a moratorium on executions.[5] The Illinois moratorium reinvigorated a national conversation over the extent to which the administration of the death penalty adequately realized due-process guarantees. In 2002, Parris N. Glendening, the governor of Maryland, imposed a moratorium on executions in that state, which was ended by his successor, Robert L. Ehrlich Jr., in 2003.[6] In January 2003, shortly before leaving office, Ryan dissolved Illinois's death row by pardoning four men whose confessions had been obtained through beating by police and by commuting the sentences of 167 inmates from death to life imprisonment. As he cleared Illinois's death row, Ryan explained: "'Because the Illinois death penalty system is arbitrary and capricious—and therefore immoral—I no longer shall tinker with the machinery of death.'"[7]

Three decades before Ryan's action, the U.S. Supreme Court had erected a new standard for the constitutional administration of the death penalty. In 1972 the court ruled five to four in *Furman v. Georgia* that the death penalty as presently administered was arbitrary and excessive and thus in violation of the Eighth Amendment's prohibition against cruel and unusual punishment.[8] However, in a 1976 decision, *Gregg v. Georgia*, the court ruled seven to two that Georgia's newly rewritten capital punishment statute, which adopted procedures that would purportedly prevent an arbitrary application of the death penalty, was constitutional.[9] The majority opinion in *Gregg*, written by Justice Potter Stewart, argued that the death penalty's enactment of retribution served the important societal function of averting social anarchy and mob law. Citing his own concurring opinion in *Furman*, Stewart echoed the southerners, westerners, and midwesterners who had argued in the late nineteenth and early twentieth centuries that a rigidly and effectively applied death penalty would confound lynchers and preserve social order: "'The instinct for retribution is part of the nature of man, and channeling that instinct in the administration of criminal justice serves an important purpose in promoting the stability of a society governed by law. When people begin to believe that organized society is unwilling or unable to impose upon criminal offenders the punishment they "deserve," then there are sown the seeds of anarchy of self-help, vigilante justice, and lynch law.'"[10]

In 1987, the U.S. Supreme Court narrowly found that the administration of capital punishment under post-*Furman* statutes met standards of racial fairness. The court ruled five to four in *McCleskey v. Kemp* that statistical evidence showing that black defendants who were convicted of murdering whites were more likely to receive a death sentence did not constitute discrimination in violation of the Eighth Amendment or the equal-protection clause of the Fourteenth Amendment. Assessing a statistical study by David Baldus of murder cases in Georgia from 1973 through 1978, Justice Lewis Powell's majority decision argued that the decisions of prosecutors and jurors in particular cases were individualized and that sufficient safeguards existed against racial bias in court procedures.[11] Powell wrote that a defendant asserting an equal-protection-clause violation must show "'the existence of purposeful discrimination'" and that there was no evidence that the Georgia state legislature enacted its death penalty statute to promote a "'racially disproportionate impact.'" Powell also dismissed McCleskey's use of racially discriminatory Georgia laws from the era of the Civil War to make his case. Powell declared that "'unless historical evidence is reasonably contemporaneous with the challenged decision, it has little probative value.'"[12]

Justice William Brennan underlined the relevance of race and history in the administration of capital punishment in a powerful dissent from the majority decision in *McCleskey*. Brennan argued that the statistical evidence of a racial disparity in the application of the death penalty showed that a "'substantial risk'" existed that punishment was being "'inflicted in an arbitrary and capricious manner.'" Thus Furman's test for the constitutional administration of the death penalty was not being met. Further, Brennan argued that a long history of a dual, racialized system of justice in Georgia should be given weight in light of the new statistical evidence of racial bias in the death penalty: "'sentencing data, history, and experience all counsel that Georgia has provided insufficient assurance of the heightened rationality we have required in order to take a human life.'" Brennan concluded by emphasizing the lessons of history for understanding the role of race and racism in the criminal justice system in contemporary America: "'we remain imprisoned by the past as long as we deny its influence in the present.'"[13]

This book argues that the history of lynching and the history of the death penalty in the United States are deeply and hopelessly entangled. One cannot be separated or understood apart from the other, for lynching came from the early modern death penalty, and the modern death penalty came from lynching. The notion that the administration of capital punishment can be individualized and particularized and that it lies outside of history and away from larger social forces and ideas is strongly rebutted by the history chronicled here, for this has never been the case in American history. This history is highly relevant and "contemporaneous" to the point of "probative value"; as recently as 1976 Justice Stewart referenced it in finding the death penalty and its performance of societal retribution beneficial and constitutional. However, the evidence arrayed here suggests that the death penalty cannot be made "rational"; the popular clamor for retribution will always be by its nature arbitrary and capricious. Nor can the death penalty be separated from larger social forces such as racism. This is because capital punishment in the United States carries the profound legacy of lynching.

The death penalty, whose geographical distribution today parallels the areas where lynching waxed in the late nineteenth and early twentieth centuries, constitutes the dubious inheritance from the struggle over rough justice and the compromise that, by reshaping the death penalty, ended lynching. The arbitrary, racialized, and performative characteristics of today's death penalty carry on what was most important to the advocates of rough justice: that the guilt, innocence, or humanity of an executed person matter less than the collective vengeance satisfied by the ritualized taking of their life. The excessive and all-too-often deadly force wielded by the police, particularly against African Americans and Latinos, also pursues tactics and goals inherited from the antebellum slave patrol and postbellum lynch mob. Brutal, racialized policing, which exists more as an informal, ritualized set of practices than as a written or formalized set of policies, asserts that the arbitrary and lethal use of force is the most appropriate response to the resistance and criminality of blacks and Hispanics. Perhaps in an era when the death penalty and racially motivated policing are being reexamined, we might wonder if the price of order was too high and whether the values of rough justice exceed the costs or, indeed, if they ever have.

APPENDIX

Confirmed Lynchings and Near Lynchings, 1874–1947

Each incident is referred to in at least one reliable primary source that I have identified, and if possible two or more independent primary sources. I thank E. M. Beck for sharing the Georgia Lynching Project's data with me. The Georgia Lynching Project's lists of mob victims and citations for Louisiana proved invaluable for the compilation of my database.

Lynching Victims in Iowa

Race: B = Black; I = American Indian; W = White

Date	Race	Name	County	Alleged Offense	Mob Type
12/15/1874	W	Charles Howard	Polk	Murder	Mass
05/09/1875	W	George W. Kirkman	Story	Arson	Private
06/29/1875	W	Archie Smith	Wapello	Murder	Unknown
06/03/1883	W	John Anderson	Cass	Attempted murder	Private
06/03/1883	W	Frank Brown	Cass	Attempted murder	Private
06/03/1883	W	John Hamner	Madison	Murder	Private
06/08/1883	W	William Barber	Bremer	Murder	Mass
06/08/1883	W	Isaac Barber	Bremer	Murder	Mass
07/15/1883	W	Simpson Tylor Crawford	Shelby	Murder	Posse
07/24/1883	W	William Hardy	Shelby	Murder	Private
12/29/1884	W	Pleasant Anderson	Wapello	Murder	Private
02/04/1885	W	Cicero Jellerson	Audubon	Murder	Private
02/04/1885	W	John Smyth	Audubon	Murder	Private
02/04/1885	W	Joel Wilson	Audubon	Murder	Private
06/05/1885	W	Finley Rainsbarger	Hardin	Murder	Private
06/05/1885	W	Emmanuel Rainsbarger	Hardin	Murder	Private
04/03/1887	W	John McKenzie	Adams	Murder	Private
08/14/1887	W	James Reynolds	Decatur	Rape	Private
06/29/1889	I	Olaf	Taylor	Rape	Private
03/22/1893	W	William Frazier	Monroe	Murder	Mass
11/21/1893	W	Frank Johnson, alias Gustaveson	Wapello	Rape	Mass
04/30/1894	W	Reddy Wilson	Harrison	Murder	Private
03/06/1895	W	Orlando Wilkins	Dallas	Robbery	Posse
01/09/1907	W	James Cullen	Floyd	Murder	Mass

Near Lynching Victims in Iowa

Race: B = Black; W = White

Date	Race	Name	County	Alleged Offense	Mob Type
03/1878	W	Henry Weese	Lee	Murder	Mass
06/10/1878	W	William Hicks	Benton	Theft	Private
06/10/1878	W	Jones	Benton	Theft	Private
07/1878	W	Unidentified	Greene	Attempted rape	Unknown
07/02/1879	W	Henry Abel	Washington	Murder	Posse
07/03/1879	W	William Pickering	Louisa	Murder	Mass
10/01/1880	W	Jerome West	Jones	Murder	Mass
04/14/1882	W	John Weise	Polk	Murder	Mass
04/14/1882	W	John Gwinn	Polk	Murder	Mass
04/14/1882	W	Charles Errickson	Polk	Murder	Mass
05/22/1882	W	H. C. Cohee	Washington	Horse theft	Mass
06/06/1883	W	William Barber	Bremer	Murder	Unknown
06/06/1883	W	Isaac Barber	Bremer	Murder	Unknown
07/1883	W	William Hardy	Shelby	Murder	Mass
08/02/1887	W	James Reynolds	Decatur	Rape	Unknown
06/30/1891	W	Frank Pierce	Polk	Murder	Mass
07/02/1891	W	Albert Parmitzke	Van Buren	Murder, attempted rape	Posse
10/16/1893	W	Edward Walton	Wapello	Murder	Mass
01/19/1894	W	Leon Lozier	Pottawatamie	Rape	Mass
05/1894	W	John Hamil	Polk	Murder	Mass
05/1894	W	John Krout	Polk	Murder	Mass
05/1894	W	George Weems	Polk	Murder	Mass
05/31/1894	W	"A Tramp"	Pottawatamie	Rape	Mass
03/06/1895	W	Charles Crawford	Dallas	Robbery	Private
04/04/1896	W	R. E. Martin	Wapello	Rape	Mass
08/28/1896	W	Wilbur Smith	Wapello	Rape	Mass

Near Lynching Victims in Iowa (cont.)

Race: B = Black; W = White

Date	Race	Name	County	Alleged Offense	Mob Type
08/28/1896	W	Charles Harris	Wapello	Rape	Mass
08/28/1896	W	Ralph Duncan	Wapello	Rape	Mass
02/09/1898	W	A. D. Storms	Des Moines	Murder	Mass
10/1900	B	Alva Brooker	Monroe	Rape	Unknown
11/24/1900	B	Alva Brooker	Monroe	Rape	Mass
12/19/1900	W	Charles Arnett	Webster	Theft	Mass
09/01/1901	B	Seymour Washington	Polk	Rape	Mass
02/1902	W	Edward Davidson	Wapello	Rape	Unknown
03/28/1903	B	Frank Brown	Muscatine	Attempted murder	Mass
12/21/1903	W	W. L. Horn	Appanoose	Murder	Posse
12/28/1903	B	Burk	Pottawatamie	Sexual assault, robbery	Mass
12/28/1903	B	Zimmerman	Pottawatamie	Sexual assault, robbery	Mass
04/18/1904	W	Harry Thompson	Woodbury	Attempted murder	Private
11/10/1904	B	James Price	Boone	Murder	Posse
09/27/1905	W	Frank Brothers	Polk	Assault	Mass
07/16/1906	B	Robert Hyde	Polk	Pushed white woman off sidewalk	Mass
07/16/1906	B	Chas. Martin	Polk	Pushed white woman off sidewalk	Mass
01/22/1907	B	Thomas Grimes	Henry	Murder	Mass
08/30/1907	B	Walker	Louisa	Attempted murder	Mass
08/30/1907	B	Johnson	Louisa	Attempted murder	Mass
08/30/1907	B	Unidentified man	Louisa	Attempted murder	Mass
01/25/1908	B	Ray Edwards	Wapello	Rape	Mass
02/1909	B	John Junkin	Des Moines	Rape, murder	Mass
02/21/1909	B	John Junkin	Wapello	Rape, murder	Mass
03/12/1909	B	John Junkin	Wapello	Rape, murder	Mass
06/01/1909	B	John Junkin	Appanoose	Rape, murder	Mass

Lynching Victims in Wyoming

Race: B = Black; I = American Indian; S = "A Spaniard"; W = White

Date	Race	Name	County	Alleged Offense	Mob Type
10/31/1878	W	Billy Mansfield	Albany	Robbery	Private
10/31/1878	W	Archie McLaughlin	Albany	Robbery	Private
01/05/1879	W	Dutch Chorley	Carbon	Murder	Mass
Autumn 1879	W	Lacey	Carbon	Robbery, assault	Terrorist
Autumn 1879	W	Unidentified man	Carbon	Robbery, assault	Terrorist
Autumn 1879	W	Unidentified man	Carbon	Robbery, assault	Terrorist
03/22/1881	W	Big Nose George Parrott	Carbon	Murder, assault	Private
09/16/1883	W	Henry Mosier	Laramie	Murder	Mass
05/20/1884	W	William Maloney	Laramie	Murder	Private
08/08/1885	W	Si Partridge	Albany	Horse theft	Terrorist
12/1886	S	Gus Kernwood	Unknown	Horse theft, murder	Terrorist
10/10/1888	W	N. L. Adams	Carbon	Poaching	Private
10/10/1888	W	Charles Putzier	Carbon	Poaching	Private
07/20/1889	W	Ellen Watson	Carbon	Rustling	Terrorist
07/20/1889	W	James Averill	Carbon	Rustling	Terrorist
06/18/1891	W	Tom Waggoner	Crook	Rustling	Terrorist
04/09/1892	W	Nick Ray	Johnson	Rustling	Terrorist
04/09/1892	W	Nate Champion	Johnson	Rustling	Terrorist
10/12/1892	W	Jack Bedford	Johnson	Rustling	Terrorist
10/12/1892	W	Dad Burch	Johnson	Rustling	Terrorist
03/28/1902	W	Charles Woodard	Natrona	Murder	Private
07/1902	W	Sheepherder	Sweetwater	Sheep range conflict	Terrorist
05/27/1903	W	W. C. Clifton	Weston	Murder	Private
07/19/1903	W	James Gorman	Big Horn	Murder	Private
07/19/1903	W	J. P. Walters	Big Horn	Murder	Private
10/31/1903	I	Black Kettle	Weston	Murder, stock theft	Posse

Lynching Victims in Wyoming (cont.)

Race: B = Black; I = American Indian; S = "A Spaniard"; W = White

Date	Race	Name	County	Alleged Offense	Mob Type
10/31/1903	I	Eagle Feather	Weston	Murder, stock theft	Posse
10/31/1903	I	Unidentified Lakota	Weston	Murder, stock theft	Posse
10/31/1903	I	Unidentified Lakota	Weston	Murder, stock theft	Posse
08/30/1904	B	Joseph Martin	Albany	Attempted sexual assault	Mass
04/1909	W	Joe Allemand	Big Horn	Sheep range conflict	Terrorist
04/1909	W	Joe Emge	Big Horn	Sheep range conflict	Terrorist
04/1909	W	Joe Lazier	Big Horn	Sheep range conflict	Terrorist
10/02/1912	B	Frank Wigfall	Carbon	Rape	Private
12/14/1917	B	Wade Hamilton	Sweetwater	Attempted rape	Private
12/09/1918	B	Joel Woodson	Sweetwater	Murder	Mass

Lynching Victims in Louisiana

Race: B = Black; M = Mexican; S = Sicilian; U = Unknown; W = White

Date	Race	Name	Parish	Alleged Offense	Mob Type
04/24/1878	U	Unidentified man	Unidentified Sugar Parish	Arson	Unknown
07/30/1878	B	Jim Beaty	Ouachita	Unknown	Private
07/30/1878	B	Ples Phillips	Ouachita	Unknown	Private
07/30/1878	B	Tom Ross	Ouachita	Unknown	Private
07/30/1878	B	Henry Atkinson	Ouachita	Unknown	Private
09/14/1878	U	Valcour St. Martin	St. Charles	Murder	Unknown
10/1878	B	Joshua Hall	Ouachita	Unknown	Mass
10/1878	B	Sam Wallace	Ouachita	Unknown	Mass
11/05/1878	B	Unidentified man	Ouachita	Unknown	Unknown
11/05/1878	B	Unidentified man	Ouachita	Unknown	Unknown
11/05/1878	B	Unidentified man	Ouachita	Unknown	Unknown
11/05/1878	B	Unidentified man	Ouachita	Unknown	Unknown
11/05/1878	B	Unidentified man	Ouachita	Unknown	Unknown
12/03/1878	B	Moustand	St. Mary	Attempted rape	Private
12/15/1878	B	Victor Bryan	Pointe Coupee	Murder	Private
08/20/1879	B	Ed. Rabun	Union	Attempt to rape	Unknown
09/01/1879	B	George Williams	Ouachita	Threats against white	Private
10/29/1879	W	W. J. Overstreet	Union	Murder	Mass
12/28/1879	B	Dick Smith	Tangipahoa	Murder	Private
12/28/1879	B	Geo. Carroll	Tangipahoa	Murder	Private
12/28/1879	B	Harrison Johnson	Tangipahoa	Murder	Private
12/28/1879	B	Unknown	Tangipahoa	Murder	Private
01/06/1880	W	James Brown	East Carroll	Murder	Private
04/01/1880	B	J. Tucker	St. Helena	Murder	Private
11/20/1880	W	Thornhill	Sabine	Horse theft	Private

Lynching Victims in Louisiana (cont.)

Race: B = Black; M = Mexican; S = Sicilian; U = Unknown; W = White

Date	Name	Race	Parish	Alleged Offense	Mob Type
11/20/1880	Fields	W	Sabine	Horse theft	Private
12/1880	Dr. Jones	U	East Carroll	Political causes	Unknown
12/20/1880	Garnett Thompson	B	West Feliciana	Insulted, shot white man	Unknown
07/17/1881	Spence	B	Caddo	Attempted criminal assault	Unknown
07/19/1881	Unidentified man	B	Desoto	Murder, robbery	Private
07/20/1881	Unidentified man	B	Lincoln	Attempted rape	Unknown
08/22/1881	Alec Wilson	B	Ouachita	Murder	Unknown
08/22/1881	Perry Munson	B	Ouachita	Murder	Unknown
08/31/1881	Caleb Jackson	B	Jackson	Arson	Unknown
09/26/1881	Ben Robertson	B	Iberia	Theft	Private
11/17/1881	Stanley	W	Pointe Coupee	Murderous assault	Private
05/15/1882	Joseph Jenkins	W	St. Martin	Murder	Unknown
05/15/1882	Eugene Azar	B	St. Martin	Murder	Unknown
06/20/1882	Ingram	U	St. Tammany	Desperado	Unknown
06/20/1882	Howard	U	St. Tammany	Desperado	Unknown
06/20/1882	Mack Taylor	B	Webster	Murderous assault	Mass
10/28/1882	Wm. Harris	B	Lincoln	Attempted rape	Posse
11/07/1882	Unidentified man	B	Lincoln	Murderous assault	Unknown
11/07/1882	Unidentified man	B	Lincoln	Murderous assault	Unknown
11/18/1882	N. David Lee	B	Franklin	Hog theft	Private
12/08/1882	Tim Robinson	B	Morehouse	Murderous assault	Unknown
12/08/1882	Wm. Cephas	B	Morehouse	Murderous assault	Unknown
12/08/1882	Wesley Andrews	B	Morehouse	Murderous assault	Unknown
01/23/1883	Henry Solomon	B	Bossier	Arson, horse theft	Private

Lynching Victims in Louisiana (cont.)

Race: B = Black; M = Mexican; S = Sicilian; U = Unknown; W = White

Date	Race	Name	Parish	Alleged Offense	Mob Type
05/13/1883	W	D. C. Hutchins	Bossier	Murder	Mass
07/09/1883	B	Henderson Lee	Morehouse	Larceny	Private
10/12/1883	B	Louis Woods	Calcasieu	Rape	Unknown
04/27/1884	W	John Mullican	Ouachita	Murder, robbery	Mass
04/27/1884	W	John Clark	Ouachita	Murder, robbery	Mass
04/27/1884	U	King Hill	Ouachita	Murder	Mass
10/21/1884	W	Charles McLean	Bossier	Arson	Private
10/24/1884	B	Unidentified man	St. Tammany	Murder	Unknown
10/24/1884	B	Unidentified man	St. Tammany	Murder	Unknown
10/24/1884	B	Unidentified man	St. Tammany	Murder	Unknown
10/24/1884	B	Unidentified man	St. Tammany	Murder	Unknown
12/22/1884	W	Wm. Fleitas	St. Tammany	Murderous assault	Unknown
01/01/1885	U	Unidentified man	Madison	Train-wrecking	Unknown
01/01/1885	U	Unidentified child	Madison	Train-wrecking	Unknown
03/05/1885	U	Unidentified man	St. Landry	Murder	Private
03/05/1885	U	Unidentified man	St. Landry	Murder	Private
04/22/1885	B	Abe Jones	Pointe Coupee	Murder	Unknown
04/22/1885	W	William Pierce Mabry	Union	Defended black woman from beating	Unknown
07/22/1885	B	Cicero Green	Webster	Murderous assault	Mass
07/22/1885	B	John Figures	Webster	Murder	Mass
09/30/1885	B	Sampson Harris	Winn	Threat to give evidence against whitecappers	Terrorist
02/16/1886	B	George Robinson	Ouachita	Murder	Mass
05/06/1886	B	Robert Smith	St. Bernard	Murder	Private
10/18/1886	B	Reeves Smith	Desoto	Attempted rape	Mass

Lynching Victims in Louisiana (cont.)

Race: B = Black; M = Mexican; S = Sicilian; U = Unknown; W = White

Date	Race	Name	Parish	Alleged Offense	Mob Type
12/28/1886	W	John Elia	Bienville	Murder	Private
01/08/1887	B	Ike Brumfield	Tangipahoa	Unknown	Unknown
04/28/1887	B	Gracy Blanton	West Carroll	Arson, robbery	Private
04/28/1887	B	Richard Goodwin	West Carroll	Arson, robbery	Private
06/06/1887	B	M. W. Washington	Desoto	Burglary with intent to rape	Unknown
06/30/1887	B	James Walden	Lincoln	Larceny	Private
08/09/1887	W	Thomas Scott	Morehouse	Murder	Private
08/11/1887	B	Daniel Pleasants, alias Hoskins	St. Mary	Murder	Posse (mixed race)
08/13/1887	B	Green Hosley	Union	Asserted self-respect in dispute with white	Private
10/20/1887	B	Perry King	Franklin	Attempted rape	Mass
10/20/1887	B	Drew Green	Franklin	Attempted rape	Mass
11/07/1887	B	Unidentified man	Caddo	Miscegenation	Unknown
12/09/1887	B	Andrew Edwards	Webster	Voodoism	Private (black)
01/28/1888	B	Ben Edwards	Tangipahoa	Criminal assault	Mass
02/09/1888	B	Unidentified man	Tangipahoa	Attempted rape	Private
05/06/1888	W	Dave Southall	Pointe Coupee	Attempted murder, political causes	Private
09/1888	B	Unidentified Woman	St. Martin	Unknown	Terrorist
09/17/1888	B	Louis Alfred (Jean Pierre Salet)	St. Landry	Incendiary language	Terrorist
09/17/1888	B	Jno. Johnson (Sidairo)	St. Landry	Incendiary language	Terrorist
11/09/1888	B	Lulin	St. Landry	Unknown	Terrorist
11/13/1888	B	Unidentified man	Ascension	Rape	Mass

Lynching Victims in Louisiana (cont.)

Race: B = Black; M = Mexican; S = Sicilian; U = Unknown; W = White

Date	Race	Name	Parish	Alleged Offense	Mob Type
11/22/1888	B	Jerry Taylor	St. Helena	Rape	Private
01/25/1889	B	Samuel Wakefield	Iberia	Murder	Posse
01/29/1889	B	James Rosemond	Iberia	Theft	Private
02/08/1889	B	Haygood Handy	Bossier	Murder, hog stealing	Unknown
04/14/1889	U	Steve McIntosh	Ouachita	Rape	Unknown (black)
04/16/1889	B	Hector Junior	Iberia	Murderous assault	Posse
05/18/1889	B	Unidentified man	Caldwell	Burglary	Unknown
07/11/1889	B	Felix Keys	Lafayette	Murder	Mass (mixed race)
11/16/1889	B	Ed Gray	Concordia	Arson	Private
12/31/1889	B	Henry Holmes	Bossier	Murderous assault	Unknown
01/08/1890	B	Henry Ward	West Feliciana	Murder	Private
02/18/1890	W	R. F. Emerson	Tensas	Murderous assault	Unknown
05/13/1890	B	Phillip Williams	Assumption	Attempted rape	Mass
06/16/1890	W	George Swayze	East Feliciana	Political causes	Private (possibly black)
06/26/1890	B	John Coleman	Caddo	Murder	Unknown (black)
08/21/1890	B	Wm. Alexander	East Baton Rouge	Attempted rape	Private
10/12/1890	B	Frank Wooten	Claiborne	Arson	Unknown
11/20/1890	B	Unidentified man	East Baton Rouge	Bulldozing	Terrorist
03/14/1891	S	Antoino Scoffedi	Orleans	Conspiracy to murder	Mass (mixed race)
03/14/1891	S	Joseph Macheca	Orleans	Conspiracy to murder	Mass (mixed race)
03/14/1891	S	Pietro Monasterio	Orleans	Conspiracy to murder	Mass (mixed race)
03/14/1891	S	James Caruso	Orleans	Conspiracy to murder	Mass (mixed race)
03/14/1891	S	Rocco Gerachi	Orleans	Conspiracy to murder	Mass (mixed race)
03/14/1891	S	Frank Romero	Orleans	Conspiracy to murder	Mass (mixed race)
03/14/1891	S	Antonio Marchesi	Orleans	Conspiracy to murder	Mass (mixed race)
03/14/1891	S	Charles Traina	Orleans	Conspiracy to murder	Mass (mixed race)

Lynching Victims in Louisiana (cont.)

Race: B = Black; M = Mexican; S = Sicilian; U = Unknown; W = White

Date	Name	Race	Parish	Alleged Offense	Mob Type
03/14/1891	Loretto Comitz	S	Orleans	Conspiracy to murder	Mass (mixed race)
03/14/1891	Antonio Bagnetto	S	Orleans	Conspiracy to murder	Mass (mixed race)
03/14/1891	Manuel Politz	S	Orleans	Conspiracy to murder	Mass (mixed race)
05/21/1891	Tennis Hampton	B	Bienville	Murder	Private
05/23/1891	William Anderson	B	Caddo	Murder	Posse
05/23/1891	John Anderson	B	Caddo	Murder	Posse
06/02/1891	Samuel Hummell	B	Pointe Coupee	Murder	Unknown
06/02/1891	Alex Campbell	B	Pointe Coupee	Murder	Unknown
06/02/1891	Unidentified man	B	Pointe Coupee	Murder	Unknown
09/08/1891	Unidentified man	B	Bienville	Rape	Posse
10/19/1891	John Rush	W	Caldwell	Murder	Private
10/28/1891	Jack Parker	B	St. Tammany	Murder	Mass (black)
10/29/1891	Unidentified man	B	Bossier	Outrageous act	Mass (black)
11/04/1891	J. T. Smith	B	Morehouse	Murder	Mass
11/04/1891	W. S. Felton	B	Morehouse	Murder	Mass
11/10/1891	John Cagle	B	Claiborne	"Bad Negro"	Unknown
11/27/1891	John Maxey	B	Sabine	Criminal assault	Private
12/27/1891	Unidentified man	B	Concordia	Accessory to murder	Unknown
01/07/1892	Horace Dishroon	B	Richland	Murder, robbery	Mass
01/07/1892	Eli Foster	B	Richland	Murder, robbery	Mass
01/09/1892	Nathan Andrews	B	Bossier	Murder	Posse
01/11/1892	Unidentified man	B	Bossier	Murder, robbery	Private (black)
03/12/1892	Ella	B	Richland	Attempted murder	Private
03/26/1892	Dennis Cobb	B	Bienville	Unknown	Terrorist
03/27/1892	Jack Tillman	B	Jefferson	Argued with, shot white men	Terrorist

Lynching Victims in Louisiana (cont.)

Race: B = Black; M = Mexican; S = Sicilian; U = Unknown; W = White

Date	Race	Name	Parish	Alleged Offense	Mob Type
04/06/1892	B	Unidentified man	Grant	Murder	Posse
04/06/1892	B	Unidentified man	Grant	Murder	Posse
04/06/1892	B	Unidentified man	Grant	Murder	Posse
04/06/1892	B	Unidentified man	Grant	Murder	Posse
04/23/1892	W	Freeman	Pointe Coupee	Murder, extortion	Posse
05/28/1892	B	Walker	Bienville	Improper relations with white girl	Unknown
09/02/1892	B	Edward Laurent	Avoyelles	Aiding murderer	Terrorist
09/05/1892	B	Gabriel Magliore	Avoyelles	Threats to kill	Terrorist
09/07/1892	B	Henry Dixon	Jefferson	Murder, theft	Private
09/13/1892	B	Eli Lindsey	Morehouse	Murder	Unknown (black)
09/27/1892	B	Benny Walkers	Concordia	Attempted criminal assault	Mass
10/21/1892	B	Thomas Courtney	Iberville	Shot man	Posse
11/01/1892	B	Daughter of Hastings	Catahoula	Daughter of murderer	Private
11/01/1892	B	Son of Hastings	Catahoula	Son of murderer	Private
11/04/1892	B	John Hastings	Catahoula	Murder	Private
11/29/1892	B	Richard Magee	Bossier	Murder	Unknown
11/29/1892	B	Carmichael	Bossier	Complicity in murder	Unknown
12/28/1892	B	Lewis Fox	St. Charles	Murder, robbery	Private
12/28/1892	B	Adam Gripson	St. Charles	Murder, robbery	Private
01/08/1893	B	Unidentified man	Union	Murderous assault	Unknown
01/20/1893	B	Robert Landry	St. James	Murder, robbery	Private
01/20/1893	B	Chicken George	St. James	Murder, robbery	Private
01/20/1893	B	Richard Davis	St. James	Murder, robbery	Private
01/25/1893	B	Wm. Fisher	Orleans	Stabbing of white woman, murder	Posse

Lynching Victims in Louisiana (cont.)

Race: B = Black; M = Mexican; S = Sicilian; U = Unknown; W = White

Date	Race	Name	Parish	Alleged Offense	Mob Type
05/06/1893	B	Israel Holloway	Assumption	Rape	Unknown
07/13/1893	B	Meredith Lewis	Tangipahoa	Murder	Private (black)
09/16/1893	B	Valsin Julian	Jefferson	Brother of murderer	Private
09/16/1893	B	Paul Julian	Jefferson	Brother of murderer	Private
09/16/1893	B	Basile Julian	Jefferson	Brother of murderer	Private
09/29/1893	B	Henry Coleman	Bossier	Attempted assassination	Mass
10/19/1893	B	Unidentified man	Bossier	Stock theft	Unknown (mixed race)
10/19/1893	B	Unidentified man	Bossier	Stock theft	Unknown (mixed race)
12/27/1893	B	Tillman Green	Caldwell	Attempted rape	Private
01/18/1894	B	Unidentified man	West Feliciana	Arson, murder	Unknown
04/23/1894	B	Samuel Slaughter	Madison	Murder, insurrection	Mass
04/23/1894	B	Thomas Claxton	Madison	Murder, insurrection	Mass
04/23/1894	B	David Hawkins	Madison	Murder, insurrection	Mass
04/27/1894	B	Shell Claxton	Madison	Murder, insurrection	Mass
04/27/1894	B	Tony McCoy	Madison	Murder, insurrection	Mass
04/27/1894	B	Pomp Claxton	Madison	Murder, insurrection	Mass
04/27/1894	B	Scott Harvey	Madison	Murder, insurrection	Mass
05/23/1894	B	George Paul	Pointe Coupee	Offended white man	Unknown
06/10/1894	B	Mark Jacobs	Bienville	Unknown	Terrorist
06/14/1894	W	John Day	Ouachita	Arson	Unknown
07/23/1894	B	Vance McClure	Iberia	Attempted rape	Private
09/09/1894	W	Link Waggoner	Webster	Murderous assault	Private
09/10/1894	B	Robert Williams	Concordia	Murder	Unknown (black)
11/09/1894	M	Charlie Williams	West Carroll	Murder, robbery	Unknown
11/09/1894	B	Lawrence Younger	West Carroll	Murder	Unknown
12/23/1894	B	George King	St. Bernard	Threat to kill, resisted arrest, shot at whites	Mass

Lynching Victims in Louisiana (cont.)

Race: B = Black; M = Mexican; S = Sicilian; U = Unknown; W = White

Date	Race	Name	Parish	Alleged Offense	Mob Type
12/28/1894	B	Scott Sherman	Concordia	Brother of murderer	Posse (possibly black)
06/24/1895	W	John Frey	Jefferson	Arson	Private
07/19/1895	B	Ovide Belizaire	Lafayette	Shot at whites	Terrorist
09/18/1895	B	Unidentified man	Bossier	Rape	Mass
09/21/1895	B	Edward Smith	Tangipahoa	Murder, robbery	Mass
09/25/1895	B	Aleck Francis	Jefferson	Dangerous character	Private
01/10/1896	B	Abraham Smart	Ouachita	Murder	Unknown
01/12/1896	B	Charlotte Morris	Jefferson	Miscegenation	Private
01/12/1896	W	Patrick Morris	Jefferson	Miscegenation	Private
02/28/1896	B	Gilbert Francis	St. James	Rape, burglary	Private
02/28/1896	B	Paul Francis	St. James	Rape, burglary	Private
03/11/1896	B	Bud Love	Morehouse	Theft	Private
03/24/1896	B	Louis Senegal	Lafayette	Rape	Private
05/17/1896	B	Unidentified man	Bossier	Insulted white woman	Posse
05/19/1896	B	James Dandy	St. Bernard	Attempted rape	Private
06/09/1896	B	Wallis Starks	St. Mary	Rape, robbery	Posse
07/11/1896	B	James Porter	Webster	Murder	Private
07/11/1896	B	Monch Dudley	Webster	Murder	Private
07/24/1896	B	Isom McGee	Claiborne	Attempted rape	Unknown
07/31/1896	W	Louis Mullens	Avoyelles	Attempted rape	Private
08/04/1896	B	Hiram Weightman	Franklin	Murder, rape	Mass
08/08/1896	S	Lorenzo Saladino	St. Charles	Murder, robbery	Mass
08/08/1896	S	Decino Sorcoro	St. Charles	Murder, robbery	Mass
08/08/1896	S	Angelo Marcuso	St. Charles	Murder, robbery	Mass
09/12/1896	B	Jones McCauley	Ouachita	Sexual assault	Unknown (mixed race or black)

Lynching Victims in Louisiana (cont.)

Race: B = Black; M = Mexican; S = Sicilian; U = Unknown; W = White

Date	Race	Name	Parish	Alleged Offense	Mob Type
09/24/1896	B	Jim Hawkins	Jefferson	Assaulted boy	Private
10/01/1896	B	Lewis Hamilton	Bossier	Arson	Unknown
12/22/1896	B	Jerry Burke	Livingston	Attempted murder	Posse
01/17/1897	B	Unidentified man	Iberville	Attempted murder, robbery	Unknown
01/19/1897	B	Gustave Williams	Tangipahoa	Murder	Mass
01/19/1897	B	Archie Joiner	Tangipahoa	Murder	Mass
01/19/1897	B	John Johnson	Tangipahoa	Murder	Mass
05/11/1897	B	Charles Johnson	East Feliciana	Attempted train-wrecking	Private
07/21/1897	B	Jack Davis	St. Mary	Criminal assault	Posse
09/28/1897	B	Wm. Oliver	Jefferson	Ferry Law violation, dangerous weapon charge	Private
10/02/1897	B	Wash Ferren	Ouachita	Rape	Mass
10/15/1897	B	Douglas Boutte	Jefferson	Violated quarantine, resisted arrest	Private
12/13/1897	B	Joseph Alexander	Iberville	Murder	Mass
12/13/1897	B	Charles Alexander	Iberville	Murder	Mass
12/13/1897	B	James Thomas	Iberville	Murder	Mass
04/02/1898	B	Wm. Bell	Tangipahoa	Accessory to murder	Private
04/23/1898	B	Columbus Lewis	Lincoln	Impudence to white man	Private
06/04/1898	B	Wm. Steake	Webster	Rape	Mass
06/11/1898	B	Unidentified man	Morehouse	Murderous assault	Posse
11/03/1898	B	Charles Morrell	St. John	Robbery	Private
12/05/1898	B	Bedney Hearn	Bossier	Murder	Unknown

Lynching Victims in Louisiana (cont.)

Race: B = Black; M = Mexican; S = Sicilian; U = Unknown; W = White

Date	Race	Name	Parish	Alleged Offense	Mob Type
12/05/1898	B	John Richardson	Bossier	Murder	Unknown
06/14/1899	B	Edward Gray	St. John	Burglary	Private
07/11/1899	B	George Jones	St. Charles	Horse theft	Private (black)
07/21/1899	S	Joseph Cereno	Madison	Shooting man	Mass
07/21/1899	S	Charles Defatta	Madison	Shooting man	Mass
07/21/1899	S	Frank Defatta	Madison	Shooting man	Mass
07/21/1899	S	Joseph Defatta	Madison	Shooting man	Mass
07/21/1899	S	Sy Deferroch	Madison	Shooting man	Mass
08/02/1899	B	Man Singleton	Grant	Attempted rape	Unknown
08/08/1899	B	Echo Brown	Tangipahoa	Unknown	Unknown
10/10/1899	W	Basile LaPlace	St. Charles	Political causes, illicit liaison	Private
10/15/1899	W	James Smith	East Feliciana	Cattle rustling, desperadoism	Private
12/13/1899	B	Unidentified man	Morehouse	Rape	Unknown
04/21/1900	B	John Humely	Bossier	Conspiracy to murder	Mass
04/21/1900	B	Edward Amos	Bossier	Conspiracy to murder	Mass
05/12/1900	B	Henry Harris	Rapides	Attempted criminal assault	Mass
06/12/1900	B	Ned Cobb	West Baton Rouge	Murder	Unknown
06/23/1900	W	Frank Gilmour	Livingston	Murder	Private
08/29/1900	B	Thomas Amos	Rapides	Murder	Mass
09/21/1900	B	George Beckham	Tangipahoa	Robbery	Private
09/21/1900	B	Nathaniel Bowmam	Tangipahoa	Robbery	Private
09/21/1900	B	Charles Elliot	Tangipahoa	Robbery	Private
09/21/1900	B	Izaih Rollins	Tangipahoa	Robbery	Private

Lynching Victims in Louisiana (cont.)

Race: B = Black; M = Mexican; S = Sicilian; U = Unknown; W = White

Date	Race	Name	Parish	Alleged Offense	Mob Type
10/19/1900	B	Melby Dotson	West Baton Rouge	Murder	Mass
01/24/1901	B	Larkington	Webster	Attempted criminal assault	Unknown
02/17/1901	B	Thomas Jackson	St. John	Murder	Mass
02/21/1901	B	Thomas Vital	Calcasieu	Criminal assault	Unknown
02/21/1901	B	Samuel Thibodaux	Calcasieu	Defending rapist	Unknown
03/06/1901	B	William Davis	Caddo	Rape	Private
05/01/1901	B	Grant Johnson	Bossier	Desperate Negro gambler	Private
05/03/1901	B	Felton Brigman	Caddo	Rape	Private (black)
06/19/1901	B	Frank Smith	Bossier	Complicity in murder	Mass
06/19/1901	B	F. D. McLand	Bossier	Complicity in murder	Mass
07/15/1901	B	Lewis Thomas	Richland	Murderous assault	Unknown
07/19/1901	B	Unidentified man	Acadia	Homicide, shot officer	Posse
10/25/1901	B	Wm. Morris	Washington	Assault, robbery	Unknown
11/02/1901	B	Connelly	Washington	Threats against whites	Posse
11/02/1901	B	Parker	Washington	Threats against whites	Posse
11/02/1901	B	Low	Washington	Threats against whites	Posse
11/02/1901	B	Connelly's daughter	Washington	Threats against whites	Posse
11/02/1901	B	Woman	Washington	Threats against whites	Posse
11/02/1901	B	Child	Washington	Threats against whites	Posse
11/02/1901	B	Unidentified person	Washington	Threats against whites	Posse
11/24/1901	B	Frank Thomas	Bossier	Murder	Mass (Black)
12/08/1901	B	Sol Paydras	Calcasieu	Assault	Private
01/25/1902	B	Unidentified man	West Carroll	Murder, theft	Posse
01/25/1902	B	Unidentified man	West Carroll	Murder, theft	Posse
01/25/1902	B	Unidentified man	West Carroll	Murder, theft	Posse

Lynching Victims in Louisiana (cont.)

Race: B = Black; M = Mexican; S = Sicilian; U = Unknown; W = White

Date	Race	Name	Parish	Alleged Offense	Mob Type
03/19/1902	B	John Woodward	Concordia	Murder	Unknown
03/31/1902	B	George Franklin	Claiborne	Murderous assault	Unknown
04/12/1902	B	Unidentified man	Natchitoches	Murder	Unknown
05/04/1902	W	John Simms	Morehouse	Complicity in murder	Unknown
05/09/1902	B	Nicholas Deblanc	Iberia	Attempted rape	Posse
08/07/1902	B	Henry Benton	Claiborne	Criminal assault	Posse
10/13/1902	B	Unidentified man	Calcasieu	Attempted murder	Posse
11/25/1902	B	Joseph Lamb	West Feliciana	Attempted robbery, criminal assault	Private
01/26/1903	B	John Thomas	St. Charles	Murder	Posse
02/24/1903	B	Jim Brown	Bossier	Attempted murder	Posse
03/27/1903	B	Frank Robertson	Bossier	Arson	Unknown
06/12/1903	B	Frank Dupree	Rapides	Murder	Unknown
06/25/1903	B	Lamb Whitley	Catahoula	Murderous assault	Unknown
07/26/1903	B	Jennie Steer	Caddo	Murder	Private
10/18/1903	B	George Kennedy	Bossier	Attempt to kill	Posse
11/02/1903	B	Joseph Craddock	Bossier	Murder	Mass (black)
11/30/1903	B	Walter Carter	Caddo	Murderous assault	Mass (black)
11/30/1903	B	Phillip Davis	Caddo	Murderous assault	Mass (black)
11/30/1903	B	Clinton Thomas	Caddo	Murderous assault	Mass (black)
01/14/1904	B	Butch Riley	Madison	Murderous assault	Unknown
05/29/1904	B	Frank Pipes	Rapides	Shooting man	Private
04/26/1905	W	Richard Craighead	Claiborne	Murder	Mass
06/01/1905	B	Henry Washington	Pointe Coupee	Murder	Posse
08/12/1905	B	Unidentified man	Jackson	Murderous assault	Posse
11/26/1905	B	Monroe Williams	Tangipahoa	Criminal assault	Unknown

Lynching Victims in Louisiana (cont.)

Race: B = Black; M = Mexican; S = Sicilian; U = Unknown; W = White

Date	Race	Name	Parish	Alleged Offense	Mob Type
02/24/1906	B	Willis Page	Bienville	Rape	Mass
03/18/1906	B	Wm. Carr	Iberville	Theft	Private
03/28/1906	B	Cotton	West Carroll	Attempted criminal assault	Unknown
05/06/1906	B	George Whitner	East Feliciana	Insulted white woman	Unknown
05/22/1906	B	Thomas Jackson	Caddo	Robbery	Private
05/29/1906	W	Robert Rogers	Madison	Murder	Private
07/11/1906	B	Unidentified man	Claiborne	Attempted criminal assault	Unknown
08/26/1906	B	Alfred Schaufriet	Ouachita	Attempted criminal assault	Posse
11/25/1906	B	Antone Domingue	Lafayette	Fought whitecappers	Terrorist
03/15/1907	B	Flint Williams	Ouachita	Murder, murderous assault, robbery	Unknown
03/15/1907	B	Henry Gardner	Ouachita	Murder, murderous assault, robbery, rape	Unknown
04/16/1907	B	Charles Straus	Avoyelles	Attempted criminal assault	Private
04/18/1907	B	Frederick Kilbourne	East Feliciana	Attempted rape	Mass
05/03/1907	B	Silas Faly	Bossier	Rape	Unknown
06/01/1907	B	Henry Johnson	Rapides	Attempted criminal assault	Private
06/08/1907	B	James Wilson	Claiborne	Attempted criminal assault	Unknown
06/27/1907	B	Ralph Dorans	Rapides	Rape	Unknown
06/28/1907	B	Mathias Jackson	Rapides	Rape	Private

Lynching Victims in Louisiana (cont.)

Race: B = Black; M = Mexican; S = Sicilian; U = Unknown; W = White

Date	Race	Name	Parish	Alleged Offense	Mob Type
12/05/1907	B	Unidentified man	Morehouse	Murderous assault	Unknown
12/15/1907	S	Unidentified man	Jackson	Being an Italian worker	Unknown
12/15/1907	S	Unidentified man	Jackson	Being an Italian worker	Unknown
02/06/1908	B	Robert Mitchell	West Carroll	Murder	Mass
06/04/1908	B	Bird Cooper	Claiborne	Murder	Unknown
07/16/1908	B	Miller Gaines	Catahoula	Arson	Unknown
07/16/1908	B	Sam Gaines	Catahoula	Arson	Unknown
07/16/1908	B	Albert Godlin	Catahoula	Inciting arson	Unknown
07/26/1908	B	Andrew Harris	Caddo	Attempted rape	Private
09/16/1908	B	John Miles	Pointe Coupee	Murderous assault, robbery	Mass
07/30/1909	B	Emile Antoine	St. Landry	Robbery, shot white man	Private
07/30/1909	B	Onezime Thomas	St. Landry	Robbery, shot white man	Private
09/06/1909	B	Henry Hill	Franklin	Attempted rape	Posse
10/07/1909	B	Ap Ard	St. Helena	Murderous assault	Unknown
10/07/1909	W	Mike Rodrigauez	Vernon	Robbery	Unknown
10/28/1909	B	Joseph Gilford	West Carroll	Murder, theft	Mass
10/28/1909	B	Alexander Hill	West Carroll	Murder, theft	Mass
11/20/1909	B	Wm. Estes	Richland	Murder	Posse
11/27/1909	B	Simmie Thomas	Caddo	Rape	Mass
07/10/1910	W	J. C. Freeman	Richland	Murder	Private
01/20/1911	B	Oval Poulard	Evangeline	Shot deputy sheriff	Private
07/24/1911	B	Miles Taylor	Claiborne	Murder	Posse
04/09/1912	B	Thomas Miles	Caddo	Insulted white woman in letters	Private
04/23/1912	B	Unidentified man	Richland	Threats against whites	Mass

Lynching Victims in Louisiana (cont.)

Race: B = Black; M = Mexican; S = Sicilian; U = Unknown; W = White

Date	Race	Name	Parish	Alleged Offense	Mob Type
05/02/1912	B	Ernest Allums	Bienville	Writing insulting letters to white women	Private
09/25/1912	B	Samuel Johnson	Desoto	Murder	Private
11/28/1912	B	Mood Burks	Bossier	Murderous assault	Private
11/28/1912	B	Jim Hurd	Bossier	Murderous assault	Private
11/28/1912	B	Silas Jimmerson	Bossier	Murderous assault	Private
12/23/1912	B	Norm Cadore	West Baton Rouge	Murder	Private
02/14/1913	B	Charles Tyson	Caddo	Unknown	Unknown (possibly black)
08/27/1913	B	James Comeaux	Jefferson Davis	Assault	Private
10/22/1913	B	Warren Eaton	Ouachita	Improper proposal	Private
12/16/1913	B	Ernest Williams	Caddo	Murder, robbery	Private
12/16/1913	B	Frank Williams	Caddo	Murder, robbery	Private
05/08/1914	B	Sylvester Washington	St. James	Murder	Posse
05/12/1914	B	Earl Hamilton	Caddo	Rape	Mass
08/05/1914	B	Oli Romeo	St. Tammany	Murder	Mass
08/06/1914	B	Henry Holmes	Ouachita	Murder, robbery	Private
08/07/1914	B	Dan Johnson	Ouachita	Complicity in murder	Mass
08/07/1914	B	Louis Pruitt	Ouachita	Complicity in murder	Mass
08/09/1914	B	Unidentified man	Ouachita	Murder	Unknown
12/02/1914	B	Jobie Lewis	Caddo	Murder, robbery, arson	Private
12/02/1914	B	Elijah Durden	Caddo	Murder, robbery, arson	Private
12/11/1914	B	Charles Washington	Caddo	Murder, robbery	Private
12/11/1914	B	Beard Washington	Caddo	Murder, robbery	Private
12/12/1914	B	Watkins Lewis	Caddo	Murder, robbery	Mass
07/15/1915	B	Thomas Collins	Avoyelles	Murderous assault	Posse

Lynching Victims in Louisiana (cont.)

Race: B = Black; M = Mexican; S = Sicilian; U = Unknown; W = White

Date	Race	Name	Parish	Alleged Offense	Mob Type
08/21/1915	B	Bob	Red River	Attempted rape	Unknown
08/26/1916	B	Jesse Hammett	Caddo	Attempted rape	Mass
11/15/1916	B	James Grant	St. Landry	Murder	Private
02/28/1917	B	Emma Hooper	Tangipahoa	Murderous assault	Unknown
07/29/1917	B	Daniel Rout	Tangipahoa	Murder	Private
07/29/1917	B	Jerry Rout	Tangipahoa	Murder	Private
01/26/1918	B	James Nelson	Bossier	Living with white woman	Private
02/26/1918	B	James Jones	Richland	Murder	Unknown
02/26/1918	B	Wm. Powell	Richland	Murder	Unknown
02/26/1918	B	James Lewis	Richland	Murder	Unknown
03/16/1918	B	George McNeal	Ouachita	Rape	Private
04/22/1918	B	Clyde Williams	Ouachita	Murderous assault, robbery	Private
06/18/1918	B	George Clayton	Richland	Murder	Posse
08/07/1918	B	Bubber Hall	Morehouse	Criminal assault	Unknown
01/18/1919	B	Henry Thomas	Red River	Murder	Posse
01/29/1919	B	Sampson Smith	Caldwell	Murder	Unknown
02/14/1919	B	Will Faulkner	Bossier	Murder	Private
04/29/1919	B	George Holden	Ouachita	Wrote insulting note to white woman	Unknown
08/26/1919	B	Jesse Hammett	Caddo	Attempted rape	Mass
08/31/1919	B	Lucius McCarty	Washington	Attempted rape	Mass
09/06/1919	B	Unidentified man	Morehouse	Attempted criminal assault	Private
09/13/1919	B	Unidentified man	Catahoula	Hiding under bed	Unknown
01/31/1921	B	George Werner	Iberville	Shot man	Unknown

Lynching Victims in Louisiana (cont.)

Race: B = Black; M = Mexican; S = Sicilian; U = Unknown; W = White

Date	Race	Name	Parish	Alleged Offense	Mob Type
09/14/1921	B	Gilmon Holmes	Caldwell	Murder	Unknown
03/11/1922	W	Brown Culpeper	Franklin	Unknown	Unknown
07/06/1922	B	Joe Pemberton	Bossier	Murderous assault	Unknown
08/24/1922	W	F. Watt Daniel	Morehouse	Angered Klan	Unknown
08/24/1922	W	Thomas F. Richards	Morehouse	Angered Klan	Unknown
08/26/1922	B	Thomas Rivers	Bossier	Attempted rape	Private
01/03/1923	B	Leslie Leggett	Caddo	Intimate with white girl	Private
02/26/1925	B	Joseph Airy	Bossier	Murder	Unknown
08/04/1926	B	Johnny Norris	Desoto	Improper advances to girl	Posse
04/16/1927	B	Willie Autrey	Calcasieu	Peeping Tom	Private
06/02/1928	B	Lee Blackman	Rapides	Brother of murderer	Private
06/02/1928	B	David Blackman	Rapides	Brother of murderer	Private
02/19/1933	B	Nelson Cash	Bienville	Murder, robbery	Unknown
08/26/1933	B	John White	St. Landry	Unknown	Unknown
09/11/1933	B	Freddy Moore	Assumption	Murder	Unknown
07/21/1934	B	Jerome Wilson	Washington	Murder	Private
10/13/1938	B	W. C. Williams	Lincoln	Murder, murderous assault	Mass
08/08/1946	B	John Jones	Webster	Intent to rape	Private

Lynching Victims in New York State

Race: B = Black

Date	Race	Name	County	Alleged Offense	Mob Type
06/02/1892	B	Robert Lewis, alias Jackson	Orange	Assault	Mass

Lynching Victims in California

Race: B = Black; C = Chinese; I = American Indian; M = Mexican; U = Unknown; W = White

Date	Race	Name	County	Alleged Offense	Mob Type
12/22/1875	M	Jose Antonio Ygarra	Mendocino	Murder	Private
06/10/1876	W	Charles W. Henley	Sonoma	Murder	Private
05/03/1877	M	Francisco Arias	Santa Cruz	Murder	Private
05/03/1877	M	Jose Chamalis	Santa Cruz	Murder	Private
07/13/1877	M	Justin Arayo	Monterey	Murderous assault, murder	Private
12/22/1877	M	Anthony Maron	Kern	Horse theft	Private
12/22/1877	M	Francisco Ensinas	Kern	Horse theft	Private
12/22/1877	M	Miguel Elias	Kern	Horse theft	Private
12/22/1877	M	Fermin Eldeo	Kern	Horse theft	Private
12/22/1877	M	Bessena Ruiz	Kern	Horse theft	Private
05/02/1878	W	Christian Mutchler	Colusa	Arson	Private
05/07/1878	I	Modoc Charlie	Mendocino	Rape	Mass
07/06/1878	M	Rufugio Boca	San Bernardino	Murder	Unknown
05/28/1879	W	Thomas Yoakum	Kern	Murder	Private
05/28/1879	W	William Yoakum	Kern	Murder	Private
09/04/1879	W	Elijah Frost	Mendocino	Theft	Private
09/04/1879	W	Bige Gibson	Mendocino	Theft	Private
09/04/1879	W	Tom McCracken	Mendocino	Theft	Private
01/17/1881	W	Joseph Da Roche	Mono	Murder	Private
04/05/1881	I/M	Francisco Jimeno	Santa Barbara	Rape, murder	Mass
08/07/1881	W	T. J. Noakes	Butte	Murder	Unknown
06/17/1883	M	Incarnacion Garcia	Santa Clara	Murder or murderous assault	Private
12/30/1883	W	William Richardson	Humboldt	Rape	Private
12/04/1884	W	William Pitts	San Bernardino	Murder	Unknown

Lynching Victims in California (cont.)

Race: B = Black; C = Chinese; I = American Indian; M = Mexican; U = Unknown; W = White

Date	Name	Race	County	Alleged Offense	Mob Type
06/10/1885	James Delaney	W	Plumas	Murder	Private
08/12/1885	Henry D. Benner	W	Humboldt	Murder	Mass
01/23/1886	Holden Dick	I	Lassen	Murder	Unknown
01/23/1886	Vicente Olivas	M	Lassen	Murder	Unknown
04/01/1886	Peter Hemmi	W	San Luis Obispo	Murder, murderous assault	Private
04/01/1886	James Hemmi	W	San Luis Obispo	Murder, murderous assault	Private
05/05/1886	George Vuga	W	Amador	Murder	Private
07/11/1887	Hong Di	C	Colusa	Murder, murderous assault	Mass
11/26/1887	Frank McCutcheon	W	Stanislaus	Arson	Unknown
05/05/1888	John Wright	W	Napa	Murder	Private
04/30/1890	Tacho	I	San Diego	Horse theft	Private
05/12/1890	E. L. Chriswell	W	Santa Barbara	Murder	Private
06/10/1891	Ah Quong Tis/Tia/Tai	C	Mono	Murder	Mass
07/24/1892	Charles Ruggles	W	Shasta	Murder, robbery	Private
07/24/1892	John Ruggles	W	Shasta	Murder, robbery	Private
08/21/1892	Francisco Torres	M	Orange	Murder	Private
09/30/1892	J. W. Smith	W	Shasta	Murder	Private
04/07/1893	Jesus Fuen (Quien)	M	San Bernardino	Murder	Mass
12/12/1894	William Dean	I	Siskiyou	Murder	Private
07/26/1895	Victor Adams	W	Madera	Murder	Private
08/26/1895	L. H. Johnson	W	Siskiyou	Murder	Private
08/26/1895	William Null	W	Siskiyou	Murder	Private
08/26/1895	Luis Moreno	M	Siskiyou	Murder	Private

Lynching Victims in California (cont.)

Race: B = Black; C = Chinese; I = American Indian; M = Mexican; U = Unknown; W = White

Date	Race	Name	County	Alleged Offense	Mob Type
08/26/1895	W	Garland Stemler	Siskiyou	Murder	Private
09/23/1895	I	William Archer	Kern	Murder	Private
05/31/1901	W	Calvin Hall	Modoc	Theft, burglary	Private
05/31/1901	I	James Hall	Modoc	Theft, burglary	Private
05/31/1901	I	Frank Hall	Modoc	Theft, burglary	Private
05/31/1901	I	Martin Wilson	Modoc	Theft, burglary	Private
05/31/1901	I	Daniel Yantis	Modoc	Theft, burglary	Private
07/09/1901	C	Yung Fook (Ah Sing)	Kern	Murderous assault	Mass
03/11/1904	B	James Cummings	Kern	Rape of boy	Private
04/15/1904	W	B. H. Harrington	Siskiyou	Rape	Mass
04/22/1908	W	Joseph Simpson	Inyo	Murder	Private
12/10/1920	W	George Boyd	Sonoma	Murder	Private
12/10/1920	W	Terrence Fitts	Sonoma	Murder	Private
12/10/1920	W	Charles Valento	Sonoma	Murder	Private
11/26/1933	W	John M. Holmes	Santa Clara	Kidnapping, murder	Mass
11/26/1933	W	Thomas H. Thurmond	Santa Clara	Kidnapping, murder	Mass
08/03/1935	W	Clyde Johnson	Siskiyou	Murder	Private
01/06/1947	B	Unknown	Siskiyou	Cattle rustling	Private

Lynching Victims in Washington Territory and State

Race: I = American Indian; W = White

Date	Race	Name	County	Alleged Offense	Mob Type
01/18/1882	W	James Sullivan	King	Murder	Mass
01/18/1882	W	William Howard	King	Murder	Mass
01/18/1882	W	Benjamin Payne	King	Murder	Mass
06/1882	W	Aldy (Oldie) Neal	Spokane	Horse theft	Private
08/1884	W	Louis A. Knott	Whitman	Murder	Private
08/1889	W	Fred Trotman	Kittitas	Murder	Mass
01/05/1891 or					
01/06/1891	I	Stephen (Indian Steve)	Okanagan	Murder	Private
04/11/1891	W	John B. Rose	Pacific	Murder	Private
04/11/1891	W	John Edwards	Pacific	Murder	Private
04/25/1891	W	A. J. Hunt	Walla Walla	Murder	Private
06/02/1894	W	George Parker	Whitman	Murder	Private
06/02/1894	W	Ed Hill	Whitman	Murder	Private
08/14/1895	W	Sam Vinson	Kittitas	Murder	Mass
08/14/1895	W	Charles Vinson	Kittitas	Murder	Mass
08/1896	I	Frank Viles	Asotin	Rape	Private
01/08/1898	W	"Blackey" Chadwick Marshall	Whitman	Murder	Private
08/05/1903	W	William Hamilton	Asotin	Murder, attempted rape	Mass
11/11/1919	W	Wesley Everest	Lewis	Murder, being a Wobbly	Private

Lynching Victims in Wisconsin

Race: W = White

Date	Race	Name	County	Alleged Offense	Mob Type
11/19/1881	W	Edward Maxwell (alias Williams)	Pepin	Murder	Mass
10/16/1884	W	Nathaniel "Scotty" Mitchell	La Crosse	Murder	Mass
06/08/1888	W	Andrew Grandstaff	Vernon	Murder	Mass
11/24/1889	W	Hans Jacob Olsen	Trempeleau	Violence against his family	Private
09/21/1891	W	Anton Sieboldt	Lafayette	Murder	Mass

NOTES

Abbreviations

SHSI-IC	State Historical Society of Iowa, Iowa City
SHSI-DM	State Historical Society of Iowa, Des Moines
WSM-C	Wyoming State Museum, Cheyenne
WSA	Wyoming State Archives
HRS	Wyoming State Archives–Historical Research Section
LSUSC	Special Collections, Hill Memorial Library, Louisiana State University, Baton Rouge
LSA-BR	Louisiana State Archives, Baton Rouge
NYSA	New York State Archives, Albany

Introduction

1. For the "informal, often rough, and highly democratic" criminal justice of colonial America and its reform from the revolution through the postbellum era into a professionalized, bureaucratic system committed to due process, see Walker, *Popular Justice*, 13–111, and Friedman, *Crime and Punishment in American History*, 22–82. Walker argues in regard to colonial America: "The norms of the local majority, rather than abstract legal principles, dictated criminal justice policy" (15). Gilded Age reform and the postbellum national debate over due process are analyzed in Brown, *Strain of Violence*, 144–79, Keller, *Affairs of State*, 493–95, and Paul, *Conservative Crisis and the Rule of Law*.

2. Richard Maxwell Brown, following Herbert L. Packer, has argued that nineteenth-century Americans divided in their perceptions of law and vigilantism into camps advocating either crime control, that is, the harsh repression of crime, or a respect for due-process law and the rights of a defendant. Some nineteenth-century legal scholars allied with law officers and vigilantes in trying to reform the criminal justice system for the purpose of swift and sure punishment regardless of legal niceties. Their opponents worried that repressive law enforcement and courts and widespread lynching mocked the American legal system's guarantee of justice. Brown, *Strain of Violence*, 144–79.

3. For elites who supported vigilantism, see ibid. and Ingalls, *Urban Vigilantes in the New South*. The 1891 lynching of eleven Sicilians by a mob that included elite New Orleanians is analyzed in chapter 1.

4. This movement's origin in the revolutionary-era Northeast is analyzed in Masur, *Rites of Execution*.

5. Between 1866 and 1899, 185 legal executions occurred in Pennsylvania, 155 in New York State, fifty-five in New Jersey, twenty-four in Massachusetts, and sixteen in Connecticut. By comparison, authorities in the same years executed four in Iowa, none in Wisconsin (which did not have a death penalty), six in Wyoming, twenty in Washington Territory and State, 127 in California, and 135 in Louisiana. Espy and Smykla, *Executions in the United States.* The dynamic persistence of older cultural traits in American regions may also help to explain why midwesterners, westerners, and southerners lynched and northeasterners did not. David Hackett Fischer argues that the roots of American regionalism can be found in the distinctive traits brought by particular waves of immigrants from Britain in the seventeenth and eighteenth centuries; these traits had special salience in the context of the far-reaching social and legal changes of the nineteenth century and the transition from rough justice to due process. Cavaliers from southern and western England and borderers from North Britain brought folkways to the American South that were skeptical of centralized authority and stressed the harsh and violent punishment of affronts to personal and collective honor. Their descendants carried these ordering folkways to the lower Midwest and parts of the West. In contrast, Puritans from eastern England and Quakers from the north of England brought legal folkways to New England and the mid Atlantic that emphasized consensus, public order, individual rights, and a disinclination toward violence. Their descendants populated the upper Midwest and portions of the West. Fischer, *Albion's Seed,* 189–96, 398–405, 584–89, 765–76, and 889–95.

6. Wright, *Racial Violence in Kentucky;* Brundage, *Lynching in the New South;* Brundage, ed., *Under Sentence of Death;* Tolnay and Beck, *Festival of Violence.* Also see several recent dissertations: Finnegan, "'At the Hands of Parties Unknown'"; Pfeifer, "Lynching and Criminal Justice in Regional Context"; Carrigan, "Between South and West"; Feimster, "'Ladies and Lynching.'" Popular treatments can be found in Allen, Als, Lewis, and Litwack, *Without Sanctuary,* and Dray, *At the Hands of Persons Unknown.*

7. Brown, *Strain of Violence;* Brown, *No Duty to Retreat;* Bancroft, *Popular Tribunals.* Gard, *Frontier Justice,* posits a transition from "savagery" to "social stability" in the West, with vigilantism serving as the transitional device (v–vi).

8. For an insightful work analyzing lynching in the South and the West, see Ross, "At the Bar of Judge Lynch." For a valuable bibliography of sources on southern and western collective violence, see Moses, *Lynching and Vigilantism in the United States.*

9. Brundage, *Lynching in the New South,* 101–2. For a useful analysis of white southerners' justification of lynching as "informal justice," see Jean and Brundage, "Legitimizing 'Justice.'"

10. Tolnay and Beck, *Festival of Violence,* 86–118.

11. Brown, *Strain of Violence,* analyzes the roots, components, and uses of the ideology of vigilantism (113–18).

12. For a valuable interpretation that takes the ideology of western lynchers seriously but overstates the decline of lynching in California after 1875, see Johnson, "Vigilance and the Law." For accounts that emphasize the nefarious and ephemeral nature of western lynching, see Vyzralek, "Murder in Masquerade," and Grimsted, "Making Violence Relevant." The best interpretation of the influential vigilante movements in San Francisco is Senkewicz, *Vigilantes in Gold Rush San Francisco.* A recent attempt at surveying western vigilantism can be found in Gordon, *Great Arizona Orphan Abduction,* 254–74. For a comprehensive study of lynching in a western state, see Leonard, *Lynching in Colorado.*

13. For an influential view that the West was not particularly violent, see Dykstra, *Cattle Towns.* Hollon, *Frontier Violence,* documents western bloodshed but asserts that

frontier mayhem was overstated. For an argument that the "trans-Sierra frontier was unmistakably violent and lawless, but only in special ways" (247), see McGrath, *Gunfighters, Highwaymen, and Vigilantes*, 247–60. McKanna, *Homicide, Race, and Justice in the American West*, finds high rates of homicide in counties in Nebraska, Colorado, and Arizona.

14. Quoted in Brundage, *Lynching in the New South*, 291.

15. For an essential, insightful discussion of the historical problem of definition and the way in which the Tuskegee definition was crafted, see Waldrep, "Word and Deed," Waldrep, "War of Words," and Waldrep, *Many Faces of Judge Lynch*. Waldrep persuasively argues that historians of violence have not appreciated the problematic nature of the word "lynching." He highlights the role of technological changes, including the rise of the newspaper industry and political factors, such as the particular ways in which antilynching advocates publicized the violence, in the evolution of the usage and understanding of the term. Waldrep neglects the practice of collective violence itself, however, which remained relatively consistent from the 1860s through the 1930s, and which was in all regions characterized as "lynching" by those who chronicled its occurrence. Moreover, lynching never required the uniform support of the community, as Waldrep asserts in "Word and Deed," based upon his reading of James Elbert Cutler's definition: "'A lynching may be defined as an illegal and summary execution at the hands of a mob, or a number of persons, who have in some degree the public opinion of the community behind them'" (245). As study of the local dynamics of the violence in the Midwest, West, and South reveals, portions of the populace often opposed the violence, but local editors still called it "lynching."

16. Black, "Lynchings in Iowa," 152.

17. I am indebted to David Baldus for this point.

18. For early arguments that Americans lynched because of an ambivalence toward law, particularly because of the criminal justice system's unreliability, see Cutler, *Lynch-Law*, 267–79, and Black, "Lynchings in Iowa," 162–63.

19. Popspisil, *Anthropology of Law*, 107.

20. Brundage, *Lynching in the New South*, 14–16, 48; Tolnay and Beck, *Festival of Violence*, 50.

21. Wood, *Radicalism of the American Revolution*, esp. 229–34.

22. Brown, *Strain of Violence*, 5–7, 39–66, 71–73.

23. Wood, *Radicalism of the American Revolution*, 192–93; Friedman, *Crime and Punishment in American History*, 61–82; Masur, *Rites of Execution*.

24. Analysis of popular violence in early modern Europe can be found in Davis, "Reasons of Misrule," and Thompson, "'Rough Music,'" 286–87. Early treatments of the origins of lynching and the lethal transformation of collective violence in the antebellum period can be found in Cutler, *Lynch-Law*, 1–136, and Shay, *Judge Lynch*, 15–69. For recent analyses of the parallel transformation of rioting, large-scale crowd actions against persons and property, often in urban areas, see Gilje, *Rioting in America*, 60–86, and Grimsted, *American Mobbing*. Gilje's analysis is especially persuasive on the relation between shifts in patterns of violence and antebellum social and cultural changes.

Chapter 1: Mobs across Time and Space

1. These processes are analyzed in Foner, *Reconstruction*.

2. The southwestern parish of St. Landry was the scene of one of the worst incidents of Reconstruction political violence in the South. In September 1868, members of the

Seymour Knights, a paramilitary club of conservative whites, attacked a white Republican schoolteacher in Opelousas. African Americans in the parish, a number of them armed, responded by flooding into the town. The Knights of the White Camelia, another paramilitary organization of conservative whites that was extremely strong in the region, interpreted this as a "Negro Revolt," took command of Opelousas, and ordered the African Americans to surrender their weapons. A massacre ensued, eventually extending into the countryside. Whites murdered at least 150 black Republicans. For succinct accounts of these events, see Tunnell, *Crucible of Reconstruction*, 153, 156, and Brasseaux, Fontenot, and Oubre, *Creoles of Color in the Bayou Country*, 99–103.

3. George C. Wright, who has studied lynching in Kentucky during Reconstruction, argues that the chaotic period following emancipation witnessed a dramatic surge in lynching violence in that border slave state, even exceeding that which occurred in the "nadir" of postbellum race relations in the early to mid 1890s. Wright, *Racial Violence in Kentucky*, 41–42.

4. For the 1859 lynchings of four slaves in central Missouri's "Little Dixie," see Dyer, "A Most Unexampled Exhibition of Madness and Brutality." The descendants of French, English, and African settlers and slaves made this rugged transition in southwestern Louisiana in the 1850s and 1860s. An extensive vigilante movement in 1859 led by Acadian landholders targeted lower-class white deviants and sparked antivigilante campaigns by landless and yeomen whites and an ensuing bloodbath in 1859–60. Eventually local vigilantes also directed their efforts against free persons of color. During the Civil War, the region saw prolonged guerilla violence between "Jayhawkers," who supported the Union and allied with Creoles of Color and ex-slaves, and Confederate supporters. During the war and after, vigilante bands also made freedpeople their targets, seeking to reassert the racial control altered by emancipation. For the 1859 Attakapas vigilante movements and ensuing collective violence in southwestern Louisiana, consult Brasseaux, *Acadian to Cajun*, 112–49, and Brasseaux, Fontenot, and Oubre, *Creoles of Color in the Bayou Country*, 85. The role of lynching and vigilantism in the transition from slavery to Redemption in Louisiana is also perceptively analyzed in Vandal, *Rethinking Southern Violence*, 90–109.

5. Christopher Waldrep makes this important argument in *Roots of Disorder*, esp. 172–74.

6. Black, "Lynchings in Iowa," 187–200. Mid-nineteenth-century midwestern vigilantism is treated perceptively in Nolan, "Vigilantes on the Middle Border."

7. For this movement in the Northeast, see Masur, *Rites of Execution*.

8. *New Orleans Picayune*, September 30, 1893.

9. One hundred fifty-five of 263 lynching victims (59 percent).

10. For accounts of the lynching of the eleven Sicilians in New Orleans, see *New Orleans Picayune*, March 14, 15, and 16, 1891, Hair, *Kingfish and His Realm*, 12–15, Jackson, *New Orleans in the Gilded Age*, 247–53, and Scarpaci, "Italian Immigrants in Louisiana's Sugar Parishes," 246–48.

11. *New Orleans Picayune*, March 15, 1891.

12. *Baton Rouge Weekly Advocate*, April 16, 1892.

13. Hair, *Kingfish and His Realm*, 14.

14. Lynchers in South Louisiana killed 159 persons between 1878 and 1946, at least 132 of them African Americans.

15. Scarpaci, "Italian Immigrants in Louisiana's Sugar Parishes," 251.

16. One hundred fifty-nine lynching victims out of a total of 422 deaths (38.6 percent) by lynching in Louisiana.

17. One hundred fourteen of 159 lynchings in southern Louisiana occurred before 1900 (72 percent).

18. Black, "Lynching Research Notes," box 2, folders by county, Manuscript Collection, SHSI-IC. Also see Black, "Lynchings in Iowa," and Black, "Attempted Lynchings in Iowa."

19. Lynchers in Iowa murdered sixteen in the 1880s, four in the 1890s, and a single person in the early twentieth century. At least eighteen additional mobs gathered in the first decade of the twentieth century, but these dispersed before killing their intended victims.

20. Whites made up three-fourths of all persons (fifty-seven of seventy-six) sought by mobs in Iowa.

21. See Pfeifer, "Iowa's Last Lynching."

22. U.S. Bureau of the Census, *Tenth Census of the United States*; State of Iowa, *Census of 1905*, 511–20. Residents born in Missouri, Kentucky, Virginia, Ohio, and Indiana comprised 25 percent of the population in Taylor County, 28.6 percent in Decatur County, 24 percent in Wapello County, 28 percent in Appanoose County, and 23.5 percent in Monroe County. Yeoman traditions of honor and violence thrived in the southern Butternut regions of Ohio and Indiana, and many settlers born in those areas migrated to southern Iowa in the mid-nineteenth century. By contrast, a much smaller percentage of Ohioans and Indianans settled in northern Iowa counties, where persons born in mid-Atlantic states such as New York and Pennsylvania contributed greater numbers and a lesser tendency toward extralegal violence. For the antebellum formation of "cornbelt culture" in Indiana and Ohio, see Power, *Planting Cornbelt Culture*. On the nineteenth-century evolution of agricultural production and the emergence of a market-driven corn-hogs combination, see Bogue, "Farming in the Prairie Peninsula." For southern cultural attributes stressing honor and personal and collective violence, see Wyatt-Brown, *Southern Honor*, and Ayers, *Vengeance and Justice*.

23. *Atlanta Constitution* quoted in *Ottumwa (Iowa) Daily Democrat*, December 9, 1893. For additional partisan wrangling over lynching and its sectional dimensions, see *Des Moines Weekly Leader*, December 7, 1893, and *Oskaloosa (Iowa) Times*, March 31, 1893.

24. *Burlington (Iowa) Hawkeye*, February 11, 1898.

25. Among many examples of this kind of exposition, see *Dubuque Times*, June 7, 1883, and *(Des Moines) Iowa State Register*, July 25, 1883.

26. *(Des Moines) Iowa State Register*, July 24, 1883. Among other expressions of the view that lynching was a form of atavism, see *Burlington (Iowa) Saturday Evening Post*, February 12, 1898. In an exceptional circumstance, though, "progressive" business attitudes might coincide with support for lynching; see Pfeifer, "Iowa's Last Lynching," 320, 326–27.

27. The abolition of the death penalty in Wisconsin is analyzed in Current, *History of Wisconsin*, 190–91.

28. Coroner's Inquest on Charles Woodard, March 29, 1902, Natrona County, WSA, WSM-C; Motions for Change of Venue and New Trial, *State of Wyoming v. Charles F. Woodard*, filed February 7 and March 3, 1902, Natrona County, "Crime and Criminals File," HRS, WSM-C; *Natrona County (Wyo.) Tribune*, January 2, 9, 16, 23, 30, February 6, 13, 20, 27, March 6, 18, 20, 29, 31, and April 3, 1902; *(Casper) Wyoming Derrick*, March 27, 28, and April 3, 1902; *Cheyenne Daily Leader*, March 25, 26, 27, and 28, 1902. Woodard had been originally imprisoned for stealing from ranchers. He escaped from the Natrona County jail in December 1901 and murdered the sheriff in January as a posse attempted to capture him.

29. Although oil drilling began in the 1880s, Casper would not become a major oil center until the 1910s. Mokler, *History of Natrona County*, 58, 116, 245–63.

30. For Sheriff W. C. Ricker's long-standing role in fraternal organizations and municipal politics in Casper, see ibid., 57, 120, 123, 153, and *Natrona County (Wyo.) Tribune*, January 9, 1902.

31. *Natrona County (Wyo.) Tribune*, January 9, 1902.

32. The *Natrona County (Wyo.) Tribune* bears some responsibility for the lynching of Woodard. The *Tribune* histrionically covered the story beginning with Woodard's escape from jail and suggested at several points that a lynching might be appropriate. *Natrona County (Wyo.) Tribune*, January 2, 9, 16, 23, 30, February 6, 13, 20, 27, March 6, 18, 20, 29, 31, and April 3, 1902.

33. *Natrona County (Wyo.) Tribune*, April 3, 1902. The majority of the townspeople in Casper, the town's two newspapers, a number of small-town editors throughout the state, and a district judge, C. W. Bramel, defended the mob killing. See the *Cheyenne Daily Leader*, March 28, 1902; *Natrona County (Wyo.) Tribune*, March 29, 31, and April 3, 1902.

34. For vigilantism in early territorial Wyoming, see Larson, *History of Wyoming*, 36–63, and Gustafson, "History of Vigilante and Mob Activity in Wyoming," 41–94.

35. A parallel shift in Colorado to lynching on allegations of homicide and the coalescence of a "respectable" social bloc that opposed lynching in more established towns and cities is charted in Leonard, *Lynching in Colorado*, 73–96, 98, 155–60.

36. *Olympia (Wash.) Transcript*, January 21, 1882.

37. For an analysis of accounts of the episode, many from oral history, see Stevens, *Vigilantes Ride in 1882*.

38. The social alterations in the Pacific Northwest in the last two decades of the nineteenth century are analyzed in Schwantes, *Pacific Northwest*, 184–206.

39. I thank Gilbert Gia of Bakersfield, California, for his well-researched account of the 1879 lynching of the Yoakums. E-mail correspondence with the author, November 20, 22, 24, December 11 and 12, 2002. Webb, "History of Lynching in California since 1875," 24–27; my gratitude to William Dean Carrigan for this highly valuable source.

40. *Kern County (Calif.) Gazette*, June 7, 1879, and *Kern County (Calif.) Courier*, June 15, 1879, are quoted in Webb, "History of Lynching in California since 1875," 26–27.

41. *Redding (Calif.) Free Press*, April 16, 1904; *San Francisco Chronicle*, April 17, 1904; *San Francisco Examiner*, April 17, 1904.

42. Schwantes, "Concept of the Wageworkers' Frontier." For the 1901 Lookout lynching, see *San Francisco Chronicle*, June 1, 2, and 4, 1901, *Yreka Journal*, June 4, 7, 11, 14, 18, 21, 25, 26, August 16, November 5 and 8, 1901, and *San Francisco Examiner*, June 1, 2, 3, 4, and July 12, 1901. I am also indebted to Glennda Bradley, the great-granddaughter of the white man who was lynched, Calvin Hall, for information concerning this incident. E-mail correspondence with the author, March 17 and 18, 2002.

43. *Middletown (N.Y.) Daily Press*, June 3, 4, 6, 7, 8, 9, 10, 11, and 14, 1892; *Middletown (N.Y.) Argus*, June 3, 4, 6, 7, and 8, 1892; *New York Evening Post*, June 3, 1892; *New York Times*, June 3 and 4, 1892. Robert Lewis was variously identified as being twenty-two or twenty-nine years of age and also went by the surname Jackson.

44. *Middletown (N.Y.) Daily Press*, June 3, 4, 6, 7, 8, 9, 10, 11, and 14, 1892; *Middletown (N.Y.) Argus*, June 3, 4, 6, 7, and 8, 1892; *New York Evening Post*, June 3, 1892; *New York Times*, June 3 and 4, 1892. Lewis had relatives in Port Jervis and Middletown, N.Y., and Paterson, N.J., and his family had lived in the region for at least sever-

al generations. In 1890, blacks contributed 119 of Port Jervis's population of 9,327 (1.2 percent). U.S. Bureau of the Census, *Eleventh Census of the United States*.

45. *Middletown (N.Y.) Daily Press*, June 4, 6, 7, 8, 9, 10, and 11, 1892; *Middletown (N.Y.) Argus*, June 6 and 7, 1892; *New York Times*, June 3, 1892; Murlin, *New York Red Book*.

46. *Middletown (N.Y.) Daily Press*, June 4 and 14, 1892; *Middletown (N.Y.) Argus*, June 4 and 8, 1892. Port Jervis authorities buried Lewis in the plot bought by African Americans. For the history of the small African American community in southern New York, derived from slavery in seventeenth- and eighteenth-century New York, escaped southern slaves in the antebellum period, and the migration of southern blacks after emancipation, see Banner-Haley, "Extended Community"; Quynne, "'The Hills' in the Mid-Nineteenth Century"; Watkins, "Survey of the African American Presence in the History of the Downstate New York Area." For an interpretation arguing that the novella, "The Monster," authored by Judge William Crane's brother Stephen, may have been inspired by the Port Jervis lynching, see Marshall, "'The Monster' Seen in the Light of Robert Lewis's Lynching."

47. *Middletown (N.Y.) Argus*, June 4 and 7, 1892; *New York Times*, June 4, 1892.

48. An instructive comparison is the August 1911 lynching of an African American, Zachariah Walker, in Coatesville, Pennsylvania. Walker had murdered a white police officer. Unlike Robert Lewis in Port Jervis, Walker was a newcomer to Coatesville and had few ties to the ethnically and racially mixed coal-mining community. Downey and Hyser, *No Crooked Death*.

49. The lynching of African Americans in the New York City Draft Riots in July 1863 by Irish laborers is analyzed in Bernstein, *New York City Draft Riots*, 27–31. Most of the lynchers convicted in Newburgh, New York, had Irish surnames. The *Middletown Argus* emphasized the fact that some of the 1863 lynchers had been eventually punished, although for riot, not "for taking the life of a human being." *Middletown (N.Y.) Argus*, June 3 and 7, 1892.

50. An earlier Pennsylvania lynching is chronicled in *The Murder of the Geogles and the Lynching of the Fiend Snyder*. An 1873 lynching in northern Maine of a white man, Jim Cullen, who had murdered two men, is analyzed in York, "'They Lynched Jim Cullen.'"

Chapter 2: The Making of Mobs

1. My discussion follows Brundage's taxonomy of four mob types in *Lynching in the New South*, 17–48. The value of this taxonomy is demonstrated by its applicability not only to Louisiana but also to nonsouthern settings like Iowa, Wisconsin, Wyoming, Washington, and California, where the range of mob activity fell roughly into the same four categories, which Brundage labels as mass mobs, posses, private mobs, and terrorist mobs. Ross, "At the Bar of Judge Lynch," advances a taxonomy that includes seven kinds of mobs: those with a "permanent organization," vigilante mobs and terrorist mobs; those with "some advance planning or collusion," the organized mob, the private mob, and the secret mob; and those that were "wholly spontaneous," the hue-and-cry mob and mass mob (172–236).

2. Several interesting and important studies tend to monolithize southern mobs. These include Tolnay and Beck, *Festival of Violence*, and Finnegan, "'At the Hands of Parties Unknown,'" esp. 270–73.

3. Following Brundage, I have categorized collective killings perpetrated by search

parties as lynchings only if victims were unarmed or did not attempt to avoid arrest after being located. Brundage, *Lynching in the New South,* 17–48, 291–92.

4. Ibid.

5. *Des Moines Weekly Leader,* December 7, 1893; *Des Moines Leader,* November 23, 1893; *Ottumwa (Iowa) Daily Democrat,* November 22, 23, 24, 25, 26, 28, 29, 30, December 3, 9, 10, and 16, 1893; *Ottumwa (Iowa) Sun,* November 23 and 30, 1893; Black, "Lynching Research Notes," box 2, Wapello County Folder, Manuscript Collection, SHSI-IC.

6. Webb, "History of Lynching in California since 1875," 37.

7. Mass mobs killed six of twenty-four lynching victims in Iowa and ten of sixty-five lynching victims in California.

8. *New Orleans Picayune,* May 13 and 14, 1914; *Shreveport (La.) Times,* May 13, 14, and 17, 1914. For an interpretation focusing on spectacle lynchings in the context of the spread of mass consumption and the culture of segregation in the South in the early twentieth century, see Hale, *Making Whiteness,* 199–239. Mass mobs killed sixty-three persons in northern parishes.

9. *Des Moines Weekly Leader,* March 30 and April 3, 1893; *Oskaloosa (Iowa) Times,* March 23, 24, and 31, 1893; Black, "Lynching Research Notes," box 2, Monroe County Folder, Manuscript Collection, SHSI-IC.

10. Twenty-eight of 263 lynching victims in northern Louisiana died at the hands of posses. For posses and their often ambiguous legal status, see Brundage, *Lynching in the New South,* 33.

11. *Waverly (Iowa) Democrat,* June 8, 15, 22, and 29, 1883; *(Waterloo) Iowa State Reporter,* June 7 and 14, 1883; *Dubuque Times,* June 7, 8, 9, 10, and 13, 1883; *(Des Moines) Iowa State Register,* June 8, 9, 10, and 14, 1883; in Black, "Lynching Research Notes," box 2, Bremer County Folder, Manuscript Collection, SHSI-IC.

12. For another Iowa posse that lynched, see *(Des Moines) Iowa State Register,* March 7, 1895; *Dallas County (Iowa) Record,* March 8 and 15, 1895, in Black, "Lynching Research Notes," box 2, Dallas County Folder, Manuscript Collection, SHSI-IC. For additional near lynchings involving posses in Iowa, see *Council Bluffs (Iowa) Nonpareil,* June 1, 1894, *Ottumwa (Iowa) Weekly Sun,* August 29, 1896, *Muscatine (Iowa) Journal,* March 31, 1903, *(Des Moines) Register and Leader,* December 21, 1903, and *(Des Moines) Iowa State Register,* November 1904, in Black, "Lynching Research Notes," box 2, Boone County Folder, Manuscript Collection, SHSI-IC.

13. For examples of Iowa posses that killed in "self-defense," see *(Waterloo) Iowa State Reporter,* September 25, 1884; *Burlington (Iowa) Hawkeye,* January 31, 1892, in Black, "Lynching Research Notes," box 2, Jasper County Folder, Manuscript Collection, SHSI-IC; *Jefferson (Iowa) Bee,* June 26, 1902, in Black, "Lynching Research Notes," box 2, Greene County Folder, Manuscript Collection, SHSI-IC. Also, see Brundage, *Lynching in the New South,* on the difficulty of classifying posses that killed persons they were seeking (291).

14. *Ellensburgh (Wash.) Capital,* August 15 and 22, 1895; *Ellensburgh (Wash.) Localizer,* August 17 and 24, 1895; *Ellensburgh (Wash.) Dawn,* August 17, 1895; *San Francisco Chronicle,* August 15, 1895.

15. Quoted in *Ellensburgh (Wash.) Capital,* September 26, 1895.

16. Private mobs claimed fifty of sixty-five victims in California, fifteen of twenty-four victims in Iowa, and eleven of eighteen victims in Washington Territory and State.

17. In the Sugarland, where lynchers murdered forty-six persons, private mobs killed 38 percent of total victims; mass mobs 25 percent; posses 18 percent; and terrorist mobs 3 percent. The orientation of 19 percent of the mobs could not be determined.

18. *New Orleans Picayune,* March 19, 1906.

19. Terrorist mobs killed sixteen of Wyoming's thirty-six lynching victims.

20. *Newcastle (Wyo.) Journal,* June 19 (includes reprint of most of coroner's inquest) and 26, 1891; *Sundance (Wyo.) Gazette,* June 19, 1891.

21. *Bill Barlow's Budget* (Douglas, Wyo.), October 15, 1892. For the class consciousness of Johnson County settlers, see Larson, *History of Wyoming,* 280–83.

22. Lynch mobs claimed twenty-six victims, twenty-three of them African American, in southwestern Louisiana.

23. *New Orleans Picayune,* September 6 and November 2, 1892; *Baton Rouge Weekly Advocate,* December 17, 1892. Cajun "regulators" also lynched two black Creoles and may have killed another black man as they sought to intimidate the black Creole community in St. Landry Parish in the fall of 1888. Coroner's Inquest, September 16, 1888, Clerk of Court's Office, St. Landry Parish, Opelousas; *New Orleans Picayune,* September 18, 1888; *Opelousas (La.) Courier,* September 22, 29, October 6, 13, 20, 27, November 17, December 1 and 22, 1888.

24. Five lynchings of African Americans by whitecappers occurred in the upcountry of central and northern Louisiana and, as in southwestern parishes, these elicited condemnation from parish elites. For incidents in Bienville Parish, see *New Orleans Times-Democrat,* March 28, 1892, *Baton Rouge Weekly Advocate,* April 2, 1892, and *New Orleans Times-Democrat,* June 10, 1894. Incidents in Union Parish are described in the *New Iberia (La.) Enterprise,* April 29, 1885, and *New Orleans Weekly Pelican,* September 17, 1887. For a whitecapping in Winn Parish, see *New Orleans Picayune,* November 11, 1885. As W. Fitzhugh Brundage notes in his discussion of whitecapping in Georgia, some research suggests that white farmers of middling status who sought with frustration to become landholders, not the most impoverished white farmers, were responsible for whitecapping. Brundage, *Lynching in the New South,* 24–25. Whitecapping in Mississippi is discussed in McMillen, *Dark Journey,* 120–21.

25. *New Orleans Picayune,* September 6 and November 2, 1892; *Baton Rouge Weekly Advocate,* December 17, 1892.

26. Quoted in *New Orleans Picayune,* November 2, 1892.

27. *Baton Rouge Weekly Advocate,* December 17, 1892.

28. See, for example, the *Burlington (Iowa) Hawkeye,* February 10, 1898, and *Burlington (Iowa) Weekly Hawkeye,* September 5, 1901, in Black, "Lynching Research Notes," box 2, Polk County Folder, Manuscript Collection, SHSI-IC; *Dallas County (Iowa) News,* April 20, 1904, in Black, "Lynching Research Notes," box 2, Woodbury County Folder, Manuscript Collection, SHSI-IC; *(Des Moines) Register and Leader,* January 25, 1907, in Black, "Lynching Research Notes," box 2, Henry County Folder, Manuscript Collection, SHSI-IC.

29. Black, "Lynching Research Notes," box 2, Des Moines County Folder, Manuscript Collection, SHSI-IC; *Burlington (Iowa) Hawkeye,* February 10, 11, 12, 13, and 15, 1898.

30. W. Fitzhugh Brundage argues that scholars have overstated the ritualistic quality of mob activity. He convincingly asserts that mass mobs in the South were more overtly ritualistic than other kinds of mobs, but he may understate the extent to which the activities of private mobs were understood in a symbolic way. Brundage, *Lynching in the New South,* 17–48. For a discussion of lynching and ritual in a border state, see Pfeifer, "Ritual of Lynching," esp. 29–32.

31. The popular fascination that surrounded executions in eighteenth-century England is described in Linebaugh, *London Hanged.* For the public spectacle of an antebellum execution in Iowa attended by approximately ten thousand, see the account of the legal hanging of William Hinkle in Appanoose County on August 13, 1858, in *Pioneer History of Davis County,* 374–78.

32. *Waverly (Iowa) Democrat,* June 15, 1883; *(Des Moines) Iowa State Register,* July

25, 1883; *(Des Moines) Iowa State Register*, December 31, 1884, January 1 and 2, 1885; *(Des Moines) Iowa State Register*, July 2, 1889, in Black, "Lynching Research Notes," box 2, Taylor County Folder, Manuscript Collection, SHSI-IC; *Oskaloosa (Iowa) Times*, March 24, 1893; *Ottumwa (Iowa) Sun*, November 23, 1893; *Missouri Valley (Iowa) Daily Times*, May 1, 1894.

33. *(Des Moines) Iowa State Register*, January 31, 1884; *Des Moines Weekly Leader*, March 30, 1893; Black, "Lynching Research Notes," box 2, Taylor County Folder, Manuscript Collection, SHSI-IC.

34. *(Des Moines) Iowa State Register*, June 10, 1883; *(Des Moines) Iowa State Register*, January 1, 1885; *(Des Moines) Iowa State Register*, August 16, 1887.

35. Lynchings solely by hanging in Iowa occurred in Bremer and Shelby Counties in 1883, Wapello County in 1884, Adams and Decatur Counties in 1887, Taylor County in 1889, Monroe County in 1893, Harrison County in 1894, and Floyd County in 1907. Riddling with bullets occurred in the counties of Cass, Madison, and Shelby in 1883, Audubon and Hardin in 1885, and Dallas in 1895. Black, "Lynchings in Iowa," 233–49.

36. Ibid., 239; *Ottumwa (Iowa) Sun*, November 23, 1893; *Des Moines Leader*, November 23, 1893.

37. *Atlantic (Iowa) Daily Telegraph*, June 5, 1883; *Dubuque Times*, June 8, 1883; *Atlantic (Iowa) Daily Telegraph*, July 24, 1883; *(Des Moines) Iowa State Register*, July 25, 1883; *Council Bluffs (Iowa) Nonpareil*, February 7, 1885; *Missouri Valley (Iowa) Daily Times*, May 1, 1894; Black, "Lynchings in Iowa," 233–54.

38. *Vernon County (Wisc.) Censor*, May 30 and June 6, 1888; *Milwaukee Sentinel*, June 2, 1888.

39. *Vernon County (Wisc.) Censor*, June 6, 1888; *Milwaukee Sentinel*, June 2, 1888.

40. *Vernon County (Wisc.) Censor*, June 6, 1888. In another highly ritualistic lynching in western Wisconsin on October 16, 1884, a mob of three thousand stormed the jail in La Crosse and seized and hanged Nathaniel Mitchell, an English-born river pilot who had shot to death Frank Burton, a grain broker and prominent Republican leader, during an election victory parade earlier in the evening. Relics and trophies circulated, as far as Milwaukee, of the jail door cut into splinters, pieces of rope, and the hanging tree "ruined by jack-knives." *Milwaukee Sentinel*, October 18, 1884; *La Crosse Morning Chronicle*, October 18, 1884.

41. Coroner's Inquest on "Big Nose" George Parrott, March 23, 1881, Carbon County, and Coroner's Inquest on "Dutch Chorley," January 5, 1879, Carbon County, WSA, WSM-C; *Rawlins (Wyo.) Journal*, March 26, 1881; *Rocky Mountain (Denver) News*, September 18, 1955; "Research Memorandum," December 14, 1960, "Big Nose George" Folder, Crime and Criminals Folder, HRS, WSM-C.

42. *Carbon County (Wyo.) Journal*, October 20, November 10, 1888.

43. *Cheyenne Daily Leader*, April 23, 1892.

44. *Cheyenne Daily Leader*, March 28, 1902.

45. *Carbon County (Wyo.) Journal*, October 27, 1888.

46. *Cheyenne Daily Leader*, November 22, 1903.

47. On the similarities between western honor and southern honor, see Brown, "Western Violence," 14–17. For southern honor and the anthropological meaning of sadism in the performance of southern lynchings, including the notion of collective atonement through pollution, see Wyatt-Brown, *Southern Honor*, 453–61. Another interpretation that borrows anthropological concepts and stresses ritual and psychosexual dynamics in southern lynching is Williamson, *Crucible of Race*, 185–89, 308–9, 314–15. On masculinity in southern fighting techniques, see Gorn, "'Gouge and Bite.'"

48. Webb, "History of Lynching in California since 1875," 31–32.

49. *San Francisco Chronicle*, August 28, 1895.

50. *Yreka (Calif.) Journal*, August 27 and 30, 1895; *San Francisco Chronicle*, August 27 and 28, 1895; *San Francisco Examiner*, August 27 and 28, 1895.

51. See, for example, Hale, *Making Whiteness*, 209–15; Dray, *At the Hands of Persons Unknown*, 3–16; and Litwack, *Trouble in Mind*, 280–83.

52. For the connection between ritualistic mutilation and mobs' punishment of interracial rape, see Brundage, *Lynching in the New South*, 64–66.

53. See the independent but highly stylized accounts in *New Orleans Picayune*, September 9, 1891, and *Baton Rouge Weekly Advocate*, September 12, 1891.

54. *New Orleans Picayune*, February 25, 1906.

55. Ibid.

56. *Anamosa (Iowa) Eureka*, October 14, 1880. Also see *Burlington (Iowa) Hawkeye*, July 3, 1891, and *(Des Moines) Iowa State Register*, July 3, 1891.

57. *Atlantic (Iowa) Daily Telegraph*, July 24 and 30, 1883. For numerous examples of the older vigilantism, see Black, "Lynchings in Iowa," 153–233. In the only such case after 1880, an ethnically diverse group of more than fifty farmers attempted to hang Dr. H. C. Cohee, accused of leading a gang of horse thieves, in Washington County in 1882. Energized by a commitment to property rights and a disdain for county law enforcement, some of the Washington County mobbers were later tried but exonerated by a jury that awarded Cohee only minimal damages. O. E. Brown to Black, recd. December 15, 1910, January 4, 1911, and February 4, 1911, "Lynching Research Notes," box 2, Washington County Folder, Manuscript Collection, SHSI-IC.

58. *Dallas County (Iowa) News*, April 20, 1904; *(Des Moines) Iowa State Register*, January 20, 1894, cited in Black, "Lynching Research Notes," box 2, Manuscript Collection, SHSI-IC. Also see *Des Moines Leader*, May 24, 1894; *(Des Moines) Iowa State Register*, January 20, 1894, cited in Black, "Lynching Research Notes," box 2, Manuscript Collection, SHSI-IC.

59. For urban population figures, see State of Iowa, *Census of 1915*, xxx. For a profile of urban working-class Iowa in the early twentieth century, see Schwieder, *Iowa*, 244–45. Twenty-five out of fifty-two near lynchings in Iowa between 1878 and 1909 occurred in towns with a population greater than fifteen thousand; fifteen out of twenty-five urban near lynchings took place between 1895 and 1910.

60. *Des Moines Weekly Leader*, March 30 and 31, 1893.

61. Ibid., *Des Moines Leader*, May 24, 1894; *Burlington (Iowa) Hawkeye*, February 13 and 15, 1898.

62. *Council Bluffs (Iowa) Nonpareil*, February 7 and 12, 1885; *Atlantic (Iowa) Daily Telegraph*, August 10, 1883; Burg Brown to Governor William Larabee, April 7, 1887, Governor's Office, Records and Correspondence: Criminal Matters, box/vol. GII 579, SHSI-DM; *(Des Moines) Iowa State Register*, July 14, 1883; *Waverly (Iowa) Democrat*, June 8, 1883; *Atlantic (Iowa) Daily Telegraph*, August 10, 1883. Local officials were required by state law to make speeches to mobs requesting them to disperse. State of Iowa, *Annotated Code of the State of Iowa* (1885).

63. *Waverly (Iowa) Democrat*, June 15, 1883.

64. *Council Bluffs (Iowa) Nonpareil*, June 7, 1883.

65. *Waverly (Iowa) Democrat*, June 15, 1883.

66. See cases of John Anderson and Frank Brown, June 3, 1883, *Council Bluffs (Iowa) Nonpareil*, June 5 and 7, 1883; *Atlantic (Iowa) Daily Telegraph*, June 7, 14, and 21, 1883; *(Des Moines) Iowa State Register*, June 5 and 9, 1883. For the cases of William and Isaac Barber, June 8, 1883, see *Waverly (Iowa) Democrat*, June 8, 15, 22, and 29, 1883; *(Waterloo) Iowa State Reporter*, June 7 and 14, 1883; *Dubuque Times*, June 7, 8, 9, 10, and

13, 1883; *(Des Moines) Iowa State Register,* June 8, 9, 10, and 14, 1883, in Black, "Lynching Research Notes," box 2, Bremer County Folder, Manuscript Collection, SHSI-IC. For the cases of William Tylor Crawford and William P. (James) Hardy, July 14 and 24, 1883, see *Atlantic (Iowa) Daily Telegraph,* July 12, 13, 14, 16, 18, 19, 24, 27, 30, August 1, 8, and 10, 1883; *Council Bluffs (Iowa) Nonpareil,* July 10, 15, 17, 18, 24, 25, 26, and 27, 1883, in Black, "Lynching Research Notes," box 2, Shelby County Folder, Manuscript Collection, SHSI-IC. For the cases of Finley and Emmanuel Rainsbarger, June 5, 1885, see *(Des Moines) Iowa State Register,* June 6, 1885, in Black, "Lynching Research Notes," box 2, Hardin County Folder, Manuscript Collection, SHSI-IC. For "Reddy" Wilson, April 30, 1894, see *Missouri Valley (Iowa) Daily Times,* April 30, May 1, 2, 4, 8, 9, and 10, 1894; *Council Bluffs (Iowa) Nonpareil,* May 1 and 3, 1894; *Des Moines Weekly Leader,* May 3 and 10, 1894, in Black, "Lynching Research Notes," box 2, Harrison County Folder, Manuscript Collection, SHSI-IC.

67. *Griswold (Iowa) Advocate,* June 6, 1883; *(Des Moines) Iowa State Register,* April 5, 1887. For a theoretical discussion of the structural relation between lynch mobs and their victims, see Senechal de la Roche, "Sociogenesis of Lynching."

68. Coroner's Report on Frank Wigfall, filed October 5, 1912, Carbon County, Wyoming State Archives, Cheyenne; *Rawlins (Wyo.) Republican,* October 3 and 10, 1912; *Cheyenne State Leader,* October 3 and 5, 1912.

69. *Ellensburgh (Wash.) Capital,* August 15 and 22, 1895; *Ellensburgh (Wash.) Localizer,* August 17 and 24, 1895; *Ellensburgh (Wash.) Dawn,* August 17, 1895; *San Francisco Chronicle,* August 15, 1895.

70. *Asotin County (Wash.) Sentinel,* August 8, 1903; *Seattle Post-Intelligencer,* August 5, 1903; *Seattle Times,* August 5, 1903; *San Francisco Chronicle,* August 5, 1903.

71. For the far-flung wageworking frontier of extractive industries, see Schwantes, "Concept of the Wageworkers' Frontier."

72. *San Francisco Chronicle,* April 24, 1908; *Los Angeles Times,* April 24, 1908. On western honor and violence, see Brown, "Western Violence."

73. *San Francisco Chronicle,* June 1, 2, and 4, 1901; *Yreka (Calif.) Journal,* June 4, 7, 11, 14, 18, 21, 25, 26, August 16, November 5 and 8, 1901; *San Francisco Examiner,* June 1, 2, 3, 4, and July 12, 1901; Glennda Bradley, the great-granddaughter of the lynching victim Calvin Hall, e-mail correspondence with the author, March 17 and 18, 2002.

74. Larson, *History of Wyoming,* 268–84. For accounts of the Johnson County War written by contemporaries, neither especially objective, see David, *Malcolm Campbell,* and Mercer, *Banditti of the Plains.* The most comprehensive account of the Johnson County War can be found in Smith, *War on Powder River.* For the "Western Civil War of Incorporation," see Brown, "Western Violence" and *No Duty to Retreat.*

75. Brown, "Western Violence," 5–6, 18–19.

76. Larson, *History of Wyoming,* 268–69; Gustafson, "History of Vigilante and Mob Activity in Wyoming," 124–30.

77. For a summary of Horn's career, see Larson, *History of Wyoming,* 372–74. Larson estimates that "fifteen men and a boy and perhaps ten thousand sheep were killed" in the conflict between cattlemen and sheepmen between 1897 and 1909 (369–72). Only a minority of these killings fit the definition of lynching. Larson also argues that the cattle ranchers eventually prevailed in their economic interests over the sheepowners and their herders, even if the violence ceased; this portion of the range had been successfully incorporated. Sources on the Tensleep Raid include Gage, *Tensleep and No Rest.* For the response to the Tensleep Raid, see the editorial in the *Laramie Republican,* April 10, 1909.

78. *Laramie Daily Boomerang*, August 10 and 12, 1885; Coroner's Inquest on Si Partridge, August 10, 1885, Albany County, WSA, WSM-C.

79. Coroner's Inquest on N. L. Adams and Charles Putzier, filed October 1888, Carbon County, WSA, WSM-C; *Carbon County (Wyo.) Journal*, October 20 and November 10, 1888; Letterbook of Territorial Governor Thomas Moonlight, October 30, 31, November 8, 12, 13, December 1, 2, and 14, 1888 (microfilm stills 39, 40–41, 44, 53–56, 64–68, 83–85), WSA, WSM-C.

80. *Newcastle (Wyo.) Journal*, June 19 (includes reprint of most of coroner's inquest) and 26, 1891; *Sundance (Wyo.) Gazette*, June 19, 1891.

81. For the pattern of sociability among Wyoming ranchers in the early twentieth century, see Guenther, "'Y'all Call Me Nigger Jim Now,'" 30–35.

82. Larson, *History of Wyoming*, 268–71; Gustafson, "History of Vigilante and Mob Activity," 130. Helena Huntington Smith holds that the extent of cattle thievery in Johnson County and the ostensible failure of the criminal justice system to convict property offenders were greatly exaggerated by the Wyoming Stock Growers Association. Smith, *War on Powder River*.

83. *Laramie Boomerang*, August 10, 1885.

84. *Cheyenne Sun*, quoted in *Laramie Boomerang*, August 13, 1885.

85. *Laramie Boomerang*, August 10 and 13, 1885; Coroner's Inquest on N. L. Adams and Charles Putzier, filed October 1888, Carbon County, WSA, WSM-C; *Carbon County (Wyo.) Journal*, October 20 and November 10, 1888; Letterbook of Territorial Governor Thomas Moonlight, October 30, 31, November 8, 12, 13, December 1, 2, and 14, 1888 (microfilm stills 39, 40–41, 44, 53–56, 64–68, 83–85), WSA, WSM-C. The quotation, alluding to several Little Snake River district residents suspected in the lynching, is from the Letterbook of Territorial Governor Thomas Moonlight, to Alfred McGarvery, December 14, 1888 (microfilm still 83–85), WSA, WSM-C.

86. Black, "Lynching Research Notes," box 2, Bremer County Folder, Manuscript Collection, SHSI-IC; *Dubuque Times*, June 8, 1883; *(Des Moines) Iowa State Register*, December 23, 1884; *Ottumwa (Iowa) Daily Democrat*, November 26 and 30, 1893; Black, "Lynching Research Notes," box 2, Wapello County Folder, Manuscript Collection, SHSI-IC; *Des Moines Leader*, January 22, 1896.

87. *(Portland) Oregonian*, August 1, 1893; *Colfax (Wash.) Commoner*, August 4, 1893.

88. *Darlington (Wisc.) Democrat and Register*, September 18, 25, and October 2, 1891; *Darlington (Wisc.) Journal*, September 23, 30, and October 7, 1891; *Milwaukee Sentinel*, September 22, 23, 24, and 25, 1891.

89. *Milwaukee Sentinel*, September 24 and 25, 1891.

90. *Milwaukee Sentinel*, September 23, 1891.

91. *Richland Center (Wisc.) Republican*, October 1, 1868; *Milwaukee Sentinel*, September 30, 1868.

92. Pederson, "Gender, Justice, and a Wisconsin Lynching," 78. Pederson analyzes the Trempeleau County case from the perspective of gender, ethnicity, and law.

93. Donald G. Mathews observes that historians have said little about the nexus between the South's fundamentalist Protestantism and its propensity to lynch. For treatments of religiosity and lynching that make similar points but in rather different ways, see Mathews, "Southern Rite of Human Sacrifice," and Patterson, *Rituals of Blood*, 171–232.

94. The different contexts for lynching, including disparate religious landscapes, in southern and northern Louisiana are discussed in Pfeifer, "Lynching and Criminal Justice in South Louisiana," 156–62, esp. 160–61.

95. Overt references to Christian theology, symbols, or practices were almost entirely absent from the newspaper coverage of the 422 lynchings in Louisiana and occurred only infrequently in the reporting on mob killings in Iowa, Wisconsin, Wyoming, Washington, and California.

96. "'Should the Murderer of Miss Bishop Be Lynched.'"

97. "The Presbyterian Church in the United States of America vs. Rev. Robert A. Elwood," church court transcript, New Castle, Del., February 2, 1904; my thanks to Jeff Neberman for this source. *Chicago Record Herald*, June 24 and 29, 1903, quoted in Ginzburg, *100 Years of Lynching*, 53–58 (the quotation from Bishop is on p. 54); my gratitude to Jimee Lowe for this source. Patterson, *Rituals of Blood*, also describes the Wilmington episode, using Ginzburg (203–4).

98. *(Des Moines) Register and Leader*, January 15, 1907.

99. *Floyd County (Iowa) Advocate*, January 15, 1907.

100. Fedo, *Lynchings in Duluth*, 103–6, 120.

101. *Atlantic (Iowa) Daily Telegraph*, July 30, 1883; *Missouri Valley (Iowa) Daily Times*, April 30 and May 1, 1894. Midwestern and western mobs often acted out the "culturally defined masculine virtues" identified by Richard White in his study of social bandits of the American West. White, "Outlaw Gangs of the Middle Border," 397. Midwestern and western lynchers were also informed by the masculinist values of western honor, "the practice of aggressive, violent, self-defense embodied in the American social and legal doctrine of no duty to retreat" interpreted by Richard Maxwell Brown. Brown, "Western Violence," 16–17. For the fundamental role of women as aggressive cheerleaders, consult Pfeifer, "Ritual of Lynching," 27.

102. The lynching of women and the participation of women in mobs in the post-bellum South is analyzed in Feimster, "'Ladies and Lynching.'" For the ways in which white and black understandings of black femininity differed from notions of white femininity, see White, *Ar'n't I a Woman*, 161–67.

103. *New Orleans Picayune*, March 14, 1892.

104. *New Orleans Times-Democrat*, November 2, 1892; *New Orleans Picayune*, January 13, 1896; Letter from Alice Thrasher to Arthur Thrasher, January 13, 1896, Arthur P. Thrasher Correspondence, Special Collections, Hill Memorial Library, Louisiana State University, Baton Rouge. Six additional black women were killed by mobs in Louisiana. Gracy Blanton, collectively murdered in West Carroll Parish in April 1887, was accused of arson and robbery in collaboration with a male partner. Jennie Steers, a domestic servant hanged by a small mob in Caddo Parish in July 1903, had allegedly fatally poisoned the daughter of her employer. An unidentified African American woman died at the hands of night riders in the Cajun parish of St. Martin in September 1888. Two women, including the daughter of an African American preacher, died in Washington Parish in November 1902, as whites avenged the death of a participant in a white posse that sought to subdue an African American suspect. And a mob lynched Emma Hooper after she had shot and seriously wounded a constable in Tangipahoa Parish in December 1917. *New Orleans Times-Democrat*, May 8, 1887; *New Orleans Picayune*, September 17, 1888; *Opelousas (La.) Courier*, September 22, 1888; *(Amite City, La.) Florida Parishes*, November 2, 1901; *New Orleans Picayune*, March 1, 1917. Lynchers sent the son of Fred Karleton, who died from the wound inflicted by Emma Hooper, a piece of the rope used in the hanging; they also had invited him to the lynching. My thanks to Julia Polk, the granddaughter of Fred Karleton, for information on the 1917 lynching of Emma Hooper; e-mail correspondence with the author, July 22, 2002.

105. Hufsmith, *Wyoming Lynching of Cattle Kate*, 209–18.

106. *Salt Lake Tribune,* July 27, 1889, quoted in ibid., 225.

107. *(Des Moines) Iowa State Register,* August 16 and 20, 1887; Marion F. Stookey to Governor William Larabee, August 15, 1887, Governor's Office, Records and Correspondence: Criminal Matters, box/vol. GII 579, SHSI-DM. Rapes and murders of women in Iowa also sparked lynchings in Taylor County in 1889 and near lynchings in Van Buren County in 1891, twice in Council Bluffs in 1894, twice in Wapello County in 1896, as well as at least seven near lynchings of African Americans in the early 1900s. Black, "Attempted Lynchings in Iowa."

108. *Bakersfield Daily Californian,* March 12, 14, 15, 16, 17, 18, and 25, 1904; *Los Angeles Times,* March 13, 14, and 17, 1904; *San Francisco Chronicle,* March 13 and 15, 1904. Evidence suggests that sexual relationships between hobo boys and hobo men were common in the late nineteenth-century American West. The 1904 Mojave lynching corresponds with a historical era during which heterosexual relations were increasingly emphasized and intimate same-sex relations stigmatized. Quinn, *Same-Sex Dynamics among Nineteenth-Century Americans,* 156–57.

109. In north central Louisiana, eleven persons died at the hands of mobs after charges of rape (28 percent), and ten (26 percent) died for homicide allegations. Lynchers killed two more African American men who were accused of improper relations with a white girl and writing letters to a white woman, respectively.

110. For the Charles City, Iowa, incident, see Pfeifer, "Iowa's Last Lynching." For the Castella, California, incident, see the *Yreka (Calif.) Journal,* October 5, 1892, *San Francisco Chronicle,* October 1, 1892, and *San Francisco Examiner,* October 2, 1892. For the near lynching of R. W. Stubbs, see *(Des Moines) Iowa State Register,* April 18, 1882.

111. Wyatt-Brown, *Southern Honor,* 436–37. Honor in the postbellum South did not exist merely between social equals. Persons or groups of one status could seek to avenge their honor against a person of another social ranking, as Wyatt-Brown describes in a chapter on lynching and charivari.

112. *New Orleans Picayune,* December 27, 1881.

113. *New Orleans Picayune,* January 2, 1882.

114. Ibid.

115. Out of thirty-nine total victims (18 percent).

116. *New Orleans Picayune,* April 27, 1905.

117. *New Orleans Picayune,* June 5, 1908.

118. A discussion of how both defenders and opponents of lynching, including Ida B. Wells, deployed rhetorics of manliness can be found in Bederman, *Manliness and Civilization,* 45–76.

119. *Kern County (Calif.) Courier,* June 15, 1879, quoted in Webb, "History of Lynching in California since 1875," 27.

120. *Santa Cruz Local Item,* May 4, 1877, quoted in Webb, "A History of Lynching in California since 1875," 16–17.

121. *Daily Alta California* (San Francisco), May 4, 1877, quoted in Webb, "A History of Lynching in California since 1875," 18.

Chapter 3: Judge Lynch and the Color Line

1. Caddo, Bossier, Red River, De Soto, Natchitoches, Grant, and Rapides Parishes.

2. On Reconstruction-era violence in the Red River Delta, see Vandal, "Policy of Violence in Caddo Parish," and Vandal, "Black Violence in Post–Civil War Louisiana," esp. 56–57; Tunnell, *Crucible of Reconstruction,* 155–56, 200–204.

3. U.S. Bureau of the Census, *Eleventh Census of the United States*; U.S. Bureau of the Census, *Twelfth Census of the United States.*

4. Bossier Parish tallied thirty-seven victims, the most of any parish in Louisiana and among the highest totals of any county in the Deep South; Caddo Parish was the setting for twenty-five mob killings.

5. Brundage, *Lynching in the New South*, 159; Tolnay and Beck, *Festival of Violence*, 157–60. Additional surveys that contextualize lynchings in southern states include Carrigan, "Between South and West," Feldman, "Lynching in Alabama," and Buckelew, "Racial Violence in Arkansas." Edward L. Ayers emphasizes the factors of low population density in rural areas and high levels of black in-migration to explain the elevated levels of lynching in the cotton uplands, including north central and northwestern Louisiana. Ayers, *Promise of the New South*, 156–57. The most lynching-prone parishes in Louisiana—Bossier, Ouachita, and Caddo—had far more concentrated populations than Ayers's model predicts. In 1890, Bossier numbered 20,327 (16,225 blacks); Ouachita enumerated 17,985 (12,344 blacks); and Caddo had a population of 31,544 (23,541 blacks). U.S. Bureau of the Census, *Eleventh Census of the United States.*

6. Morehouse, Ouachita, Richland, and Franklin Parishes.

7. Hair, *Bourbonism and Agrarian Protest*, 41–42; U.S. Bureau of the Census, *Eleventh Census of the United States*; U.S. Bureau of the Census, *Twelfth Census of the United States.*

8. For parallel findings for Mississippi and South Carolina, see Finnegan, "'At the Hands of Parties Unknown,'" 189–90, 199–202. On cotton sharecropping, tenancy, and the crop-lien in Louisiana, see Hair, *Bourbonism and Agrarian Protest*, 51–53.

9. *Shreveport (La.) Journal*, February 25, 1903.

10. Ten lynchings in the Red River Delta can be directly traced to disputes over cotton labor and the violent enforcement of planters' authority; thirty lynchings across northern Louisiana can be similarly traced. No doubt this is an undercount, because in many instances the full context of a lynching cannot be clearly discerned from extant sources.

11. For corporal punishment as a white masculine prerogative in slavery, see Wyatt-Brown, *Southern Honor*, 373–75, and Genovese, *Roll, Jordan, Roll*, 63–67. For its postbellum persistence in Georgia and Mississippi, see Flynn, *White Land, Black Labor*, 63, and McMillen, *Dark Journey*, 202–3.

12. *New Orleans Picayune*, October 5, 1896. Thirteen mob murders (5 percent of the total) in northern Louisiana resulted from charges of arson. For black-white antagonism in agricultural labor and the possibility that some African Americans used arson as a form of protest, see Smith, "'Southern Violence' Reconsidered," esp. 561–64.

13. For black female domestics in postbellum Georgia, see Hunter, *To 'Joy My Freedom.*

14. *New Orleans Picayune*, July 27, 1903; *Shreveport Times*, July 26 and 28, 1903. For poisoning as resistance by antebellum plantation cooks and nurses, consult White, *Ar'n't I a Woman*, 79.

15. *New Orleans Picayune*, March 14, 1892.

16. Ayers, *Promise of the New South*, 81–103.

17. Twenty-five northern Louisiana lynchings can be directly tied to crimes involving mercantile circumstances (in a general store or against a peddler); five victims died after allegations of hog theft, four of these in Mississippi River Delta Parishes.

18. *New Orleans Times-Democrat*, November 11, 1894.

19. *New Orleans Picayune*, January 8, 1892.

20. Hair, *Bourbonism and Agrarian Protest*, 268–79; Fairclough, *Race and Democracy*, 6.

21. Fairclough, *Race and Democracy*, 6; Logsdon and Bell, "Americanization of Black New Orleans," 256–60.

22. At least fourteen lynchings of African Americans in northern Louisiana, excluding labor disputes, drew their meaning from blacks' explicit protest of racially hierarchical arrangements. In another telling incident, an African American, Thomas J. Amos, allegedly shot and killed a white store clerk in Rapides Parish in August 1900. Amos attempted to shoot at a posse that arrested him and then reportedly boasted to a mob that he would "show you how a man can die." The crowd believed this to be an imitation of Robert Charles, the African American who had shot twenty-seven whites, including members of a posse who tried to apprehend him, in New Orleans a month earlier. *New Orleans Picayune*, August 30, 1900. Robert Charles's extraordinary defiance of white authority at the nadir of African Americans' status in the state sparked the New Orleans Race Riot of 1900 and reverberated throughout black Louisiana. On Robert Charles, see Hair, *Carnival of Fury*, and Hair, *Kingfish and His Realm*, 67. For the celebration of "bad men" such as Robert Charles in African American culture, consult Levine, *Black Culture and Black Consciousness*, 410–20. Northern Louisiana had its own version of Robert Charles, W. S. Wade, an African American entrepreneur from Pine Bluff, Arkansas, who shot approximately twenty-five whites on the streets of Monroe in August 1909. After Wade died in a volley of bullets, a crowd of several hundred whites ceremonially hanged and burned his corpse. Wade had apparently been angered by two recent killings of Arkansas blacks by Monroe police. *Monroe (La.) News-Star*, August 23, 24, 25, 26, 27, and 30, 1909.

23. *New Orleans Picayune*, June 20, 1901.

24. *New Orleans Picayune*, October 10, 1903. Perhaps not coincidentally, lynchings in northern Louisiana surged in the early 1890s as the legal status of African Americans became a raging social and political issue—1890 produced three lynchings, 1891 saw fourteen mob killings, 1892 witnessed nineteen collective murders (the most in a single year), 1893 tallied five mob victims, 1894 totaled fourteen deaths by lynching, and 1895 brought one mob murder. However, the connection with social tensions brought on by the Populist political revolt is tenuous. It is true that two of the years that saw extraordinarily high rates of lynching, 1892 and 1894, were election years in which the Populists posed a significant challenge at the ballot box. Support for the Populist party among African Americans and lower-class white farmers was quite strong in the central and western parishes of northern Louisiana. Yet not a single lynching can be directly tied to retribution against supporters of the Populist party. In the year in which the Populists offered their gravest challenge to Louisiana's conservative political order through the gubernatorial candidacy of John N. Pharr, 1896, there were nine lynchings, a relatively average annual total for northern Louisiana. Hair, *Bourbonism and Agrarian Protest*, 204–67. For research that attempts to link the frequency of lynching in Louisiana with the social turmoil created by the Populist movement, see Inverarity, "Populism and Lynching in Louisiana." Inverarity's analysis relies upon flawed statistics compiled by antilynching organizations and neglects a reading of sources from actual lynching incidents. After extensive analysis of accurate statistics compiled from newspaper sources on southern lynchings, Stewart E. Tolnay and E. M. Beck argue that there is little evidence for a significant correlation between political competition, including that offered in the 1890s by the Populists, and the lynching of African Americans. Conversely, southern counties where the Republican and Populist parties received substantial support were less likely to be the settings for mob killings of blacks. Tolnay and Beck, *Festival of Violence*, 167–201.

25. East Carroll, West Carroll, Madison, Tensas, Concordia, and Point Coupee Parishes.

26. These include the north central parishes of Jackson, Winn, Caldwell, and Cata-houla; the northern parishes of Webster, Bienville, Claiborne, Lincoln, and Union; and the western parishes of Sabine and Vernon. Of these, only Webster and Claiborne had black majorities in the late nineteenth and early twentieth centuries. Caldwell Parish had a slight black majority throughout the late nineteenth century, which had become a white majority by the 1900 census. U.S. Bureau of the Census, *Twelfth Census of the United States*.

27. Hair, *Bourbonism and Agrarian Protest*, 40–41; U.S. Bureau of the Census, *Twelfth Census of the United States*.

28. *New Orleans Times-Democrat*, April 26, 1898; *New Orleans Picayune*, July 25, 1911. Conflicts between black and white workers at sites of rural industrialization, such as lumber mills and oil facilities, provided contexts for the mob killings of at least twelve persons in northern Louisiana (six in the Red River Delta, and four in upcoun-try parishes).

29. *New Orleans Times-Democrat*, June 10, 1894.

30. When the populations of the six Mississippi Delta Parishes are combined, 72,820 blacks outnumbered 8,157 whites. U.S. Bureau of the Census, *Twelfth Census of the United States*.

31. Hair, *Bourbonism and Agrarian Protest*, 78–79. Because planters had suppressed political alternatives for blacks and channelled the African American vote exclusive-ly to the Democratic party, the Populists failed to win votes in the Mississippi Delta as they did elsewhere in black Louisiana.

32. Neil R. McMillen finds that the northern Delta counties in Mississippi were some of the most lynching-prone in that state. Mob killings occurred far less often in Mis-sissippi's River lowlands counties, which adjoin Louisiana's Delta parishes. McMillen does not offer an explanation for this divergence. McMillen, *Dark Journey*, 230–32. Christopher Waldrep traces whites' abandonment of law and their turn to extralegal violence for the subordination of African Americans in the Delta county of Warren in *Roots of Disorder* (esp. 173–74).

33. Louisiana's late nineteenth- and early twentieth-century criminal law specified an extensive array of capital offenses. The death penalty could result from conviction for "willful murder"; rape; poison with intent to murder; lying in wait with intent to murder; assault with a dangerous weapon in perpetration of or attempt to perpetrate arson, rape, burglary, or robbery; arson at night of a place inhabited by humans; and armed burglary at night. Most of these statutes derived from the state's harsh 1855 legal code. State of Louisiana, *Revised Statute Laws of the State of Louisiana*; State of Lou-isiana, *Constitution and Revised Laws of Louisiana*.

34. Fifty-three legal hangings occurred in the Mississippi Delta Parishes from 1878 through 1920; the Red River Delta was the next closest subregion with forty-eight executions; all the others were far behind. Espy and Smykla, *Executions in the Unit-ed States*. M. Watt Espy's list, which is the most comprehensive extant inventory of the legal executions that have occurred in American jurisdictions, omits a significant number of Louisiana executions. I have obtained partial information concerning addi-tional executions from the record of death warrants issued by the Louisiana governor's office. State of Louisiana, Executive Department, Death Warrants, 1892–1930, LSA-BR.

35. Espy and Smykla, *Executions in the United States*; State of Louisiana, Execu-tive Department, Death Warrants, 1892–1930, LSA-BR.

36. *New Orleans Picayune*, April 5, 1880.

37. *New Orleans Picayune*, October 29, 1909.

38. *New Orleans Picayune*, April 24 and 28, 1894.

39. *New Orleans Picayune*, April 28, 1894.

40. In addition to the March 1891 episode in New Orleans in which a mass mob killed eleven Italians, which is discussed in chapter 1, and a July 1899 collective killing in Madison Parish, analyzed below, lynchers killed three Sicilians in St. Charles Parish west of New Orleans in August 1896 and two Italian workers in a logging camp in the northern parish of Jackson in 1907. The lynchers in St. Charles Parish reportedly cited the popular association of Sicilians with criminal organizations and sought to teach "the lawless Italians a salutary lesson." Scarpaci, "Italian Immigrants in Louisiana's Sugar Parishes," 248–50; *New Orleans Picayune*, August 9, 1896, and December 16, 1907. For a consideration of racialized perceptions of Italians in late nineteenth- and early twentieth-century America, see Jacobson, *Whiteness of a Different Color,* 56–62. An analysis of the lynching of Sicilians in the American South can be found in Webb, "Lynching of Sicilian Immigrants in the American South." The lynching of Italians also occurred on the western wageworking frontier in Colorado. See Leonard, *Lynching in Colorado,* 135–41.

41. *New Orleans Picayune*, July 22 and August 9, 1899. A number of variants of the Sicilians' names are given in newspaper accounts.

42. For the reconstitution of the social arrangements in the Sugarland in the post-bellum era, see Hair, *Bourbonism and Agrarian Protest,* 37–39. For Creoles of Color and black Creoles, consult Brasseaux, Fontenot, and Oubre, *Creoles of Color in the Bayou Country.* Brasseaux, *Acadian to Cajun,* examines the creation of Cajun social and cultural identity from lower-class white Creole and Acadian sources in the late nineteenth century. I use the confusing but essential term "Creole" to refer to the amalgam of French-speaking peoples in southern Louisiana.

43. I am grateful to Carl Brasseaux for this point.

44. *New Orleans Picayune*, March 20, 29, April 1 and 2, 1880; Hair, *Bourbonism and Agrarian Protest,* 171–75.

45. For a concise account of the 1887 sugar laborers' strike, see Hair, *Bourbonism and Agrarian Protest,* 176–85.

46. Ibid., 88.

47. For the complex postbellum political experience in the sugar parish of Iberia and Democrats' successful use of violence to thwart white Republican leaders and to keep African Americans from voting Republican in 1884, see Vandal, "Politics and Violence in Bourbon Louisiana."

48. See, for example, references to a black constable in St. James Parish in 1896 in *New Orleans Picayune*, March 1, 1896, and a racially balanced jury of blacks and whites in the trial of a black man charged with murdering an African American boy in St. Mary Parish in 1882 in *New Orleans Picayune*, June 23, 1882.

49. Hair, *Bourbonism and Agrarian Protest,* 268–79. The disfranchisement measures were at least partially in response to the near victory of a Republican-Populist fusion gubernatorial candidate, John N. Pharr, a sugar planter from St. Mary Parish, in 1896. Pharr carried four black majority parishes in southern Louisiana and twenty-five of thirty-two parishes throughout the state that had majorities of white voters. Massive fraud by white Democrats in black-majority parishes, especially those along the Mississippi River, deprived Pharr of victory. In addition to white sugar planters, Pharr's strength lay with African American voters and upcountry white farmers, suggesting the potential for a biracial working-class alliance contesting power with the cotton planters and New Orleans business interests that controlled the Democratic party.

50. The northwestern Red River Delta, analyzed above, tallied eighty-seven lynching victims between 1878 and 1946. For population distribution by race, see maps in Hair, *Bourbonism and Agrarian Protest.*

51. Attempting to explain southwide lynching trends, Edward Ayers argues in *The Promise of the New South:* "The only state whose Gulf Plain area had a relatively low lynching rate, close to that of the region as a whole, was Louisiana's, which did not see great black population change" (156). While I do not dismiss the importance of demographic shifts, my analysis emphasizes the interaction of labor, ethnic, legal, and political cultures in understanding the relatively low incidence of lynching in the Sugarland.

52. Logsdon and Bell, "Americanization of Black New Orleans," 201–9.

53. *New Orleans Picayune,* April 28, 1878.

54. *New Orleans Picayune,* October 23, 1892.

55. *New Orleans Picayune,* June 13, 1900.

56. *New Orleans Picayune,* December 30, 1892, and January 22, 1893. Wage-earning sugar workers bristled at wages that were payable only in script at the plantation store. See Hair, *Bourbonism and Agrarian Protest,* 87–88.

57. *New Orleans Picayune,* December 24, 1912.

58. *New Orleans Picayune,* October 20, 1900.

59. *New Orleans Picayune,* January 27, 1903.

60. *New Orleans Picayune,* December 4, 1878.

61. *New Orleans Picayune,* November 15, 1888.

62. Vandal, "Politics and Violence in Bourbon Louisiana," 23–42.

63. *New Orleans Picayune,* January 26, 27, and 31, 1889.

64. Gallic legal traditions, especially the Napoleonic Code, profoundly influenced civil law in Louisiana. However, English common law and American criminal procedure were the primary influences on Louisiana's criminal law. Billings, "Origins of Criminal Law in Louisiana."

65. I have identified three mob killings in the Sugarland that involved explicit responses to the criminal justice system: in St. James Parish in February 1896, where the lynchers of Gilbert and Paul Francis, accused of rape and burglary, cited a verdict of "guilty, without capital punishment," in a recent case where an African American had been convicted of "criminal assault" upon a white woman (*New Orleans Picayune,* March 1, 1896); in Iberville Parish in December 1897, where the mob supposedly feared that the impending removal of three African Americans, James Thomas, Joe Alexander, and Charles Alexander, to New Orleans for safekeeping meant that they might escape "the punishment the people say they deserved" for the murder of a white man (*New Orleans Picayune,* December 14, 1897); and in West Baton Rouge Parish in December 1912, where the attorney for an African American, Norm Cadore, convicted and sentenced to death for murdering a white man, had appealed his sentence to the Supreme Court (*New Orleans Picayune,* December 24, 1912).

66. Intrastate variations in the application of capital punishment in the late nineteenth century are revealing. Sugarland parishes that experienced few lynchings legally executed significant numbers of African Americans; Cotton Belt parishes that were exceedingly prone to lynching sent few blacks to the gallows. Between 1878 and 1910 in the Sugarland, West Baton Rouge Parish legally executed eight blacks (two lynching victims); St. Mary Parish tallied eight executions of blacks (four lynched); and Ascension Parish legally hanged ten blacks (one lynching victim). By comparison, in the northwest, Bossier Parish saw two legal executions of blacks (twenty-seven lynching victims), and in Caddo Parish officials hanged seven blacks (eleven lynching victims). In the north central parish of Ouachita, officials performed one legal execution of an African American (thirteen persons lynched). Espy and Smykla, *Executions in the United States;* State of Louisiana, Executive Department, Death Warrants, 1892–1930, LSA-BR. My analysis of state death warrants and newspapers indicates that more

legal executions occurred than enumerated by M. Watt Espy, but these additional numbers of legal hangings do not seem to affect the pattern of intrastate variation in the frequency of state-sponsored executions and lynchings.

67. Forty-five of the fifty-one persons reported legally executed in the twelve sugar parishes between 1878 and 1910 were African American (88 percent); four were white (8 percent); race could not determined for two of those hanged. Forty-six of those executed (90 percent) had been convicted on a murder charge (half of these exclusively on a homicide charge; the rest on combined charges of robbery/murder, rape/murder, or kidnap/murder). Six of those legally hanged (12 percent) had been convicted on a rape charge (rape, rape/murder, or attempted rape); all of these were African American. Espy and Smykla, *Executions in the United States.*

68. *New Orleans Picayune,* May 17, 1879, April 3, 1880, September 4, 1880, and December 9, 1882.

69. *New Orleans Picayune,* December 9, 1882.

70. State of Louisiana, Executive Department, Death Warrants, 1892–1930, LSA-BR; *New Orleans Picayune,* January 11, 1896.

71. Letter from Alice Thrasher to Arthur Thrasher, September 28, 1896, Arthur P. Thrasher Correspondence, Special Collections, Hill Memorial Library, LSUSC.

72. *New Orleans Picayune,* March 28, 1892.

73. Hair, *Bourbonism and Agrarian Protest,* 39.

74. *New Orleans Picayune,* March 28 and September 9, 1892, June 25, September 16 and 17, 1893, September 27, 1895, January 13 and September 24, 1896, September 30 and October 16, 1897.

75. *New Orleans Picayune,* September 16 and 17, 1893; Hair, *Kingfish and His Realm,* 5. Whites had only recently achieved a majority in Jefferson Parish, as enumerated by the census of 1890. U.S. Bureau of the Census, *Eleventh Census of the United States;* U.S. Bureau of the Census, *Twelfth Census of the United States.* Two other Jefferson Parish lynchings reflected the contest among blacks and whites over political authority. In September 1892, a small mob of masked men seized Henry Dixon from the jail at Kenner and hanged him from a nearby oak tree. Dixon had been charged three months earlier in an alleged conspiracy of African Americans to assassinate Judge Henry Long, but he had been released on bail from the Gretna jail after an energetic legal defense funded by the black community. Kenner law officers had arrested Dixon again at the corner of Jackson and St. Charles in New Orleans on a burglary warrant and conveyed him to the flimsy flatboat lumber jail across the parish line. Douglass Boutte, reportedly taken from a small jail along the Barataria Bayou and lynched, had been arrested for "going and coming" in violation of parish quarantine regulations. A *Picayune* correspondent asserted that Boutte "was a leader among his race . . . expounded the Bible to his class, and often boasted of his political influence." *New Orleans Picayune,* September 9, 1892, and October 16, 1897.

76. *New Orleans Picayune,* March 14, 15, and 16, 1891.

77. On the formation and activities of a "Committee of Public Safety" in 1881–82, see *New Orleans Picayune,* January 31, July 23, August 3, 10, 14, September 2, 3, 4, November 10 and 11, 1881, January 17, February 26, and March 16, 1882; and Jackson, *New Orleans in the Gilded Age,* 240–41.

78. Jackson, *New Orleans in the Gilded Age,* 237–41; *New Orleans Picayune,* August 21, 1879. For the New Orleans police, consult Rousey, *Policing the Southern City.* In the late nineteenth century, the Crescent City's police force was notoriously corrupt, undersized, and underfunded and had already acquired a reputation for brutality against blacks that would flourish in the twentieth century.

79. For the 1866 race riot, which claimed the lives of at least forty-six African Amer-

icans and contributed to the evaporation of political support for Andrew Johnson's presidential Reconstruction policies, see Tunnell, *Crucible of Reconstruction*, 104–7. For the life of Mississippi-born Robert Charles and the massive reprisal of whites against New Orleans's blacks for his defiance of white supremacy, see Hair, *Carnival of Fury*. As in large northern cities, popular white violence in large southern cities most often took the form of deadly race riots that indiscriminately killed or injured large numbers of African Americans instead of lynchings that targeted individual blacks. For racial violence in Atlanta, see Brundage, *Lynching in the New South*, 123–26; Ayers, *Promise of the New South*, 435–37.

80. Treatments of the relation between violence and social relations in the eastern Florida Parishes, especially Tangipahoa, can be found in Hyde, *Pistols and Politics*, and Baiamonte, *Spirit of Vengeance*.

81. Hyde, *Pistols and Politics*, 4, 7, 145, 191–98. Arriving in the 1880s, Sicilians labored on strawberry truck farms along the Illinois Central Railroad route. For discrimination and violence against Sicilians in Tangipahoa Parish in the late nineteenth century, see Baiamonte, *Spirit of Vengeance*, 3–15.

82. U.S. Bureau of the Census, *Twelfth Census of the United States*.

83. Hyde, *Pistols and Politics*, 15. For an analysis of violence in the eastern Florida Parishes, particularly in "Bloody" Tangipahoa Parish, see Hyde, *Pistols and Politics*, chapters 5 and 6. Hyde argues that the endemic violence in Tangipahoa in the late nineteenth century resulted in part from a "perverted [yeoman white] understanding of the Jefferson-Jacksonian concepts of independence and honor" (228).

84. Mobs in the eastern Florida Parishes murdered two whites; the race of two victims is not known; one of the victims was a black woman. Mobs of African Americans perpetrated two of the collective killings. For mob killings in Livingston Parish, see *New Orleans Picayune*, December 23, 1896, and June 24, 1900. For St. Helena Parish, see *New Orleans Picayune*, April 3 and 19, 1880, and *New Orleans Times-Democrat*, November 23, 1888. For St. Tammany Parish, see *New Orleans Picayune*, June 30, 1882, December 23, 1884, October 30, 1891, and August 6, 1914. For Tangipahoa Parish, see *New Orleans Picayune*, December 29 and 30, 1879, June 11, 1887, February 10, 1888, January 22 and July 16, 1893, September 23, 1895, January 21, 1897, April 3, 1898, August 9, 1899, September 22 and 23, 1900, November 27, 1905, March 1 and July 30, 1917, and *New Orleans Times-Democrat*, January 29, 1888. For Washington Parish, see *Memphis Commercial Appeal*, October 25, 1901, *Amite City (La.) Florida Parishes*, November 2, 1901, and *New Orleans Picayune*, September 1, 1919.

85. Hyde, *Pistols and Politics*, 191–262. Hyde stresses a class-related dispute over racial philosophies among whites in the Florida Parishes. The debate pitted racial "cooperationists," who sought to use blacks for their own benefit, against racial "exclusionists," who wished to avoid all interaction with African Americans (193–94).

86. Ibid., 242–60; *New Orleans Picayune*, January 21, 1897.

87. Hyde, *Pistols and Politics*, 242–60.

88. According to the list of legal executions compiled by M. Watt Espy, St. Tammany Parish executed two blacks, and Tangipahoa Parish hanged a single African American. Espy and Smykla, *Executions in the United States*. Louisiana state death warrants record one additional legal hanging in Livingston Parish, another in St. Helena Parish, and two in Washington Parish. State of Louisiana, Executive Department, Death Warrants, 1892–1930, LSA-BR.

89. Carrigan and Webb, "Muerto por Unos Desconocidos (Killed by Persons Unknown)." Diplomatic protests by Mexico led President McKinley to approve the payment of an indemnity of two thousand dollars to the heirs of Luis (Louis) Moreno,

lynched for murder along with three whites on August 26, 1895, in Yreka, California. The indemnity set a precedent cited in later cases in which Mexicans were lynched.

90. *(Bakersfield) Southern Californian* and *Kern County (Calif.) Courier,* December 27, 1877, quoted in Webb, "History of Lynching in California since 1875," 22.

91. *Los Angeles Times,* April 7, 8, 9, and 10, 1893; *San Bernardino Daily Courier,* April 7, 8, 9, 11, 13, and 14, 1893; Webb, "History of Lynching in California since 1875," 59–61.

92. *Los Angeles Times,* April 8, 1893.

93. *San Bernardino Daily Courier,* April 13 and 14, 1893.

94. Webb, "History of Lynching in California since 1875," 23–24.

95. For a case study of the lynching of two Seminole Indians accused in the murder of a white woman in Oklahoma in 1898, see Littlefield, *Seminole Burning.* Lynchers killed nine Native Americans in California and four Indians in Wyoming. For the mob killing of Modoc Charlie in Mendocino County on May 1878, see Webb, "History of Lynching in California since 1875," 22–23. For the mob killing of Willie Archer in Kern County in September 1895, see ibid., 66–67, *Bakersfield Daily Californian,* September 26 and 27, 1895, *Los Angeles Times,* September 27, 1895, and *San Francisco Examiner,* September 27, 1895. For the lynching of Holden Dick in Susanville in January 1886, see Webb, "A History of Lynching in California since 1875," 37–39. For the mob killing of Dean Case in Siskiyou County in December 1894, see ibid., 61–62. For the mob killing of Tacho in San Diego County in April 1890, see ibid., 52–53. For the mob hanging of James Hall, Frank Hall, Martin Wilson, and Daniel Yantis in Modoc County in 1901, see *San Francisco Chronicle,* June 1, 2, and 4, 1901, *Yreka (Calif.) Journal,* June 4, 7, 11, 14, 18, 21, 25, 26, August 16, November 5 and 8, 1901, *San Francisco Examiner,* June 1, 2, 3, 4, and July 12, 1901, and e-mail correspondence between Glennda Bradley and the author, March 17 and 18, 2002. For the collective killing of four Lakota Sioux in northeastern Wyoming in 1903, see Letterbook of Governor Fenimore Chatterton, November 2–6, 1903 (microfilm stills 90, 95, 96–100, 104, 105), WSA, WSM-C.

96. For the lynching of Steven, see Wilson, *Late Frontier,* 133–37, and Florin, *Washington Ghost Towns,* 82. An additional Native American and two mixed-race men were lynched by Washington whites. For the February 1884 lynching of Louie Sam, a fifteen-year-old Stòlô (Coast Salish) youth accused of murder, by white residents of the Whatcom County town of Nooksack who crossed the border into British Columbia to perform the lynching, see Carlson, "Lynching of Louie Sam." For the lynching of the Indian "half-breed" Frank Viles, accused of rape, at Asotin in August 1896, see *Lewiston (Idaho) Tribune,* March 17, 2002. For the lynching of the Indian "half-breed" Jim Shell, accused of murder, at Tacoma in April 1873, see Hunt, "Judge Lynch in Old Tacoma."

97. Black, "Lynchings in Iowa," 243–44.

98. *Iowa City Republican,* July 2, 1889, and B. F. Reed to Paul W. Black, recd. December 15, 1910, in Black, "Lynching Research Notes," box 2, Taylor County Folder, Manuscript Collection, SHSI-IC.

99. *Iowa City Republican,* July 2, 1889, and *(Des Moines) Iowa State Register,* July 2, 1889, in Black, "Lynching Research Notes," box 2, Taylor County Folder, Manuscript Collection, SHSI-IC; Black, "Lynchings in Iowa," 243–44.

100. Riley, *Women and Indians on the Frontier,* describes whites' racialized and sexualized perception of Native American men (249). For a brief history of Native Americans in Iowa that emphasizes the period of white settlement and dispossession in the early nineteenth century, see Schwieder, *Iowa,* 3–20.

101. See Schwantes, "Concept of the Wageworkers' Frontier."

102. *Bakersfield Daily Californian,* July 10, 11, 12, 16, and 19, 1901; *San Francisco Chronicle,* July 10 and 11, 1901; *San Francisco Examiner,* July 10, 1901; Webb, "History of Lynching in California since 1875," 73. See Takaki, *Strangers from a Different Shore,* 99–103, and Saxton, *Indispensable Enemy,* for the social relations of Chinese labor and the development of working-class white anti-Chinese sentiment and its sexual and gender dimensions in postbellum California.

103. In June 1891, Paiute Indians in Mono County, California, collectively murdered Ah Tai, a Chinese merchant accused of killing a Native American. The Paiutes reportedly seized Ah Tai at the courthouse after his preliminary examination. *Bridgeport (Calif.) Chronicle Union,* June 6, 1891; *San Francisco Chronicle,* June 15, 1891; *San Francisco Examiner,* June 14, 1891. In Colusa County, California, in July 1887, a mob of 150 whites seized and hanged Hong Di, a Chinese house boy who had shot and killed his white employer, Julia Billiou. The mob was enraged by a jury's failure to impose a death sentence after convicting Di of the crime. Webb, "History of Lynching in California since 1875," 41–47. In Rock Springs, Wyoming, in September 1885, culminating a decade-long conflict with Union Pacific management over the employment of Chinese labor, white miners attacked the Chinese district, shooting some Chinese and setting fire to dwellings, some of them occupied. An estimated fifty-one Chinese died in the Rock Springs Massacre, approximately half perishing from exposure in the hills outside Rock Springs where they fled. Storti, *Incident at Bitter Creek.* Anti-Chinese violence also flared in the Puget Sound region of western Washington in the winter of 1885–86, with the most egregious episode being an incident in which a band of American Indians and whites murdered three Chinese hops workers by setting their shack afire. Liestman, "Horizontal Inter-Ethnic Relations," 339–40.

104. *(Cheyenne) Wyoming Tribune,* December 10 and 11, 1918; *Green River (Wyo.) Star,* December 10, 1918; *Salt Lake City Semi-Weekly Tribune,* December 13, 1918.

105. *Natrona County (Wyo.) Tribune,* September 1, 1904; *Laramie Boomerang,* September 1 and 20, 1904; Coroner's Report on Joseph Martin, August 31, 1904, Albany County, WSA-C. Todd Guenther, in his analysis of the life of Jim Edwards, an African American rancher in Wyoming in the early 1900s, notes that Edwards conspicuously avoided contact with white women, aware of the stigma white westerners attached to contact between black men and white women. Guenther, "'Y'all Call Me Nigger Jim Now,'" 23, 35.

106. Wigfall was born in Charleston, South Carolina, in 1862. Beginning in 1878, he traveled around the upper South laboring in various kinds of unskilled work, and in 1887 he came to Wyoming. Between his arrival and his incarceration in the late 1890s, Wigfall worked as a domestic servant, a stableworker, and a "stationary boiler fireman" in Rawlins and Laramie and was convicted of assault at a saloon in Cheyenne and served a brief sentence. The details of Wigfall's biography come from his application for parole, July 19, 1911, Wyoming State Penitentiary, WSA-C. Gov. Joseph Carey to Ida B. Wells-Barnett, October 18, 1912, Governor Joseph Carey's Outgoing Correspondence, WSA-C; Coroner's Report on Frank Wigfall, filed October 5, 1912, Carbon County, WSA-C; *Rawlins (Wyo.) Republican,* October 3 and 10, 1912; *Cheyenne State Leader,* October 3 and 5, 1912.

107. Several additional lynchings of African Americans occurred on the West's "wage-workers' frontier." In September 1902, a mob in Marshfield (now Coos Bay), Oregon, shot and dragged to death an African American, Alonzo Tucker, whom they accused of raping Mrs. Benjamin Dennis, the wife of a white miner. McLagan, *Peculiar Paradise,* 135–37. On June 18, 1925, whites in Price, Utah, collectively murdered Robert Marshall, an itinerant African American coal miner accused of killing the night watchman for the Utah Fuel Company. See Gerlach, "Justice Denied." Lynchers had previ-

ously killed an itinerant African American, Sam Joe Harvey, in Salt Lake City on August 25, 1883. Gerlach, "Vengeance vs. the Law." Nine lynchings of African Americans in Colorado between 1867 and 1902 are analyzed in Leonard, *Lynching in Colorado,* 123–30, 144–50.

108. An analysis of the experience of African Americans in the West in this era, although without an emphasis on a qualitative shift in race relations after 1900, can be found in Taylor, *In Search of the Racial Frontier,* 192–227.

109. Guenther, "'Y'all Call Me Nigger Jim Now,'" 23. Guenther notes that another Wyoming law permitted segregated schools. In 1882, as the result of the efforts of a Kentucky-born black legislator, William Jefferson Hardin, the Wyoming territorial legislature had repealed an antimiscegenation clause in the 1869 constitution. Hardaway, "William Jefferson Hardin."

110. See *(Cheyenne) Wyoming Tribune,* December 19, 26, and January 1, 1917, which printed bold headlines such as, "Negroes Murder Casper Men," "Negro Women at Casper Face Trial for Murder," and "11 Murders Occur in 'Wet' Cheyenne." For an analysis that interprets an early twentieth-century antigambling campaign as a precursor of Wyoming progressivism, see Moore, "Progressivism and the Social Gospel in Wyoming." Moore argues that Wyoming reformers shared a preoccupation with vices such as "the brothel, saloon, and gambling parlor" with Progressives elsewhere. Although Moore does not mention it, Progressive rhetoric in Wyoming also contained a strong racial element.

111. In Wyoming, the census of 1890, the year of statehood, enumerated 922 blacks, or 1.6 percent of the population; the percentage slipped to just over 1 percent in 1900, climbed again to 1.6 percent in 1910, and declined to less than 1 percent in 1920. U.S. Bureau of the Census, *Twelfth Census of the United States;* State of Wyoming, *Census of Wyoming, 1905;* State of Wyoming, *Census of the State of Wyoming, 1915.*

112. *(Cheyenne) Wyoming Tribune,* December 19, 1918.

113. *(Cheyenne) Wyoming Tribune,* December 13, 1917.

114. *Burlington (Iowa) Hawkeye,* October 31, 1900; *Des Moines Daily Leader,* October 31 and November 24, 1900.

115. For brief accounts of these episodes, see Black, "Lynchings in Iowa," 249–54, and Black, "Attempted Lynchings in Iowa."

116. A growing literature documents and analyzes the lynchings and race riots that targeted African Americans in the Midwest. For Missouri, see Pfeifer, "Ritual of Lynching," Huber, "Lynching of James T. Scott," Capeci, *Lynching of Cleo Wright,* and Navarro, "Racial Violence in the Midwest." For Illinois, see Downey, "Many Headed Monster," Cha-Jua, "'Join Hands and Hearts with Law and Order,'" Cha-Jua, "'Warlike Demonstration,'" Pratt, "'Outrageous Proceeding,'" and Senechal, *Sociogenesis of a Race Riot.* For Ohio, see Howard, "Black Lynching in the Promised Land." For Indiana, see Madison, *Lynching in the Heartland.* For Minnesota, see Fedo, *Lynchings in Duluth.* For Nebraska, see Menard, "Tom Dennison, the *Omaha Bee,* and the 1919 Race Riot."

117. Bergman, *Negro in Iowa,* 35–40; Schwieder, *Iowa,* 83–89.

118. Bergman, *Negro in Iowa,* 40–42; Schwieder, *Iowa,* 194. In 1905, African American miners composed half of the town of Buxton in Monroe County, which also included African American professionals, entrepreneurs, and various black community institutions. On Buxton, see Schwieder, Hraba, and Schwieder, *Buxton.*

119. Bergman, *Negro in Iowa,* 48–60. For examples of sympathetic newspaper coverage of African American communities in Iowa, some of which reflects the importance of African Americans as a political constituency in the late nineteenth century, see *(Des Moines) Iowa State Register,* July 18 and August 10, 1883, *Ottumwa (Iowa)*

Daily Democrat, January 7, 1885, and *Des Moines Weekly Leader,* April 6, 1893. For the older paternalistic race relations in the Midwest and their decline, consult Spear, *Black Chicago,* 29–49, Kusmer, *Ghetto Takes Shape,* 3–31, 99–108, 174–89, and Senechal, *Sociogenesis of a Race Riot.*

120. In Iowa, the U.S. Census counted African Americans as 0.6 percent of Iowa's population in 1890 and 1900, 0.7 percent in 1910, and 0.8 percent in 1920. U.S. Bureau of the Census, *Twelfth Census of the United States;* U.S. Bureau of the Census, *Thirteenth Census of the United States;* U.S. Bureau of the Census, *Fourteenth Census of the United States.* For the migration and employment patterns of African Americans in nineteenth- and early twentieth-century Iowa, see Bergman, *Negro in Iowa,* 36–60.

121. Black, "Lynchings in Iowa," 249–54; Black, "Attempted Lynchings in Iowa."

122. The most accurate available enumeration, that of Stewart E. Tolnay and E. M. Beck, maintains that nearly twenty-five hundred African Americans died at the hands of lynch mobs from 1882 through 1930 in the ten southern states of Mississippi, Georgia, Louisiana, Alabama, South Carolina, Florida, Tennessee, Arkansas, Kentucky, and North Carolina. Tolnay and Beck, *Festival of Violence,* ix.

Chapter 4: Rough Justice and the Revolt against Due Process

1. *South Bend (Wash.) Journal,* April 17, 24, and June 5, 1891; "Bad News"; "Justice Triumphs"; "Fredericksen Story."

2. *Seattle Post-Intelligencer,* April 25, 26, 27, 28, and 29, 1891; *Walla Walla Daily Union,* April 24, 25, 26, 28, and 29, 1891; *South Bend (Wash.) Journal,* May 1 and June 5, 1891.

3. Quoted in *Walla Walla Daily Union,* April 28, 1891.

4. Quoted in ibid.

5. Quoted in ibid.

6. *Seattle Post-Intelligencer,* April 26, 1891.

7. *Seattle Post-Intelligencer,* April 14, 1891.

8. *South Bend (Wash.) Journal,* April 10, 1891.

9. Ibid.

10. *South Bend (Wash.) Journal,* April 17, 1891.

11. Quoted in *South Bend (Wash.) Journal,* April 24, 1891 (my emphasis).

12. *Colfax (Wash.) Commoner,* January 14, 1898; also quoted, with slight variation, in *Colfax (Wash.) Gazette,* January 14, 1898.

13. *Colfax (Wash.) Commoner,* April 2, 1898.

14. *Colfax (Wash.) Commoner,* January 14, 1898.

15. *Walla Walla Daily Union,* April 25, 1891. Newspapers around the region similarly noted the irony of the army's lawlessness in editorials reprinted in succeeding issues by the *Walla Walla Daily Union.* For example, the *Salt Lake Times,* perhaps with memories of the U.S. army's confrontation with Latter-Day Saints in Utah, noted that lynchings were often winked at, but this one must be punished, because "'soldiers are regarded as the embodiment of law and lawless actions on their part cannot be tolerated.'" Quoted in *Walla Walla Daily Union,* April 30, 1891.

16. *Seattle Post-Intelligencer,* April 30, 1891.

17. Ibid.

18. *Olympia (Wash.) Transcript,* January 29, 1870.

19. Ibid.

20. Ibid.

21. Athow, "A Brief History of the Adam Byrd Branch of the Byrd Family," Tacoma Public Library. Firsthand accounts of the 1863 lynching can be found in Light, "Early Times in Pierce County," Tacoma Public Library, and William D. Vaughan, "The Byrd Murder," *Tacoma Weekly Ledger*, February 17, 1893.

22. *Puget Sound Herald*, January 29, 1863, quoted in Athow, "A Brief History of the Adam Byrd Branch of the Byrd Family," Tacoma Public Library.

23. Vaughan, "Byrd Murder."

24. For an analysis of lynchings in a setting where the law was absent and distant, the western Overland Trail in the 1840s, 1850s, and 1860s, as well as of the uneven ways in which emigrants sought to replicate the forms of Anglo-American law, see Reid, *Policing the Elephant*, 117–208. Also see the analysis of the important precedent set by the extralegal proceedings of "People's Courts," which conducted informal trials and executions of accused criminals in Denver and other Colorado towns that lacked legal institutions between 1859 and the formation of Colorado Territory in 1861, in Leonard, *Lynching in Colorado*, 15–29.

25. Hunt, *Distant Justice*, 254–58. Jack London later fictionalized the lynching of Severts in his story "The Unexpected." Typically "miner's courts" informally administered disputes without recourse to violence.

26. *Seattle Post-Intelligencer*, February 3, 1898. I am indebted to Larry Lashway for this information.

27. As in Washington Territory, extensive vigilantism in the early years of American settlement in California bequeathed important precedents for the lynching violence employed by Californians in succeeding decades. For an analysis of some of this violence in the context of Gold Rush society, see Johnson, *Roaring Camp*, 218, 320–21. For the influential vigilante committees in San Francisco, see Senkewicz, *Vigilantes in Gold Rush San Francisco*. For how early vigilantism was remembered in the late nineteenth century in California, see, for example, a Yreka editor's recollection of "the early fifties when the Vigilance Committee attended to the criminal element" following the August 26, 1895, lynching of William Null, Lawrence H. Johnson, Louis Moreno, and Garland Stemler. The editor rejected the image of the "wild and wooly west" held by "the Eastern states" and defended the revival of lynching as a protest against due-process mechanisms that drained county coffers and thwarted "justice" for murderers. *Yreka (Calif.) Journal*, August 30, 1895.

28. *Redding (Calif.) Weekly Republican Free Press*, June 11, 18, 25, July 16, 23, 30, August 6 and 13, 1892; *San Francisco Chronicle*, July 25 and 26, 1892; *San Francisco Examiner*, July 25 and 26, 1892. The Ruggleses' father, L. B., was a rancher and former chairman of the board of supervisors of Yolo County. Supporters of the lynching cited the considerable funds L. B. Ruggles could employ for the legal defense of his sons.

29. *San Francisco Chronicle*, July 26, 1892; *Redding (Calif.) Weekly Republican Free Press*, July 30, 1892.

30. *Redding (Calif.) Weekly Republican Free Press*, July 30, 1892.

31. *Yreka (Calif.) Journal*, July 27, 1892.

32. Quoted in *Redding (Calif.) Weekly Republican Free Press*, July 30, 1892.

33. *Yreka (Calif.) Journal*, August 9, 16, 20, 27, 30, September 3 and 6, 1895; *San Francisco Chronicle*, August 27 and 28, 1895; *San Francisco Examiner*, August 27, 28, and 29, 1895.

34. *San Francisco Examiner*, August 27, 1895.

35. *West Coast Star*, January 8, 1876, quoted in Webb, "History of Lynching in California since 1875," 13. A similar defense of "peremptory justice" that cited the "re-

cent operation of the law in Madera county" was offered following the collective kill-ing by sixty mountaineers of the mountain "bad man" Victor Adam, who had mur-dered a magistrate in a property dispute, in July 1895. *Fresno Morning Republican,* July 28, 1895.

36. Extensive vigilantism in Wyoming's early territorial period had established an influential blueprint for collective violence as an integral aspect of the region's approach to the social control of crime. The record of lynching in the railroad towns in 1868 is a mixed one, and it belies simple explanations. The burgeoning railroad towns possessed a semblance of government and law enforcement. Although evidence concerning the 1868 mob killings is sparse, it is obvious that political factionalism, economic com-petition, and a struggle over social status and the definition of respectability in newly formed and relatively unstable communities motivated much of the collective kill-ing. For a more extended discussion, see Pfeifer, "Lynching and Criminal Justice in Regional Context," 96–100. Also on the early territorial period and vigilantism in Wyoming, see Larson, *History of Wyoming,* 36–63, and Gustafson, "History of Vigi-lante and Mob Activity in Wyoming," 41–94.

37. For the cattle baron aristocracy, composed of American and British elements, and its ostentatious style of recreation and conviviality in Cheyenne, see Frink, *Cow Coun-try Cavalcade,* 109–16.

38. *Cheyenne Daily Leader,* September 17, 18, and 19, 1883; Coroner's Inquest on John H. Wensel, September 13, 1883, Laramie County, WSA, WSM-C; Gustafson, "History of Vigilante and Mob Activity," 113–17.

39. *Cheyenne Daily Leader,* September 19, 1883.

40. *Cheyenne Daily Leader,* September 21, 1883.

41. Of newspaper opinion sampled following the lynching of Mosier, only the *Chey-enne Daily Leader* expressed equivocal opposition; editors in Laramie, Denver, and Ft. Collins defended the collective murder. *Cheyenne Daily Leader,* September 19, 22, 23, and 25, 1883.

42. See the account of the execution of Toussaint Kensler in *Cheyenne Daily Lead-er,* November 20, 1874, and "Laws of Wyoming, 1869," in "Executions in Wyoming," Subject File, WSA, WSM-C.

43. Bramel's philosophy can be found in statements he made in the trial of Charles Woodard, lynched in 1902, and in response to the mob murder in *Natrona County (Wyo.) Tribune,* February 27 and April 3, 1902, and after the trial of James Keffer, exe-cuted in 1903, in *Laramie Boomerang,* September 26, 1903.

44. Frank Bond to Governor Amos Barber, February 20, 1892, Pardon File, Charles Miller, WSA, WSM-C.

45. Alfred S. Peabody to Governor F. E. Warren, February 19, 1890, in Pardon File, George Black, WSA, WSM-C. For examples of a critique of the administration of crim-inal justice voiced in support of lynching in the neighboring state of Colorado, see Leonard, *Lynching in Colorado,* 61–63. A traveler from Scotland, Dr. William Bell, argued after an 1867 Colorado lynching that "although Europeans might consider such 'rough justice barbarous and uncivilized,' it might be better than the 'systematic eva-sion of justice which is commonly practiced throughout the western country'" (quot-ed in ibid., 63).

46. Laramie County Coroner's Inquest, WSA, WSM-C; Laramie County Criminal Court Journal, WSA, WSM-C.

47. Sweetwater County Criminal Court Journal and Criminal Files, WSA, WSM-C.

48. Clare V. McKanna finds elevated levels of violence and homicide, far exceeding the rates in northeastern cities such as New York and Philadelphia, in Douglas Coun-

ty, Nebraska, Las Animas County, Colorado, and Gila County, Arizona. These jurisdictions experienced extraordinary amounts of industrial growth and ethnic and racial interaction and cannot be considered representative of most western counties. McKanna, *Homicide, Race, and Justice in the American West*, esp. 39–44.

49. *Laramie Boomerang*, August 4, 1903.

50. Governor Amos Barber to Charles Miller and Frank D. Taggart, Pardon File, Charles Miller, WSA, WSM-C.

51. Espy and Smykla, *Executions in the United States*. T. A. Larson makes an explicit connection between a dormant death penalty and the incidence of lynching in the territorial period in *History of Wyoming*, 230–31. In Colorado, a flurry of lynchings followed the abolition of the death penalty in 1897 and contributed to its restoration in 1901. Moreover, legal executions were relatively rare in Colorado in the postbellum era, and proponents of lynching cited this in their defense of mob killings. Leonard, *Lynching in Colorado*, 62.

52. "Laws of Wyoming, 1869," in "Executions in Wyoming," Subject File, WSA, WSM-C.

53. *Cheyenne Daily Leader*, April 23, 1892.

54. Kensler was convicted of murder at Ft. Laramie. *Cheyenne Daily Leader*, November 20, 1874. For the execution of George Black, see *Laramie Boomerang*, February 24, 1890.

55. For the transformation of the gallows from a public ritual to a concealed and carefully controlled procedure in the northeastern United States during the antebellum period, see Masur, *Rites of Execution*, esp. 93–116.

56. *(Casper) Wyoming Derrick*, March 27, 28, and April 3, 1902.

57. *Cheyenne Daily Leader*, May 27, 1903; *Crook County (Wyo.) Monitor*, May 29, 1903.

58. *Cheyenne Daily Leader*, July 20, 1903; *Laramie Boomerang*, July 30, August 4, 7, 18, and 20, 1903; *Wyoming Stockgrower and Farmer* 1.44 (July 21, 1903), in "Crime and Criminals," HRS, WSA-C.

59. *Cheyenne Daily Leader*, May 28, 1903.

60. *(Casper) Wyoming Derrick*, March 28, 1902. The *Natrona County (Wyo.) Tribune* and *Cheyenne Daily Leader* printed slightly varying versions of this rhyme in their March 28 editions.

61. *Natrona County (Wyo.) Tribune*, April 3, 1902.

62. *Cheyenne Daily Leader*, March 29, 1902.

63. *Cheyenne Daily Leader*, July 20, 1903; *Laramie Boomerang*, July 30, August 4, 7, 18, and 20, 1903; *Wyoming Stockgrower and Farmer* 1.44 (July 21, 1903), in "Crime and Criminals," HRS, WSA-C. Threats of lynching also erupted in Lander in central Wyoming in August 1903, as punitive-justice proponents protested "delays" in the execution of James Keffer and "demand[ed] a quick trial and execution of [the double murderer James] Dollard." Governor Fenimore Chatterton wrote to officials in Lander and pleaded that they intervene to prevent a lynching. The "mayor and other leading citizens" counseled townspeople to avoid mob violence, and county officials legally executed James Keffer the following month. *Laramie Boomerang*, August 18 and September 26, 1903; Letterbook of Governor Fenimore Chatterton, to James F. Vidal, August 21, 1903 (microfilm still 46), WSA, WSM-C.

64. Letterbook of Governor Fenimore Chatterton, to the Honorable Board of County Commissioners, Big Horn County, Basin, Wyo., July 20 and 21, 1903 (microfilm stills 17, 20–21); to John P. Arnott, Prosecuting Attorney, Basin, Wyo., July 20 and 21, 1903 (microfilm stills 18, 24); to James F. Vidal, August 21, 1903 (microfilm still 46), WSA,

WSM-C. For Chatterton's fruitless efforts to prevent the Casper lynching and his futile request that county authorities thoroughly investigate the affair, see *Cheyenne
Daily Leader,* March 28, 1902, and *Natrona County (Wyo.) Tribune,* February 6, 1902.

65. *(Des Moines) Iowa State Register,* June 12, 1883; State of Iowa, *Iowa Official
Register.*

66. District Court Indices, Wapello County District Court, Clerk of Court's Office,
Ottumwa, Iowa; Monroe County District Court, Clerk of Court's Office, Albia, Iowa.

67. State of Iowa, *Annotated Code of the State of Iowa* (1885 and 1897).

68. State of Iowa, *Census of 1905,* 794–96.

69. For Judge McGill, see *(Des Moines) Iowa State Register,* June 12, 1883. For Judge
Loofbourow, see *(Des Moines) Iowa State Register,* February 7, 1885, *Council Bluffs
(Iowa) Nonpareil,* February 3, 1885, and *Audubon (Iowa) Times,* February 12, 1885.
For Judge McHenry, see *(Des Moines) Iowa State Register,* February 10 and 18, 1885.

70. For a few examples of numerous editorials that treated due-process themes in
the context of lynching, see *Dubuque Times,* June 10, 1883, *(Des Moines) Iowa State
Register,* June 10, 1883, May 2, 1884, January 13, and February 13, 1885, and *Burlington (Iowa) Hawkeye,* February 11, 1885.

71. *Anita (Iowa) Times,* June 21, 1883. Other statements urging fiscal conservatism
in the expenditure of county funds on criminal justice can be found in *Atlantic (Iowa)
Daily Telegraph,* July 12, 1883, and *Ottumwa (Iowa) Democrat,* January 25, 1885.
Richard Maxwell Brown stresses fiscal prudence as a major component of the American ideology of vigilantism. Brown, *Strain of Violence,* 155–56.

72. Among many instances of critical commentary on juries and proposals for reform,
see *(Des Moines) Iowa State Register,* January 24, February 20 and 21, 1885.

73. For a sampling of opinions along these lines, see *(Des Moines) Iowa State Register,* February 10 and 13, 1885.

74. For the national debate over criminal procedure and its reform in the Gilded Age
and Progressive Era, see Brown, *Strain of Violence,* 144–79, and Walker, *Popular Justice,* 103–19, 127–30.

75. *(Des Moines) Iowa State Register,* February 13, 1885. Also see *Dubuque Times,*
June 7, 1883, and *Washington (Iowa) Press,* quoted in *(Des Moines) Iowa State Register,* June 14, 1883.

76. For the debate over the supposed failure of Iowa officials to enforce the death
penalty, the encouragement this ostensibly offered to murderers, and the defense it
offered to lynchers, see *(Des Moines) Iowa State Register,* February 10, 13, and 18, 1885,
and Pfeifer, "Iowa's Last Lynching," 315–17.

77. *(Des Moines) Iowa State Register,* June 5, 1883.

78. *Burlington (Iowa) Hawkeye,* February 21, March 12, and June 1, 1909, in Black,
"Lynching Research Notes," box 2, Wapello County Folder, Manuscript Collection,
SHSI-IC.

79. *Burlington (Iowa) Hawkeye,* February 9, 1895; Governor's Office, Records and
Correspondence: Criminal Matters, J. K. Cumberland File, box/vol. GII 434, SHSI-DM.

80. James Munns to Governor Frank Jackson, June 7, 1894, in Governor's Office,
Records and Correspondence: Criminal Matters, James Dooley File, box/vol. GII 432,
SHSI-DM.

81. See C. C. Stiles's lists of those sentenced to life compiled for Paul W. Black and
Black's lists of life sentences in Black, "Lynching Research Notes," box 1, Manuscript
Collection, SHSI-IC.

82. A. F. Truax to Paul W. Black, November 12, 1910, and F. J. Ives to Paul W. Black,
November 22, 1910, in Black, "Lynching Research Notes," box 1, Manuscript Collection, SHSI-IC.

83. C. C. Stiles's lists in Black, "Lynching Research Notes," box 1, Manuscript Collection, SHSI-IC.

84. See petitions for pardon in the files of death-row inmates in Governor's Office, Records and Correspondence: Criminal Matters, SHSI-DM.

85. *Floyd County (Iowa) Advocate,* January 15 and February 1, 1907.

86. Trial transcript, Governor's Office, Records and Correspondence: Criminal Matters, John Junkin File, box/vol. GII 475, folder 2, SHSI-DM.

87. *(Des Moines) Iowa State Register,* February 21, 1885.

88. The hesitancy with which juries applied the death penalty was something of a universal, as Michael Hindus discovered this tendency in both antebellum Massachusetts and South Carolina. Hindus, *Prison and Plantation,* 250.

89. For the abolition of Wisconsin's death penalty, see Current, *History of Wisconsin,* 190–91. Four legal executions in the state and territory between 1836 and 1851 had preceded abolition. Two of the four executed were American Indians. The movement's origin in the Northeast is described in Masur, *Rites of Execution.*

90. *Sunday Telegraph,* quoted in the *Vernon County (Wisc.) Censor,* June 6, 1888. The editor of the *Lancaster (Wisc.) Herald* similarly found a direct explanation for lynching in Wisconsin's disavowal of the death penalty, after a mob hanged the accused murderer Anton Sieboldt in Darlington in September 1891. See *Lancaster (Wisc.) Herald,* quoted in *Darlington (Wisc.) Herald,* September 30, 1891.

91. For the Guiteau case in sociomedical context, see Rosenberg, *Trial of the Assassin Guiteau.*

92. *La Crosse Morning Chronicle,* October 17, 1884.

93. Klatt, *They Died at Their Posts.* A picturesque narrative of the Williams brothers and the Durand lynching can be found in Percy, *Twice Outlawed.* Brantner, "Executed on Behalf of the Public Good?" is a case study of the Durand lynching.

94. Quoted in Klatt, *They Died at Their Posts,* 39.

95. Quoted in ibid.

96. Quoted in ibid., 33.

97. Cutler, *Lynch-Law,* 223–25.

98. *New Orleans Times-Democrat,* August 10, 1887. See, by comparison, an editorial that denounced the lynching of three alleged African American arsonists in Catahoula Parish by arguing that only the punishment of rape could justify lynching. *Lafayette (La.) Gazette,* quoted in *Opelousas (La.) Courier,* August 8, 1908.

99. On the rape myth, see, for example, Hall, *Revolt against Chivalry,* 148–49.

100. State of Louisiana, *Revised Statute Laws of the State of Louisiana;* State of Louisiana, *Constitution and Revised Laws of Louisiana.*

101. District Court Minute Book, Clerk of Court's Office, St. Landry Parish, Opelousas.

102. Letters from Edward P. Veazie, July 16 and 22, 1905, in Ozeme Fontenot Papers, LSUSC.

103. *New Orleans Picayune,* October 20, 1917; Criminal Suit, *State of Louisiana v. Eli Carrier,* Clerk of Court's Office, St. Landry Parish, Opelousas. Carl Brasseaux argues that mid-nineteenth-century Acadians went to court more often than Anglo-American southerners, displaying a preference for litigious solutions of disputes. Brasseaux, *Acadian to Cajun,* 113.

104. These parishes tallied thirty-seven, thirty-four, and twenty-five lynching victims, respectively.

105. For parallel observations about legal systems in Mississippi, see McMillen, *Dark Journey,* 203–5. Michael Hindus similarly argues that nineteenth-century South Carolinians were ambivalent toward formal authority and that extralegal violence offset

limited legal institutions in preserving order and social cohesion. Hindus, *Prison and Plantation,* xxvi, 1–2, 250–53.

106. See Coroner's Inquests, filed September 6, 1879, and March 23, 1885, in Clerk of Court's Office, Ouachita Parish, Monroe; *New Orleans Picayune,* April 18, 1884, and January 11, 1896. Also, see Richland Parish lynchings in *New Orleans Picayune,* January 8, 1892, July 17, 1901, November 21, 1909, April 26, 1912, and June 19, 1918. For similar findings from early twentieth-century Mississippi, where the patronage relationship between African Americans and the white planters they worked for often defined the nature of their treatment by the formal legal system, see McMillen, *Dark Journey,* 205.

107. District Court Minute Book, Clerk of Court's Office, Ouachita Parish, Monroe; *New Orleans Picayune,* April 15, 1889, and October 3, 1897; *New Orleans Times-Democrat,* September 15, 1896.

108. *New Orleans Times-Democrat,* September 15, 1896.

109. District Court Minute Book, Clerk of Court's Office, St. Landry Parish, Opelousas; Book of Indictments, District Court, Natchitoches Parish, LSUSC. Between 1878 and 1930, St. Landry claimed eight lynching victims, at last six of them African American; Natchitoches tallied one.

110. *New Orleans Picayune,* October 9, 1897.

111. The race of defendants is not specified in court documents, so it is not possible to devise a racial breakdown of those charged with murder in Ouachita Parish. District Court Minute Book, Clerk of Court's Office, Ouachita Parish, Monroe. In the 1890s, one lynching on an allegation of homicide occurred in Ouachita Parish. In January 1896, a mob murdered an African American, Abraham Smart, who was accused of killing a French peddler. *New Orleans Picayune,* January 11, 1896.

112. District Court Minute Book, Clerk of Court's Office, Ouachita Parish, Monroe; Espy and Smykla, *Executions in the United States;* State of Louisiana, Executive Department, Death Warrants, 1892–1930, LSA-BR.

113. Thirteen of 263 lynching victims. The Red River Delta led Louisiana with eight mobs composed of blacks that killed eight blacks; in the Ouachita River Valley, two African American mobs claimed the lives of two blacks. Three more black mobs lynched in northern Louisiana, one each in Bienville, Webster, and Concordia Parishes. Twelve black or mixed-race mobs in northern Louisiana lynched four black men on allegations of homicide, three on accusations of sexual assault or rape, one for murder and robbery, and one for rape and murder. Additionally, African American mobs lynched two blacks on allegations of stock theft, one for an "outrageous act," and one for "voodooism." *New Orleans Picayune,* May 14 and 24, 1881, December 11 and April 15, 1887, June 27, 1890, October 30, 1891, January 12, 1892, October 25, 1893, September 14, 1894, and November 3, 1903; *New Orleans Times-Democrat,* September 15, 1896; *Shreveport Times,* November 25, 1901.

114. *Shreveport Times,* November 25, 1901.

115. *New Orleans Picayune,* November 3, 1903.

116. W. Fitzhugh Brundage cites several examples of private and terrorist mobs composed of African Americans and indicates that their actions were sporadic instances of private vengeance or economically motivated violence among blacks. Brundage, *Lynching in the New South,* 23–24, 29–30, 45. The four mass mobs of African Americans that lynched in Bossier and Caddo Parishes belie this hypothesis. Stewart E. Tolnay and E. M. Beck found that 6.7 percent of all African American lynching victims in the cotton South died at the hands of black mobs. Tolnay and Beck, *Festival of Violence,* 135. For an extended discussion of black-on-black lynchings that largely parallels mine, see Tolnay and Beck, "When Race Didn't Matter." For mobs of African

Americans that lynched blacks outside of the South, see Pfeifer, "Ritual of Lynching," 29, for a lynching in February 1895 in Kingston, Missouri; and Howard, "Black Lynching in the Promised Land," 94–99, for a lynching on August 13, 1887, in Greene County, Ohio.

117. For descriptions of the public spectacle of executions in Louisiana before the statutory privatization of the death rite, see, for example, *New Orleans Picayune,* April 3 and 5, 1880.

118. State of Louisiana, Executive Department, Death Warrants, 1892–1930, LSA-BR.

119. *New Orleans Picayune,* October 9, 1897. Pat Paine was the only person legally executed in Ouachita Parish in the late nineteenth century; only two more died on the gallows in this lynching-prone parish before 1920. Espy and Smykla, *Executions in the United States;* State of Louisiana, Executive Department, Death Warrants, 1892–1930, LSA-BR. In a similar pattern, the exceedingly lynching-prone Bossier Parish staged a mere two legal executions between 1878 and 1899, a period during which mobs killed eighteen victims.

120. State of Louisiana, Executive Department, Death Warrants, 1892–1930, LSA-BR.

Chapter 5: Judge Lynch's Demise

1. Ellis, Frost, Syrett, and Carman, *History of New York State,* 166–93, 244–66; Cross, *Burned-Over District;* Berthoff, *Unsettled People,* 246–50. For analysis of the evolution of race in New England, see Melish, *Disowning Slavery.* Melish argues that white New Englanders erased the memory of blacks from their region's history amid the gradual emancipation of slaves after the revolution and asserts that whites in mid-Atlantic states such as New York and New Jersey remained more conscious that slavery had been part of their region's past (224–25).

2. For the waves of prison reform in New York State, which were influenced by "Arminianism, perfectionism, and millenialism," see Lewis, *From Newgate to Dannemora,* esp. 56–100, 203, 231–40. Masur, *Rites of Execution,* analyzes the philosophical and rhetorical alterations behind the shift from public to private execution in the antebellum northeastern United States. Masur argues that, in the 1820s and 1830s, authorities were increasingly anxious about threats to public order, and elites began arguing that public executions were "festivals of disorder"; that the period saw a new elite concern with privacy, associated with a trend toward "class segmentation and exclusion"; and that the fashionable pseudoscience of phrenology led some thinkers to posit that witnessing an execution could excite dangerous sensations in the emotionally weak (93–116). For a general treatment of social reform movements and the trend toward institutional solutions to social problems in the Northeast in the early nineteenth century, see Rothman, *Discovery of the Asylum.*

3. For an overview of rioting in American history, see Gilje, *Rioting in America.* On nineteenth-century urban rioting, see Gordon, *Orange Riots,* esp. 1–5, Bernstein, *New York City Draft Riots,* Runcie, "'Hunting the Nigs' in Philadelphia," and Brown, *Strain of Violence,* appendix 4, 321–24. Grimsted, *American Mobbing,* argues that agitation over issues that led to the Civil War provoked much of the collective violence in the antebellum North and South. The Progressive Era "race riots" in cities like East St. Louis in 1917, Chicago in 1919, and Tulsa in 1921 displayed a different pattern; white rioters killed significant numbers of African Americans (thirty-nine, twenty-three, and seventy-five or more African Americans, respectively), but whites also perished in the

violence (nine, fifteen, and ten, respectively). For case studies of these episodes, see Tuttle, *Race Riot*, Rudwick, *Race Riot at East St. Louis*, and Ellsworth, *Death in a Promised Land*. In a "race riot" in New York City in August 1900, working-class whites and police systematically beat and inflicted severe injuries on hundreds of African Americans after a white police officer died of stabbing wounds inflicted by an African American he was clubbing. Various accounts neglect to estimate the number of deaths. Moss, *Story of the Riot Published by the Citizen's Protective League*; Osofsky, *Harlem*, 46–52; Johnson, *Black Manhattan*, 128–30.

4. For the transformation of the police into a professional instrument for crime control, see Miller, *Cops and Bobbies*, Steinberg, *Transformation of Criminal Justice*, and Monkkonen, *Police in Urban America*.

5. By comparison, M. Watt Espy enumerates 596 legal executions in New York from 1891 through 1946. Espy and Smykla, *Executions in the United States*. For the technocratic cultural context in which the electric chair was introduced at Sing Sing, see Martschukat, "'Art of Killing by Electricity.'"

6. The data used here is compiled from the Sing Sing admission register and includes the 357 death row prisoners who were sentenced between October 1889 and October 1933 and were eventually electrocuted and the 191 death row inmates who escaped execution through a judicial reversal of judgment or a governor's commutation in the same years. Nineteen additional persons were admitted to death row, but they committed suicide, died, escaped, or were sent elsewhere because of illness and are not included in my database. Admission Register, Log of Actions, Sing Sing Prison, BO 147, NYSA; *Sing Sing Prison Electrocutions*. For summary accounts of all of the executions in New York's history, see Hearn, *Legal Executions in New York State*. Martha Place, a forty-four-year-old housekeeper who was convicted in Kings County for smothering her female victim with a pillow, was electrocuted on March 20, 1899; Ruth Snyder, a thirty-three-year-old Queens housewife who allegedly killed her husband for insurance money, died in the electric chair on January 12, 1928. Of the prisoners executed, 175 (49 percent) were convicted for murdering men, ninety-three (26.1 percent) for killing women, and the sex of the victim(s) could not be determined for eighty-nine (24.9 percent). Of those who avoided execution, eighty-seven (45.6 percent) were convicted for killing men, thirty-three (17.3 percent) for murdering women, and the sex was not given for seventy-one (37.1 percent) of the victims. Two hundred sixty-five (74.2 percent) of the persons who were electrocuted were sentenced from the nine-county region surrounding New York City, including the counties of New York (104), Kings (Brooklyn, fifty-nine), Bronx (thirty-three), Westchester (twenty-nine), Queens (eighteen), Nassau (ten), Suffolk (five), Rockland (four), and Richmond (three); 142 (74.3 percent) of the prisoners who left death row were from this region. Interestingly, in an earlier period, from 1878 through 1890, when executions were performed in the counties and by hanging, the New York City area contributed less than half (twenty-five) of the state's fifty-nine executions. Pennsylvania's death penalty was also substantially rooted in the social relations of urbanization, although less so than in New York. Of the 532 persons executed from 1880 through 1933, 54.9 percent had been sentenced from the Philadelphia, Pittsburgh, Reading, Scranton, Erie, and Allentown areas; 41.9 percent from the Philadelphia and Pittsburgh areas alone. But several rural counties in southwestern and south central Pennsylvania also produced large numbers of death sentences, especially in proportion to their smaller populations. The total numbers of persons executed in other northeastern states from 1866 through 1935 were as follows: Maine, six; Massachusetts, seventy-three; Rhode Island, zero; New Hampshire, twelve; Vermont, sixteen; Connecticut, sixty-two; and New Jersey, 198. Espy and Smykla, *Executions in the United States*.

7. Admission Register, Log of Actions, Sing Sing Prison, BO 147, NYSA. Religious affiliation of the executed broke down as follows: Catholic, 188 (52.8 percent); Protestant, seventy-six (21.3 percent); None Given, forty (11.2 percent); Jewish, twenty-four (6.7 percent); Baptist, fourteen (3.9 percent); Methodist, four (1.1 percent); Lutheran, three (0.8 percent); Greek Catholic, two (0.6 percent); Atheist/Freethinker, two (0.6 percent); Episcopal, one (0.3 percent); Heathen, one (0.3 percent); and Christian Science, one (0.3 percent). Forty-five percent (160) of the persons executed were between the ages of twenty and twenty-seven. I have grouped occupations for those electrocuted into the following general categories, listed with their distribution: Unskilled, 106 (29.6 percent); Skilled, ninety-two (25.8 percent); Service, seventy-three (20.4 percent); None Given, twenty-nine (8.1 percent); Entrepreneurial/mercantile/managerial, twenty-two (6.2 percent); Clerical, ten (2.8 percent); Detective/Law Officer, eight (2.2 percent); Professional, four (1.1 percent); Agricultural, four (1.1 percent); Military, four (1.1 percent); Student, two (0.6 percent); Housewife, two (0.6 percent); and Entertainment, one (0.3 percent). Interestingly, the occupational distribution was similar for the 191 death row inmates who averted execution, except that those citing entrepreneurial/mercantile/managerial occupations expanded to twenty-one (11 percent), indicating that those who got off were, overall, a slightly wealthier and more middling group. Race for those executed broke down as follows: White, 292 (81.8 percent); Black, sixty (16.8 percent); Asian, four (1.1 percent); and Brown, one (0.3 percent). For the condemned who escaped execution: White, 168 (87.9 percent); Black, nineteen (9.9 percent); and Asian, four (2.1 percent). Place of birth for the electrocuted was distributed as follows: New York State, 125 (35 percent); Italy, seventy-one (19.9 percent); American South, forty-three (12 percent); Russia-Poland, twenty-one (5.9 percent); New England, twenty (5.6 percent); Germany, fourteen (3.9 percent); Elsewhere in the United States, twelve (3.4 percent); Not Given, ten (2.8 percent); West Indies, seven (2 percent); Austria, five (1.4 percent); Puerto Rico, four (1.1 percent); United Kingdom, three (0.8 percent); Sweden, two (0.6 percent); Philippines, two (0.6 percent); Argentina, two (0.6 percent); Japan, two (0.6 percent); Canada, one (0.3 percent); Ireland, one (0.3 percent); Armenia, one (0.3 percent); Switzerland, one (0.3 percent); Holland, one (0.3 percent); Finland, one (0.3 percent); Belgium, one (0.3 percent); Mexico, one (0.3 percent); China, one (0.3 percent); Virgin Islands, one (0.3 percent); Norway, one (0.3 percent); Liberia, one (0.3 percent); Spain, one (0.3 percent); and Portugal, one (0.3 percent). The distribution was similar for the 191 prisoners who left death row through an appellate route, except that Italian nativity was claimed by an even greater proportion (26.7 percent), while fewer (5.2 percent) cited a birthplace in the American South. In 1930, blacks contributed 3.3 percent (412,814) of the state's population; persons of Italian birth constituted 12 percent (1,552,469). U.S. Bureau of the Census, *Fifteenth Census of the United States.*

8. Curiously, in light of the Italian immigrants who filled the ranks of Sing Sing's death row in the 1910s, 1920s, and 1930s, a WPA account of the Italian community in New York City blamed the maladjustment of second-generation Italians rather than the folkways of their sturdy and hard-working parents for the problem of criminal activity among Italian Americans. Works Progress Administration, Federal Writer's Project, *Italians of New York,* 51–53. For an editorial that analyzes the problem of "Italian crime," see *New York Times,* February 26, 1907. In 1930, there were at least 1.07 million persons of Italian ancestry, the majority with roots in southern Italy, in metropolitan New York. For the experience of Italians in New York, see Cohen, *Workshop to Office,* 2–11. For Italians and organized crime, see Nelli, *Business of Crime.* On the racial dimensions of conceptions of ethnicity in fin-de-siècle America, see Jacobson, *Whiteness of a Different Color.* For a controversial interpretation that ties urban black violence to severe economic, social, legal, and political discrimination, which limited

African Americans' encounter with the urban-industrial revolution and its values, see Lane, *Roots of Violence in Black Philadelphia*. Lane finds that Italian immigrants initially were very violent, with a homicide rate that even exceeded that of blacks early in the twentieth century. He notes that Italy had the highest murder rate in Europe and that Italians came as single young men into an "urban gun culture" (163–64). But Lane argues that Italians quickly adjusted in the first decades of the twentieth century, as their position in the urban labor market improved and as a "family culture" took root in Italian Philadelphia.

9. Admission Register, Log of Actions, Sing Sing Prison, BO 147, NYSA; *Sing Sing Prison Electrocutions*. For DeMaio's case, see *Peekskill (N.Y.) Evening Star*, August 21, 1926. Semions is listed as an alternative spelling for Emilio Semione's surname. For southern black and Caribbean black migration to New York City and the emergence of Harlem, see Osofsky, *Harlem*, 105–35, and Watkin-Owens, *Caribbean Immigrants and the Harlem Community*, 1–26, 41.

10. An 1835 statute privatized the death penalty in New York by stipulating that executions must occur within prison walls or within the yard or inclosure of a county prison. Witnesses were limited to county officials, immediate relatives of the prisoner, several clergy, and twelve citizens. State of New York, *Revised Statutes of the State of New York*. For the statutory changes that occurred with the introduction of the electric chair, see the entries for execution and the death penalty in the indices of the State of New York, *Documents of the Assembly of the State of New York, One Hundred and Twenty-Fifth Session*.

11. *New York Tribune*, April 13, 14, and 15, 1914, July 30 and 31, 1915; *New York Times*, July 30 and 31, 1915; Admission Register, Log of Actions, Sing Sing Prison, BO 147, NYSA; *Sing Sing Prison Electrocutions*. Charles Becker, forty-three years old and a native of New York, secured delays in his execution until July 30, 1915. Working-class East Siders feared that when Horowitz, Rosenberg, Seidenshner, and Corofisi were executed without Becker, the former police lieutenant would get off. Siedenshner was born in Russia or Poland, Corofisi in Italy, and Horowitz and Rosenberg in New York; all were in their twenties. Becker had reputedly arranged the murder as retaliation against Rosenthal, who would not cooperate with his graft ring.

12. *New York Tribune*, April 14, 1914.

13. Ibid. For cursory accounts of executions that suggest the routinization of the death rite, see *New York Times*, January 28 and 29, 1895, for the execution of David Hampton, sentenced from New York City; *New York Times*, February 25, 1907, and *Poughkeepsie (N.Y.) Daily Eagle*, February 25, 1907, for the execution of George Granger, sentenced from Dutchess County; *New York Times*, July 30, 1915, for the execution of Samuel Haynes, sentenced from Putnam County; *New York Tribune*, June 30, 1916, and *New York Times*, June 30, 1916, for the execution of Oresto Shilitani, sentenced from New York City; *Brooklyn Daily Eagle*, August 27, 1920, for the execution of Frank Kelley, sentenced from Kings County; *Buffalo Evening News*, September 10, 1920, and *Buffalo Courier*, September 10, 1920, for the execution of Walter Bojanowski, sentenced from Erie County; *Peekskill (N.Y.) Evening Star*, August 21, 1926, for the executions of David DeMaio, sentenced from Westchester County, and William Hoyer, sentenced from New York City; and *Niagara Falls Gazette*, June 2, 1933, for the execution of William H. Jackson, sentenced from Niagara County.

14. Fedo, *Lynchings in Duluth*; Weinberg, "'Tug of War'"; Madison, *Lynching in the Heartland*.

15. Governor's Office, Records and Correspondence: Criminal Matters, box/vols. GII 579–81, SHSI-DM.

16. For an overview of the reward system in western states, see Traub, "Rewards, Bounty Hunting, and Criminal Justice in the West."

17. For a quasi-legal self-help law enforcement organization in central Iowa in the mid 1880s, see *(Des Moines) Iowa State Register,* June 5, 1885. For a northwestern Iowa "vigilante committee," actually a quasi-legal Anti–Horse Thief Association that was active in the 1870s but dormant by the early 1880s, see Parker, "Pioneer Protection from Horse Thieves." For a discussion of the anti–horse thief movement in broad historical context, see Brown, *Strain of Violence,* 125–26.

18. State of Iowa, *Annotated Code of the State of Iowa* (1885 and 1897).

19. *Dubuque Times,* June 5, 1883.

20. Sayre, "Albert B. Cummins and the Progressives in Iowa."

21. For example, the Iowa governor's office closely coordinated strike suppression with local officials and management during the railroad strike of 1877. For the governor's correspondence on militia matters, see Governor's Office, Records and Correspondence, box/vol. GII 541, SHSI-DM.

22. *(Des Moines) Iowa State Register,* June 12, 1883. For the commentary of another state attorney general blaming the laxity of the criminal court for the popularity of lynching, see *(Des Moines) Iowa State Register,* February 6, 1885.

23. State of Iowa, *Annotated Code of the State of Iowa* (1885 and 1897); Black, "Attempted Lynchings in Iowa." For the 1893 Taylor County incident, see R. Vickery to Honorable Horace Boies, September 25, 1893, in Governor's Office, Records and Correspondence: Criminal Matters, box/vol. GII 580, SHSI-DM. Officials may have summoned militia on additional occasions.

24. For examples, see Black, "Attempted Lynchings in Iowa."

25. State of Iowa, *Annotated Code of the State of Iowa* (1897). The 1894 death penalty statute did retain some of the local interest in the execution rite by stipulating that hangings would be performed by the sheriff or deputy sheriff of the county of conviction and mandating the attendance of county officials.

26. *(Des Moines) Iowa State Register,* December 17, 1887, January 13, 1888; *Burlington (Iowa) Hawkeye,* October 19, 1894, February 9, 1895; *(Des Moines) Register and Leader,* April 20 and 21, 1906; *Des Moines Capital,* July 29, 1910.

27. For a large-scale perspective on alterations in capital punishment practices, see Masur, *Rites of Execution.*

28. William Larrabee to Paul W. Black, August 24, 1904, in Black, "Lynching Research Notes," box 2, Manuscript Collection, SHSI-IC. Several lynchings did occur after the executions in 1887 and 1888, but there was only one after 1895.

29. From 1865 through 1887, mobs murdered seventeen on homicide charges (52 percent of victims), eleven on property crime allegations (33 percent), four for attempted murder (12 percent), and one on an accusation of rape (3 percent).

30. Pfeifer, "Iowa's Last Lynching."

31. Black, "Lynchings in Iowa," 215–53. Authorities in Iowa legally hanged two African Americans in the first decade of the twentieth century and executed twelve more prisoners, five of them black, by 1931. Three of the African Americans legally hanged in Iowa were Fred Allen, Stanley Grammell, and Robert Johnson, soldiers convicted of raping a white woman at Camp Dodge. Military authorities tried and executed them in July 1918. Espy and Smykla, *Executions in the United States.*

32. *Vernon County (Wisc.) Censor,* June 6, 1888; *Milwaukee Sentinel,* June 2, 1888. The *Milwaukee Sentinel* put a kinder face on Rusk's passivity, omitting the day's earlier exchange of telegraphs. Rusk had not been reluctant to send militia to suppress labor unrest earlier in his administration.

33. *Duluth (Minn.) Daily News-Tribune,* May 6, 1893.

34. In a study of lynching in Colorado, Stephen J. Leonard argues that opinion against lynching began to coalesce in the 1880s in the state's older towns and cities. Opponents, fashioning themselves as "the responsible men of the community, the solid real estate owners," declared lynching to be inconsistent with "civilization" and cited the potentially negative effect of mob killings on investment and the attraction of new settlers. *Lynching in Colorado,* 158–60 (quote on 160).

35. *Cheyenne Daily Leader,* November 20, 1903; Letterbook of Governor Fenimore Chatterton, to Hon. T. F. Burke, Cheyenne, Wyo., October 26, 1903 (microfilm still 78), WSA, WSM-C.

36. *Cheyenne Daily Leader,* November 20, 1903; *Laramie Boomerang,* August 26 and October 26, 1903.

37. *Cheyenne Daily Leader,* November 20 and 21, 1903; *Laramie Republican,* quoted in *Cheyenne Daily Leader,* November 24, 1903.

38. *Cheyenne Daily Leader,* November 20 and 21, 1903.

39. *Laramie Republican,* quoted in *Cheyenne Daily Leader,* November 24, 1903.

40. For editorials supporting the enactment of the 1905 execution law, see *(Cheyenne) Wyoming Tribune,* January 23, 1905, *Cheyenne Daily Leader,* January 22, 1905, *Sheridan (Wyo.) Post,* January 27, 1905, and *Cody (Wyo.) Enterprise,* January 26, 1905. I am indebted to Carl Hallberg for these sources.

41. See "Session Laws of Wyoming, 1905," in "Executions in Wyoming," Subject File, WSA, WSM-C. In the mid 1910s, legislators also granted jurors the option of specifying that a person convicted of first-degree murder should suffer death or life imprisonment. See the account of the execution of Wilmer Palmer, who was the first person to whom this change applied, in *(Cheyenne) Wyoming Tribune,* August 11, 1916.

42. *(Cheyenne) Wyoming Tribune,* January 23, 1905.

43. *Cheyenne Daily Leader,* January 22, 1905.

44. Espy and Smykla, *Executions in the United States.* The *(Cheyenne) Wyoming Tribune* reported that four more prisoners resided on death row in August 1916, although only one of these, "O. W. White, colored," was eventually executed. The others, convicted from Lincoln County and sentenced to hang October 28, 1915, were "Matt Arej, Austrian, Daniel Parker, negro, and T. Ohama, a Japanese." See *(Cheyenne) Wyoming Tribune,* August 11, 1916.

45. Larson, *History of Wyoming,* 230, 290–92, 319–34, 447–48. Political historians rate Carey's "progressivism" as conservative in its outlook and achievement. William Howard Moore characterizes his governing philosophy: "Although Governor Carey supported Theodore Roosevelt in 1912, he largely restricted his own legislative proposals to direct democracy schemes, penal reform, lukewarm labor bills, and changes in federal land policy." See Moore, "Progressivism and the Social Gospel in Wyoming."

46. Governor Joseph M. Carey to Mrs. Anthony Seng, Allentown, Pa., July 15, 1911, in Pardon File, Joseph Seng, WSA, WSM-C.

47. *(Cheyenne) Wyoming Tribune,* August 11, 1916.

48. State of Wyoming, *Census of Wyoming, 1905;* State of Wyoming, *Census of the State of Wyoming, 1915;* State of Wyoming, *Wyoming State Census, 1925.* Casper and Natrona County's population exploded with the oil boom after 1915, reaching more than thirty-five thousand by 1925.

49. The last mob killing of whites in Wyoming occurred in April 1909, when a masked mob of fifteen, representing cattle interests, murdered the sheepmen Joe Allemand, Joe Emge, and Joe Lazier in Big Horn County. Wyoming lynchers killed three more African Americans in the 1910s, concluding with Joel Woodson in Green River

in December 1918. Wyoming state officials legally executed nine men between 1912 and 1933, including an African American, a Chinese American, and a Native American. Larson, *History of Wyoming*, 371–72; *(Cheyenne) Wyoming Tribune*, December 10 and 11, 1918; *Green River (Wyo.) Star*, December 10, 1918; *Salt Lake City Semi-Weekly Tribune*, December 13, 1918; Espy and Smykla, *Executions in the United States.* The fatal beating of Matthew Shepard by two men on the outskirts of Laramie in October 1998, motivated at least partially by hatred of homosexuals, in some respects resembled a lynching. *New York Times*, October 13, 1998.

50. *Colfax (Wash.) Commoner*, March 25 and April 2, 1898.

51. State of Washington, *Session Laws of the State of Washington, Eleventh Session*, 952; State of Washington, *Session Laws of the State of Washington, Sixteenth Session*, 274. Washington abolished the death penalty in 1913 and reinstated it in 1919.

52. Espy and Smykla, *Executions in the United States.*

53. *Asotin County (Wash.) Sentinel*, August 8, 1903; *Seattle Post-Intelligencer*, August 5, 1903; *Seattle Times*, August 5, 1903; *San Francisco Chronicle*, August 5, 1903. Neither of the Seattle newspapers editorialized on the Asotin lynching, although their reporting of it pointedly stressed its brutality.

54. *Asotin County (Wash.) Sentinel*, August 8, 1903.

55. Much has been written about the Centralia lynching, most of it slanted toward either the Wobblies or the Legionnaires. The best account is McLelland, *Wobbly War.*

56. Espy and Smykla, *Executions in the United States.*

57. Webb, "History of Lynching in California since 1875," 75–78.

58. Quoted in ibid., 77.

59. Quoted in ibid., 79–82.

60. Quoted in ibid., 80–81.

61. "Without Sanctuary" Web site <http://www.journale.com/withoutsanctuary/main.html>, accessed July 4, 2001; Edward J. Begley, "The Last California Lynching" (1992) <http://www.scn.org/~begley/lynching.txt>, accessed July 4, 2001.

62. Entry dated December 31, 1886, Andrew Augustus Gunby Papers, LSUSC. Gunby's distance from upper-class white Democratic opinion accelerated in ensuing years. In the 1890s he became a prominent Populist spokesperson through his newspaper, the *Monroe (La.) Bulletin.* Gunby championed liberal positions that challenged racial and class orthodoxy and opposed the softening of the Populist program through fusion tickets with conservative Republicans and Democrats. Hair, *Bourbonism and Agrarian Protest*, 231, 250, 271, 274, 278.

63. Entry dated December 31, 1886, Andrew Augustus Gunby Papers, LSUSC; *New Orleans Picayune*, February 21, 1886.

64. Entry dated December 31, 1886, Andrew Augustus Gunby Papers, LSUSC.

65. Hair, *Bourbonism and Agrarian Protest*, 41–42; U.S. Bureau of the Census, *Eleventh Census of the United States;* U.S. Bureau of the Census, *Twelfth Census of the United States.*

66. On Shreveport and Caddo Parish in the early twentieth century, see Thomson and Meador, *Shreveport*, 22–24. Only five of Caddo Parish's twenty-five lynchings occurred before 1900.

67. The historian John Cell argues analogously that middle classes in southern cities promoted Jim Crow, the statutory enactment of separate racial spaces, as a solution to the social turmoil caused by the social and spatial reconfiguration of racial arrangements engendered by urbanization. Cell, *Highest Stage of White Supremacy*, ix–x, 131–35. For the linkage of urban growth and segregation, albeit in an earlier period, see Rabinowitz, *Race Relations in the Urban South.*

68. *New Orleans Picayune,* October 3, 1897, August 27, 1906, March 15, 1907, October 22, 1913, August 7 and 8, 1914; *Monroe (La.) News-Star,* October 22 and 23, 1913, August 6, 8, and 11, 1914.

69. *New Orleans Picayune,* March 7, 1901, July 7 and December 1, 1903, May 23, 1906, August 6, 1908, November 28, 1909, April 10, 1912, February 15, December 17, 18, and 19, 1913, May 13, 14, December 3, 4, 12, and 13, 1914, and August 27, 1916; *Shreveport Times,* March 6 and 7, 1901, July 26 and 28, 1903, May 23, 1906, August 6 and 7, 1908, November 28, 29, and 30, 1909, December 16, 17, 18, 19, and 20, 1913, May 13, 14, 17, December 12, 13, 14, 15, 16, 17, 18, 19, 20, 21, 22, 23, 24, 29, 30, and 31, 1914; *Shreveport Journal,* January 4, 1923.

70. A mob of approximately five hundred, including many white railroaders, women, and children, hanged Simmie Thomas in November 1909. *New Orleans Picayune,* November 28, 1909; *Shreveport Times,* November 28, 29, and 30, 1909. In May 1914 a mob estimated at several thousand dragged Earl Hamilton from jail and stabbed and hanged him after he had allegedly raped a white girl at a downtown movie house. *New Orleans Picayune,* May 13 and 14, 1914; *Shreveport Times,* May 13, 14, and 17, 1914.

71. *Shreveport Journal,* January 4, 1923; *New Orleans Picayune,* April 10, 1912, and April 30, 1919. For urbanization and its redefinition of gender and racial roles in North Carolina, see Gilmore, *Gender and Jim Crow,* 72–76. Gilmore stresses the significance of emergent black youth and African American middle-class cultures in reconfiguring urban relations.

72. "The Shreveport People and the Law," *Natchitoches (La.) Enterprise,* Newton Blanchard Scrapbook, LSUSC.

73. For newspaper stories and editorials concerning the Charles Coleman case, see clippings in Newton Blanchard Scrapbook, LSUSC.

74. For newspaper columns concerning Blanchard's campaign against lynching, see Newton Blanchard Scrapbook, LSUSC. For example, Blanchard told a grand jury in Pointe Coupee Parish, where a lynching had recently happened, "You can not make the world believe that the names of these lynchers can not be found out."

75. Northern Louisiana lynchers killed three in 1905, six in 1906, ten in 1907, and seven in 1908.

76. "The Governor on Lynching," unattributed, undated, Newton Blanchard Scrapbook, LSUSC. Blanchard supported a bill that would have required that mob participants indicted by a grand jury be tried "in an entirely different part of the state." From a newspaper identified as the *Tribune,* May 22 (year not given).

77. See, for example, a Monroe editor's staunch defense of Blanchard after criticism of his intervention in the Coleman affair and his decision to send troops to Bienville Parish, who failed to arrive in time to prevent the lynching of Willis Page. "Unfair to Governor Blanchard," February 26, 1906, Newton Blanchard Scrapbook, LSUSC.

78. Carleton, "Newton Crain Blanchard."

79. At his inauguration, Blanchard pledged to dispatch militia in circumstances where lynchings were threatened and, if a mob killing could not be prevented, to insist on the rigorous investigation and prosecution of lynchers. "Will Oppose Lynching," unattributed, May 24, 1906, Newton Blanchard Scrapbook, LSUSC.

80. Ibid.

81. "The Governor's Message," unattributed, undated, Newton Blanchard Scrapbook, LSUSC.

82. For a discussion of disfranchisement in Louisiana, see Hair, *Bourbonism and Agrarian Protest,* 271–79. For segregation and disfranchisement, see Hair, *Kingfish and His Realm,* 60–65. As Hair explains, the state legislature racially separated railroad coaches in 1890. Streetcar companies in New Orleans initially opposed the segrega-

tion of streetcars by the legislature in 1902, arguing that color lines were unenforceable in a city with such a large racially mixed population. African Americans in New Orleans and Shreveport responded to segregation of the trolleys by organizing boycotts. In the early twentieth century, state legislators went even further, segregating an extensive array of public and private accommodations. These included saloons in 1908, residences and neighborhoods in 1912, circuses in 1914, and renters in 1921. For an analysis of the state's penal system in the late nineteenth and early twentieth centuries, see Carleton, *Politics and Punishment.*

83. Carleton, "Newton Crain Blanchard," 201.

84. *New Orleans Picayune*, December 3, 4, 12, and 13, 1914; *Shreveport Times,* December 12, 13, 14, 15, 16, 17, 18, 19, 20, 21, 22, 23, 24, 29, 30, and 31, 1914.

85. *Shreveport Times*, December 15, 1914. A rival newspaper, the aptly named *Shreveport Caucasian*, defended the lynchings. *Shreveport Times*, December 30, 1914.

86. *Shreveport Times*, December 17, 1914.

87. *Shreveport Times*, December 14, 15, 16, 17, 18, 19, 20, 21, 22, 23, 24, 29, 30, and 31, 1914. Flournoy quoted in *Shreveport Times*, December 22, 1914. The Louisiana Prison Reform Association quoted in *Shreveport Times*, December 21, 1914.

88. The yearly average of lynching victims from northern Louisiana was 5.3 in the 1880s and eight in the 1890s. Lynchers murdered fifty-one persons (fifty of them black) in the 1910s, thirteen persons (ten of them black) in the 1920s, and five blacks in the 1930s. Meanwhile, in an echo of the advice of Newton Blanchard and middle-class reformers who had eschewed lynching in favor of efficient, race-conscious capital punishment, the rate of legal execution intensified, particularly in northern Louisiana. State authorities executed at least fifty prisoners in the 1910s, forty-six in the 1920s, and sixty in the 1930s. At least half, and probably many more, of those who died on the gallows were African American. Due to incomplete data in the Espy file, a precise distribution of the race of those executed is not possible. But at least eighty-four out of 156 executed between 1910 and 1940 were African American (54 percent). Additionally, the Espy file probably understates the total number of legal executions. Espy and Smykla, *Executions in the Unites States.*

89. In the period from 1878 to 1946, fifty-five legal executions in northern parishes occurred before 1900 (25 percent). Officials hanged eighty-one between 1900 and 1919 (37 percent), and eighty-one expired on the gallows from 1920 through 1946 (37 percent). Espy and Smykla, *Executions in the United States*; State of Louisiana, Executive Department, Death Warrants, 1892–1930, LSA-BR. Stewart E. Tolnay and E. M. Beck refute the possibility of a precise statistical relationship between the decline of lynching and the rise in legal executions, the so-called substitution model. Tolnay and Beck, *Festival of Violence*, 86–118. But in northern Louisiana, the combined evidence of lynching and execution statistics and the rhetoric employed by Newton Blanchard and numerous editorialists suggests such a linkage. Neil R. McMillen discusses legal lynchings, cases of rushed judgment and extreme racial bias in the Mississippi courtroom, sometimes influenced by the threat of white violence. McMillen, *Dark Journey,* 206–17. For legal lynchings and the racially discriminatory administration of the criminal justice system in Kentucky in the first decades of the twentieth century, see Wright, *Racial Violence in Kentucky,* 251–305, and Wright, "By the Book."

90. For the important role of the NAACP and several other "interracial" organizations in fighting lynching and the ebbing of popular support for mob violence in Georgia by the 1920s, see Brundage, *Lynching in the New South,* 208–44. As with my interpretation, Brundage stresses the pivotal role of a rising urban middle class and the "progressivism" that it supported in overcoming localistic cultures that embraced lynching (208–11). Some residents of Shreveport were especially scandalized by the

national coverage of the December 1914 lynchings. *Shreveport Times*, December 22, 1914. For the NAACP's national campaign against lynching, see Zangrando, *NAACP Crusade against Lynching*. For the Great Migration of African Americans from the South to the urban North in the late 1910s, see Grossman, *Land of Hope*. Adam Fairclough adeptly analyzes several lynchings in Louisiana in the 1930s and 1940s, the mixed results achieved by the NAACP in its efforts against mob violence in the state, and the role of the ASWPL in helping to sap white support for mob murder in the 1920s and 1930s. Fairclough, *Race and Democracy*, 26–31, 113–19. The ASWPL is also analyzed in Hall, *Revolt against Chivalry*. For an analysis of how Ida B. Wells deftly argued that lynching defied civilized norms of masculinity, see Bederman, *Manliness and Civilization*, 45–76. Ida B. Wells's and Jessie Daniel Ames's condemnation of lynching as inconsistent with decent and respectable manhood assisted the formation of middle-class southern opinion that opposed lynching.

91. In August 1946 ten whites in Webster Parish fatally beat John C. Jones, a black World War II veteran who had supposedly conspired with his cousin to attempt to rape a white woman. Jones had also argued with an oil company over leases claimed on his family's land and had in other ways refused to defer to local whites. The NAACP successfully pushed for an investigation by the FBI and prosecution in federal court, marking the first federal action in a lynching case in Louisiana. Although a jury found the five defendants not guilty, the mob execution of Jones was the last recorded lynching in Louisiana. Fairclough, *Race and Democracy*, 113–19.

Epilogue

1. Wright, *Native Son*, 373.

2. For an analysis of the riots in African American inner cities in the late 1960s, see Gilje, *Rioting in America*, 158–60.

3. Analyses of the 1992 Los Angeles riots can be found in Baldassare, *Los Angeles Riots*.

4. *Cincinnati Enquirer*, April 14, 2001; *Cincinnati Post*, April 12, 2001.

5. *New York Times*, May 21, 2000.

6. *Washington Post*, March 7 and 19, 2003.

7. *Washington Post*, March 7, 2003; *Chicago Tribune*, January 12, 2003 (includes the quotation).

8. *Furman v. Georgia*, 408 U.S. 238 (1972); Latzer, *Death Penalty Cases*, 19.

9. *Gregg v. Georgia*, 428 U.S. 153 (1976); Latzer, *Death Penalty Cases*, 45. The new Georgia statute stipulates that the death penalty can only be imposed in a separate penalty hearing that follows a finding of guilt. Under the Georgia law, which was soon imitated by other states, the death penalty can only be imposed for homicides that included aggravating factors and that did not include sufficient mitigating factors.

10. Quoted in Latzer, *Death Penalty Cases*, 50.

11. *McCleskey v. Kemp*, 481 U.S. 279 (1987); Latzer, *Death Penalty Cases*, 231–35.

12. Quoted in Latzer, *Death Penalty Cases*, 234, 236.

13. Quoted in ibid., 242, 245, 249.

BIBLIOGRAPHY

Manuscript Collections

Louisiana State Archives, Baton Rouge
  Executive Department, Death Warrants, 1892–1930
New York State Archives, Albany
  Admission Register, Log of Actions, Sing Sing Prison
Special Collections, Hill Memorial Library, Louisiana State University, Baton
  Rouge
  Governor Newton Blanchard, Scrapbook
  Ozeme Fontenot Papers
  Andrew Augustus Gunby Papers
  Book of Indictments, District Court, Natchitoches Parish
  Arthur P. Thrasher Correspondence
State Historical Society of Iowa, Des Moines
  Governor's Office, Records and Correspondence
  Governor's Office, Records and Correspondence: Criminal Matters
State Historical Society of Iowa, Iowa City
  Paul Walton Black, Lynching Research Notes
Tacoma Public Library, Tacoma, Washington
  Erastus Light, "Early Times in Pierce County" (undated)
  Leland Athow, "A Brief History of the Adam Byrd Branch of the Byrd
    Family" (1953)
Wyoming State Archives, Historical Research Section
  Crime and Criminals File
  County Coroner's Inquests
  "Executions in Wyoming," Subject File
  Governor's Office, Letterbooks and Outgoing Correspondence
  Wyoming Executive Office, Pardon Files
  Albany County District Court Journal and Criminal Case Files, 1880–1920
  Sweetwater County District Court Journal and Criminal Case Files, 1891–95
Wyoming State Museum, Cheyenne

Courthouse Records

These were read at the specified courthouses:
Clerk of Court's Office, Caddo Parish, Shreveport, Louisiana
  Criminal Suits and District Court Minute Book

Clerk of Court's Office, Monroe County, Albia, Iowa
District Court Indices
Clerk of Court's Office, Ouachita Parish, Monroe, Louisiana
Coroner's Inquest, Criminal Suits, and District Court Minute Book
Clerk of Court's Office, St. Landry Parish, Opelousas, Louisiana
Coroner's Inquest, Criminal Suits, and District Court Minute Book
Clerk of Court's Office, St. Mary Parish, Franklin, Louisiana
Criminal Suits and District Court Minute Book
Clerk of Court's Office, Wapello County, Ottumwa, Iowa
District Court Indices

Published and Unpublished Primary and Secondary Sources

Allen, James, Hilton Als, John Lewis, and Leon Litwack. *Without Sanctuary: Lynching Photography in America.* Santa Fe, N.M.: Twin Palms, 2000.
Ayers, Edward. *The Promise of the New South: Life after Reconstruction.* New York: Oxford University Press, 1992.
———. *Vengeance and Justice: Crime and Punishment in the Nineteenth-Century South.* New York: Oxford University Press, 1984.
"Bad News." *The Sou'wester* (Pacific County, Wash., Historical Society) 29.3 (Autumn 1994): 14–15.
Baiamonte, John V., Jr. *Spirit of Vengeance: Nativism and Louisiana Justice, 1921–1924.* Baton Rouge: Louisiana State University Press, 1986.
Baldassare, Mark, ed. *The Los Angeles Riots: Lessons for the Urban Future.* Boulder, Colo.: Westview Press, 1994.
Bancroft, Hubert. *Popular Tribunals.* San Francisco: The History Company, 1887.
Banner-Haley, Charles T. "An Extended Community: Sketches of Afro-American History along New York State's Southern Tier, 1890–1980." *Afro-Americans in New York Life and History* 13.1 (January 1989): 5–18.
Bederman, Gail. *Manliness and Civilization: A Cultural History of Race and Gender in the United States, 1880–1917.* Chicago: University of Chicago Press, 1995.
Bergman, Leola Nelson. *The Negro in Iowa.* 1948. Reprint, Iowa City: State Historical Society of Iowa, 1969.
Bergman, Marvin, ed. *Iowa History Reader.* Ames: Iowa State University Press, 1996.
Bernstein, Iver. *The New York City Draft Riots: Their Significance in American Society and Politics in the Age of the Civil War.* New York: Oxford University Press, 1990.
Berthoff, Rowland. *An Unsettled People: Social Order and Disorder in American History.* New York: Harper and Row, 1971.
Billings, Warren M. "Origins of Criminal Law in Louisiana." *Louisiana History* 32.1 (Winter 1991): 63–76.
Black, Paul Walton. "Attempted Lynchings in Iowa." *Annals of Iowa* 11.4 (January 1914): 260–85.
———. "Lynchings in Iowa." *Iowa Journal of History and Politics* 10.2 (April 1912): 151–254.

Bogue, Allan G. "Farming in the Prairie Peninsula." In *Iowa History Reader*. Ed. Marvin Bergman. 61–85. Ames: Iowa State University Press, 1996.

Brantner, Jessica. "Executed on Behalf of the Public Good? The Lynching of Ed Maxwell in Durand, Wisconsin, 1881." Undergraduate senior thesis, University of Wisconsin–Eau Claire, 2002. In author's possession.

Brasseaux, Carl A. *Acadian to Cajun: Transformation of a People, 1803–1877*. Jackson: University Press of Mississippi, 1992.

Brasseaux, Carl A., Keith P. Fontenot, and Claude F. Oubre. *Creoles of Color in the Bayou Country*. Jackson: University Press of Mississippi, 1994.

Brown, Richard Maxwell. *No Duty to Retreat: Violence and Values in American History and Society*. New York: Oxford University Press, 1991.

———. *Strain of Violence: Historical Studies of American Violence and Vigilantism*. New York: Oxford University Press, 1975.

———. "Western Violence: Structure, Values, Myth." *Western Historical Quarterly* 24.1 (February 1993): 4–20.

Brundage, W. Fitzhugh. *Lynching in the New South: Georgia and Virginia, 1880–1930*. Urbana: University of Illinois Press, 1993.

Brundage, W. Fitzhugh, ed. *Under Sentence of Death: Lynching in the South*. Chapel Hill: University of North Carolina Press, 1997.

Buckelew, Richard Allan. "Racial Violence in Arkansas: Lynchings and Mob Rule, 1860–1930." Ph.D. dissertation, University of Arkansas, 1999.

Capeci, Dominic, Jr. *The Lynching of Cleo Wright*. Knoxville: University Press of Kentucky, 1998.

Carleton, Mark T. "Newton Crain Blanchard." In *The Louisiana Governors*. Ed. Joseph G. Dawson III. 198–203. Baton Rouge: Louisiana State University Press, 1990.

———. *Politics and Punishment: The History of the Louisiana State Penal System*. Baton Rouge: Louisiana State University Press, 1971.

Carlson, Keith Thor. "The Lynching of Louie Sam." *BC Studies* 109 (Spring 1996): 63–79.

Carrigan, William Dean. "Between South and West: Race, Violence, and Power in Central Texas, 1836–1916." Ph.D. dissertation, Emory University, 1999.

Carrigan, William D., and Clive Webb. "Muerto por Unos Desconocidos (Killed by Persons Unknown): Mob Violence against African Americans and Mexican Americans." In *Beyond Black and White: Race, Ethnicity, and Gender in the U.S. South and Southwest*. Ed. Stephanie Cole and Alison Parker. College Park: Texas A&M University Press, 2004.

Cell, John. *The Highest Stage of White Supremacy: The Origins of Segregation in South Africa and the American South*. New York: Cambridge University Press, 1982.

Chadbourn, James Harmon. *Lynching and the Law*. Chapel Hill: University of North Carolina Press, 1933.

Cha-Jua, Sundiata Keita. "'Join Hands and Hearts with Law and Order': The 1893 Lynching of Samuel J. Bush and the Response of Decatur's African American Community." *Illinois Historical Journal* 83 (Autumn 1990): 187–200.

———. "'A Warlike Demonstration': Legalism, Armed Resistance, and Black Political Mobilization in Decatur, Illinois, 1894–1898." *Journal of Negro History* 83.1 (Winter 1998): 52–72.

Cohen, Miriam. *Workshop to Office: Two Generations of Italian Women in New York City.* Ithaca, N.Y.: Cornell University Press, 1992.

Conrad, Glenn H. *The Cajuns: Essays on Their History and Culture.* Lafayette: Center for Louisiana Studies, University of Southwestern Louisiana, 1978.

Cross, Whitney R. *The Burned-Over District: The Social and Intellectual History of Enthusiastic Religion in Western New York, 1800–1850.* Ithaca, N.Y.: Cornell University Press, 1950.

Current, Richard N. *The History of Wisconsin.* Vol. 2: *The Civil War Era, 1848–1873.* Madison: State Historical Society of Wisconsin, 1976.

Cutler, James Elbert. *Lynch-Law: An Investigation into the History of Lynching in the United States.* New York: Longmans, Green, and Co., 1905.

David, Robert B. *Malcolm Campbell, Sheriff.* Casper, Wyo.: Wyomingana, 1932.

Davis, Natalie Zemon. "The Reasons of Misrule." In *Society and Culture in Early Modern France: Eight Essays by Natalie Zemon Davis.* 97–123. Stanford, Calif.: Stanford University Press, 1975.

Downey, Dennis B. "A Many Headed Monster: The 1903 Lynching of David Wyatt." *Journal of Illinois History* 2.1 (1999): 2–16.

Downey, Dennis B., and Raymond M. Hyser. *No Crooked Death: Coatesville, Pennsylvania, and the Lynching of Zachariah Walker.* Urbana: University of Illinois Press, 1991.

Doyle, Don. *New Men, New Cities, New South: Atlanta, Nashville, Charleston, Mobile, 1860–1910.* Chapel Hill: University of North Carolina Press, 1990.

Dray, Philip. *At the Hands of Persons Unknown: The Lynching of Black America.* New York: Random House, 2002.

Dyer, Thomas G. "A Most Unexampled Exhibition of Madness and Brutality: Judge Lynch in Saline County, Missouri." In *Under Sentence of Death: Lynching in the South.* Ed. W. Fitzhugh Brundage. 81–108. Chapel Hill: University of North Carolina Press, 1997.

Dykstra, Robert. *The Cattle Towns.* New York: Knopf, 1968.

Elliot, Mark, and Marie Still. *Lest We Forget: Remembrances of Cheyenne's Jews.* Cheyenne, Wyo.: Aaron Mountain Publishing, 1990.

Ellis, David M., James A. Frost, Harold C. Syrett, and Harry J. Carman. *A History of New York State.* Ithaca, N.Y.: Cornell University Press, 1967.

Ellsworth, Scott. *Death in a Promised Land: The Tulsa Race Riot of 1921.* Baton Rouge: Louisiana State University Press, 1982.

Espy, M. Watt, and John Ortiz Smykla. *Executions in the United States, 1608–1991: The Espy File.* 3d. ed. Ann Arbor, Mich.: Interuniversity Consortium for Political and Social Research, 1994.

Fairclough, Adam. *Race and Democracy: The Civil Rights Struggle in Louisiana.* Athens: University of Georgia Press, 1995.

Fedo, Michael. *The Lynchings in Duluth.* 1979. Reprint, St. Paul: Minnesota Historical Society, 2000.

Feimster, Crystal. "'Ladies and Lynching': The Gendered Discourse of Mob Violence in the New South, 1880–1930." Ph.D. dissertation, Princeton University, 2000.

Feldman, Glenn. "Lynching in Alabama, 1889–1921." *Alabama Review* 48.2 (April 1995): 114–41.

Finnegan, Terrence. "'At the Hands of Parties Unknown': Lynching in Mississippi and South Carolina, 1881–1940." Ph.D. dissertation, University of Illinois, 1993.

Fischer, David Hackett. *Albion's Seed: Four British Folkways in America.* New York: Oxford University Press, 1989.

Florin, Lambert. *Washington Ghost Towns.* Seattle: Superior Publishing Co., 1970.

Flynn, Charles L. *White Land, Black Labor: Caste and Class in Late Nineteenth-Century Georgia.* Baton Rouge: Louisiana State University Press, 1983.

Foner, Eric. *Reconstruction: America's Unfinished Revolution, 1863–1877.* New York: HarperCollins, 1989.

"The Fredericksen Story." *The Sou'wester* (Pacific County, Wash., Historical Society) 13.1 (Spring 1978): 2–12.

Friedman, Lawrence M. *Crime and Punishment in American History.* New York: Basic Books, 1993.

Frink, Maurice. *Cow Country Cavalcade.* Denver: Old West Publishing Co., 1954.

Gage, Jack R. *Tensleep and No Rest: An Historical Account of the Range War of the Big Horns in Wyoming.* Casper, Wyo.: Prairie Publishing Co., 1958.

Gard, Wayne. *Frontier Justice.* Norman: University of Oklahoma Press, 1949.

Genovese, Eugene D. *Roll, Jordan, Roll: The World the Slaves Made.* New York: Pantheon Books, 1972.

Gerlach, Larry. "Justice Denied: The Lynching of Robert Marshall." *Utah Historical Quarterly* 66.4 (1998): 355–64.

———. "Vengeance vs. the Law: The Lynching of Sam Joe Harvey in Salt Lake City." In *Community Development in the American West: Past and Present Nineteenth- and Twentieth-Century Frontiers.* Ed. Jessie L. Embry and Howard A. Christy. 201–37. Provo, Utah.: Charles Redd Monographs in Western History no. 15, Brigham Young University, 1985.

Gilje, Paul A. *Rioting in America.* Bloomington: Indiana University Press, 1996.

Gilmore, Glenda. *Gender and Jim Crow: Women and the Politics of White Supremacy, 1896–1920.* Chapel Hill: University of North Carolina Press, 1996.

Ginzburg, Ralph. *100 Years of Lynching.* 1962. Reprint, Baltimore: Black Classic Press, 1988.

Gordon, Linda. *The Great Arizona Orphan Abduction.* Cambridge, Mass.: Harvard University Press, 1999.

Gordon, Michael A. *The Orange Riots: Irish Political Violence in New York City, 1870 and 1871.* Ithaca, N.Y.: Cornell University Press, 1993.

Gorn, Elliot J. "'Gouge and Bite, Pull Hair and Scratch': The Social Significance of Fighting in the Southern Backcountry." *American Historical Review* 90 (February 1985): 18–43.

Grimsted, David. *American Mobbing, 1828–1861: Toward Civil War.* New York: Oxford University Press, 1998.

———. "Making Violence Relevant." *Reviews in American History* 4.3 (September 1976): 331–38.

Grossman, James G. *Land of Hope: Chicago, Black Southerners, and the Great Migration.* Chicago: University of Chicago Press, 1989.

Guenther, Todd R. "'Y'all Call Me Nigger Jim Now, but Someday You'll Call Me Mr. James Edwards': Black Success on the Plains of the Equality State." *Annals of Wyoming* 61.2 (Fall 1989): 20–40.

Gustafson, Carl Stanley. "History of Vigilante and Mob Activity in Wyoming." M.A. thesis, University of Wyoming, 1961.

Hair, William Ivy. *Bourbonism and Agrarian Protest; Louisiana Politics, 1877–1900.* Baton Rouge: Louisiana State University Press, 1969.

———. *Carnival of Fury: Robert Charles and the New Orleans Race Riot of 1900.* Baton Rouge: Louisiana State University Press, 1976.

———. *The Kingfish and His Realm: The Life and Times of Huey P. Long.* Baton Rouge: Louisiana State University Press, 1991.

Hale, Grace. *Making Whiteness: The Culture of Segregation in the South, 1890–1940.* New York: Pantheon Books, 1998.

Hall, Jacquelyn Dowd. *Revolt against Chivalry: Jesse Daniel Ames and the Women's Campaign against Lynching.* 2d ed. New York: Columbia University Press, 1995.

Hardaway, Roger D. "William Jefferson Hardin: Wyoming's Nineteenth-Century Black Legislator." *Annals of Wyoming* 63.1 (1991): 2–13.

Hearn, Daniel Allen. *Legal Executions in New York State: A Comprehensive Reference, 1639–1963.* Jefferson, N.C.: McFarland Press, 1997.

Hindus, Michael S. *Prison and Plantation: Crime, Justice, and Authority in Massachusetts and South Carolina, 1767–1868.* Chapel Hill: University of North Carolina Press, 1980.

Hirsch, Arnold R., and Joseph Logsdon, eds. *Creole New Orleans: Race and Americanization.* Baton Rouge: Louisiana State University Press, 1992.

The History of Muscatine County, Iowa. Chicago: Western Historical Company, 1879.

Hollon, W. Eugene. *Frontier Violence: Another Look.* New York: Oxford University Press, 1978.

Howard, Marilyn K. "Black Lynching in the Promised Land: Mob Violence in Ohio, 1876–1916." Ph.D. dissertation, Ohio State University, 1999.

Howard, Walter T. *Lynchings: Extralegal Violence in Florida during the 1930s.* Cranbury, N.J.: Associated University Presses, 1995.

Huber, Patrick J. "The Lynching of James T. Scott: The Underside of a College Town." *Gateway Heritage* 12.1 (1991): 18–37.

Hufsmith, George W. *The Wyoming Lynching of Cattle Kate, 1889.* Glendo, Wyo.: High Plains Press, 1993.

Hunt, Herbert. "Judge Lynch in Old Tacoma." In *Tacoma, Its History, and Its Builders: A Half Century of Activity.* Chicago: S. J. Clarke, 1916.

Hunt, William R. *Distant Justice: Policing the Alaska Frontier.* Norman: University of Oklahoma Press, 1987.

Hunter, Tera W. *To 'Joy My Freedom: Southern Black Women's Lives and Labor after the Civil War.* Cambridge, Mass.: Harvard University Press, 1997.

Hurst, James Willard. *The Growth of American Law: The Law Makers.* Boston: Little, Brown, 1950.

Hyde, Samuel C., Jr. *Pistols and Politics: The Dilemma of Democracy in Louisiana's Florida Parishes, 1810–1899.* Baton Rouge: Louisiana State University Press, 1996.

Ingalls, Robert P. *Urban Vigilantes in the New South: Tampa, 1882–1936.* Knoxville: University of Tennessee Press, 1988.

Inverarity, James. "Populism and Lynching in Louisiana, 1889–1896: A Test of Erikson's Theory of the Relationship between Boundary Crises and Repressive Justice." *American Sociological Review* 41 (April 1976): 262–80.

Jackson, Joy J. *New Orleans in the Gilded Age: Politics and Urban Progress.* Baton Rouge: Louisiana State University Press, 1969.

Jacobson, Matthew Frye. *Whiteness of a Different Color: European Immigrants and the Alchemy of Race.* Cambridge, Mass.: Harvard University Press, 1998.

Jean, Susan, and W. Fitzhugh Brundage. "Legitimizing 'Justice': Lynching and the Boundaries of Informal Justice in the American South." In *Informal Criminal Justice.* Ed. Dermot Feenan. 157–78. Ashgate, U.K.: Dartmouth, 2002.

Johnson, David. "Vigilance and the Law: The Moral Authority of Popular Justice in the Far West." *American Quarterly* 33 (Winter 1981): 558–86.

Johnson, James Weldon. *Black Manhattan.* 1930. Reprint, Salem, N.H: Ayer Company, 1988.

Johnson, Susan. *Roaring Camp: The Social World of the California Gold Rush.* New York: W. W. Norton, 2001.

"Justice Triumphs—Pacific County's Shame." *The Sou'wester* (Pacific County, Wash., Historical Society) 29.3 (Autumn 1994): 14–15.

Keller, Morton. *Affairs of State: Public Life in Late Nineteenth-Century America.* Cambridge, Mass.: Belknap Press of the Harvard University Press, 1977.

Klatt, Granger Christine. *They Died at Their Posts: A True Historical Account of Murder and Lynching on the Wisconsin Frontier, 1881.* Menonomie, Wisc.: Dunn County Historical Society, 1976.

Kusmer, Kenneth L. *A Ghetto Takes Shape: Black Cleveland, 1870–1930.* Urbana: University of Illinois Press, 1976.

Lane, Roger. *Roots of Violence in Black Philadelphia, 1860–1900.* Cambridge, Mass.: Harvard University Press, 1986.

Larson, T. A. *History of Wyoming.* Lincoln: University of Nebraska Press, 1965.

Latzer, Barry. *Death Penalty Cases: Leading U.S. Supreme Court Cases on Capital Punishment.* Woburn, Mass.: Butterworth-Heinemann, 1998.

Leonard, Stephen J. *Lynching in Colorado, 1859–1919.* Boulder: University Press of Colorado, 2002.

Levine, Lawrence W. *Black Culture and Black Consciousness: Afro-American Folk Thought from Slavery to Freedom.* New York: Oxford University Press, 1977.

Lewis, W. David. *From Newgate to Dannemora: The Rise of the Penitentiary in New York, 1796–1848.* Ithaca, N.Y.: Cornell University Press, 1965.

Liestman, Daniel. "Horizontal Inter-Ethnic Relations: Chinese and American Indians in the Nineteenth-Century American West." *Western Historical Quarterly* 30.3 (Autumn 1999): 327–49.

Linebaugh, Peter. *The London Hanged: Crime and Civil Society in the Eighteenth Century.* London: Penguin, 1991.

Littlefield, Daniel F., Jr. *Seminole Burning: A Story of Racial Vengeance.* Jackson: University Press of Mississippi, 1996.

Litwack, Leon F. *Trouble in Mind: Black Southerners in the Age of Jim Crow.* New York: Alfred A. Knopf, 1999.

Logsdon, Joseph, and Caryn Cosse Bell. "The Americanization of Black New Orleans, 1850–1900." In *Creole New Orleans: Race and Americanization.* Ed. Arnold R. Hirsch and Joseph Logsdon. 201–61. Baton Rouge: Louisiana State University Press, 1992.

Madison, James H. *A Lynching in the Heartland: Race and Memory in America.* New York: Palgrave, 2001.

Marshall, Elaine. "'The Monster' Seen in the Light of Robert Lewis's Lynching." *Nineteenth-Century Literature* 51.2 (September 1996): 205–24.

Martschukat, Jurgen. "'The Art of Killing by Electricity': The Sublime and the Electric Chair." *Journal of American History* 89.3 (December 2002): 900–21.

Masur, Louis P. *Rites of Execution: Capital Punishment and the Transformation of American Culture, 1776–1865.* New York: Oxford University Press, 1989.

Mathews, Donald G. "The Southern Rite of Human Sacrifice." *Journal of Southern Religion* 3 (2000), July 12, 2002 <http://jsr.as.wvu.edu/index.html>.

McGrath, Roger D. *Gunfighters, Highwaymen, and Vigilantes: Violence on the Frontier.* Berkeley: University of California Press, 1984.

McKanna, Clare V. *Homicide, Race, and Justice in the American West, 1880–1920.* Tucson: University of Arizona Press, 1997.

McLagan, Elizabeth. *A Peculiar Paradise: A History of Blacks in Oregon, 1788–1940.* Portland, Ore.: Georgian Press, 1980.

McLelland, John M., Jr. *Wobbly War: The Centralia Story.* Tacoma: Washington State Historical Society, 1987.

McMillen, Neil R. *Dark Journey: Black Mississippians in the Age of Jim Crow.* Urbana: University of Illinois Press, 1990.

Melish, Joanne Pope. *Disowning Slavery: Gradual Emancipation and "Race" in New England, 1780–1860.* Ithaca, N.Y.: Cornell University Press, 1998.

Menard, Orville D. "Tom Dennison, the *Omaha Bee*, and the 1919 Race Riot." *Nebraska History* 68.4 (1987): 152–65.

Mercer, Asa Shinn. *The Banditti of the Plains; or, the Cattlemen's Invasion of Wyoming in 1892 (the Crowning Infamy of the Ages).* 1894. Reprint, Norman: University of Oklahoma Press, 1954.

Miller, Wilbur. *Cops and Bobbies: Police Authority in New York and London, 1830–1870.* Columbus: Ohio State University Press, 1999.

Mokler, A. J. *History of Natrona County, Wyoming.* Chicago: R. R. Donnelley and Sons, 1923.

Monkkonen, Eric H. *Police in Urban America, 1860–1920.* New York: Cambridge University Press, 1981.

Moore, William Howard. "Progressivism and the Social Gospel in Wyoming: The Antigambling Act of 1901 as a Test Case." *Western Historical Quarterly* 15.3 (1984): 299–316.

Moses, Norton H. *Lynching and Vigilantism in the United States: An Annotated Bibliography.* Westport, Conn.: Greenwood, 1997.

Moss, Frank. *Story of the Riot Published by the Citizen's Protective League.* 1900. Reprint, New York: Arno Press, 1969.

The Murder of the Geogles and the Lynching of the Fiend Snyder, by the Otherwise Peaceable and Law-abiding Citizens of Bethlehem, Pa., and Its Vicinity; a Cold-blooded Murder, a Swift Retribution, a Remarkable Case, and the First Resort to Lynch Law in Pennsylvania. Philadelphia: Barclay and Co., n.d. [ca. 1881].

Murlin, Edgar L. *The New York Red Book: An Illustrated Legislative Manual.* Albany: James B. Lyon, 1898.

Nadeau, Remi. *Fort Laramie and the Sioux Indians.* Englewood Cliffs, N.J.: Prentice-Hall, 1967.

National Association for the Advancement of Colored People. *Thirty Years of Lynching in the United States, 1889–1918.* 1919. Reprint, New York: Arno Press, 1969.

Nau, John Fredrick. *The German People of New Orleans, 1850–1900*. Leiden, Neth.: E. J. Brill, 1958.

Navarro, Jason. "Racial Violence in the Midwest: Pierce City's Role in the Ethnic Cleansing of Southwest Missouri." Unpublished ms., 2001. In author's possession.

Nelli, Humbert S. *The Business of Crime: Italians and Syndicate Crime in the United States*. New York: Oxford University Press, 1976.

Nolan, Patrick Bates. "Vigilantes on the Middle Border: A Study of Self-Appointed Law Enforcement in the States of the Upper Mississippi from 1840 to 1880." Ph.D. dissertation, University of Minnesota, 1971.

Osofsky, Gilbert. *Harlem: The Making of a Ghetto, Negro New York, 1890–1930*. 2d ed. New York: Harper and Row, 1971.

Ownby, Ted. *Subduing Satan: Religion, Recreation, and Manhood in the Rural South, 1865–1920*. Chapel Hill: University of North Carolina Press, 1990.

Parker, James E. "Pioneer Protection from Horse Thieves." *Annals of Iowa* 6 (April 1903): 59–62.

Patterson, Orlando. *Rituals of Blood: Consequences of Slavery in Two American Centuries*. Washington, D.C.: Civitas Counterpoint, 1998.

Paul, Arnold M. *Conservative Crisis and the Rule of Law: Attitudes of Bar and Bench, 1887–1895*. Ithaca, N.Y.: Cornell University Press, 1960.

Pederson, Jane M. "Gender, Justice, and a Wisconsin Lynching, 1889–1890." *Agricultural History* 67.2 (Spring 1993): 65–82.

Percy, Adrian. *Twice Outlawed: A Personal History of Ed. and Lon Maxwell, Alias the Williams Brothers*. Chicago: W. R. Conkey Company, n.d. [ca. 1881].

Pfeifer, Michael James. "Iowa's Last Lynching: The 1907 Charles City Mob and Iowa Progressivism." *Annals of Iowa* 53.4 (Fall 1994): 305–28.

Pfeifer, Michael J. "Lynching and Criminal Justice in Regional Context: Iowa, Wyoming, and Louisiana, 1878–1946." Ph.D. dissertation, University of Iowa, 1998.

———. "Lynching and Criminal Justice in South Louisiana, 1878–1930." *Louisiana History* 40.2 (Spring 1999): 155–77.

———. "The Ritual of Lynching: Extralegal Justice in Missouri, 1890–1942." *Gateway Heritage* 13.3 (Winter 1993): 22–33.

Pioneer History of Davis County, Iowa. Bloomfield, Iowa: The Bloomfield Democrat, 1927.

Popspisil, Leopold. *Anthropology of Law: A Comparative Theory*. New York: Harper and Row, 1971.

Power, Richard Lyle. *Planting Cornbelt Culture: The Impress of the Upland Southerner and Yankee in the Old Northwest*. Indianapolis: Indiana Historical Society, 1953.

Pratt, Stacey McDermott. "'An Outrageous Proceeding': A Northern Lynching and the Enforcement of Anti-lynching Legislation in Illinois, 1905–1910." *The Journal of Negro History* 84.1 (Winter 1999): 61–78.

Quinn, D. Michael. *Same-Sex Dynamics among Nineteenth-Century Americans*. Urbana: University of Illinois Press, 1996.

Quynne, Edythe Ann. "'The Hills' in the Mid-Nineteenth Century: The History of a Rural Afro-American Community in Westchester County, New York." *Afro-Americans in New York Life and History* 14.2 (July 1990): 35–50.

Rabinowitz, Howard N. *Race Relations in the Urban South, 1865–1890.* New York: Oxford University Press, 1978.

Raper, Arthur. *The Tragedy of Lynching.* Chapel Hill: University of North Carolina Press, 1933.

Reid, John Phillip. *Policing the Elephant: Crime, Punishment, and Social Behavior on the Overland Trail.* San Marino, Calif.: Huntington Library, 1987.

Riley, Glenda. *Women and Indians on the Frontier, 1825–1915.* Albuquerque: University of New Mexico Press, 1984.

Rosenberg, Charles E. *The Trial of the Assassin Guiteau: Psychiatry and Law in the Gilded Age.* Chicago: University of Chicago Press, 1968.

Ross, John. "At the Bar of Judge Lynch: Lynching and Lynch Mobs in America." Ph.D. dissertation, Texas Tech University, 1983.

Rothman, David J. *The Discovery of the Asylum: Social Order and Disorder in the New Republic.* Boston: Little Brown, 1971.

Rousey, Dennis C. *Policing the Southern City: New Orleans, 1805–1899.* Baton Rouge: Louisiana State University Press, 1996.

Rudwick, Elliot M. *Race Riot at East St. Louis, July 2, 1917.* Carbondale: Southern Illinois University Press, 1964.

Runcie, John. "'Hunting the Nigs' in Philadelphia: The Race Riot of August 1834." In *Lynching, Racial Violence, and Law.* Ed. Paul Finkelman. 271–302. New York: Garland Press, 1992.

Saxton, Alexander P. *The Indispensable Enemy: Labor and the Anti-Chinese Movement in California.* Berkeley: University of California Press, 1971.

Sayre, Ralph Mills. "Albert B. Cummins and the Progressives in Iowa." Ph.D. dissertation, Columbia University, 1958.

Scarpaci, Jean Ann. "Italian Immigrants in Louisiana's Sugar Parishes." Ph.D. dissertation, Rutgers University, 1972.

Schwantes, Carlos A. "The Concept of the Wageworkers' Frontier: A Framework for Future Research." *Western Historical Quarterly* 18.1 (January 1987): 39–55.

———. *The Pacific Northwest: An Interpretive History.* Lincoln: University of Nebraska Press, 1989.

———. "Protest in a Promised Land: Unemployment, Disinheritance, and the Origin of Labor Militancy in the Pacific Northwest, 1885–1886." *Western Historical Quarterly* 13 (1982): 373–90.

Schwieder, Dorothy. *Black Diamonds: Life and Work in Iowa's Coal Mining Communities, 1895–1925.* Ames: Iowa State University Press, 1987.

———. *Iowa: The Middle Land.* Ames: Iowa State University Press, 1996.

Schwieder, Dorothy, Joseph Hraba, and Elmer Schwieder. *Buxton: Work and Racial Equality in a Coal Mining Community.* Ames: Iowa State University Press, 1987.

Senechal, Roberta. *The Sociogenesis of a Race Riot: Springfield, Illinois, in 1908.* Urbana: University of Illinois Press, 1990.

Senechal de la Roche, Roberta. "The Sociogenesis of Lynching." In *Under Sentence of Death: Lynching in the South.* Ed. W. Fitzhugh Brundage. 48–76. Chapel Hill: University of North Carolina Press, 1997.

Senkewicz, Robert M. *Vigilantes in Gold Rush San Francisco.* Stanford, Calif.: Stanford University Press, 1985.

Shay, Frank. *Judge Lynch: His First Hundred Years.* New York: Ives Washburn, 1938.

"'Should the Murderer of Miss Bishop be Lynched.'" Pamphlet (Sermon by Rev. R. A. Elwood, June 21, 1903). Wilmington, Del.: Wilmington Morning News, 1903.

Sing Sing Prison Electrocutions, 1891–1963. Ossining, N.Y.: Ossining Historical Society, n.d.

Smith, Albert C. "'Southern Violence' Reconsidered: Arson as Protest in Black-Belt Georgia, 1865–1910." *Journal of Southern History* 51.4 (November 1985): 527–64.

Smith, Helena Huntington. *The War on Powder River*. New York: McGraw-Hill, 1966.

Southern Commission on the Study of Lynching. *Lynchings and What They Mean*. Atlanta: Southern Commission on the Study of Lynching, 1931.

Spear, Allan H. *Black Chicago: The Making of a Negro Ghetto*. Chicago: University of Chicago Press, 1967.

State of Iowa. *Annotated Code of the State of Iowa*. Des Moines: Mills, 1885; F. R. Conaway, 1897.

———. *Census of 1885*. Des Moines: G. E. Roberts, 1885.

———. *Census of 1895*. Des Moines: F. R. Conaway, 1896.

———. *Census of 1905*. Des Moines: B. Murphy, 1905.

———. *Census of 1915*. Des Moines: R. Henderson, 1916.

———. *Iowa Official Register*. Des Moines: N.p., 1882.

State of Louisiana. *Revised Statute Laws of the State of Louisiana*. New Orleans: B. Bloomfield and Co., 1876.

———. *Constitution and Revised Laws of Louisiana*. New Orleans: F. F. Hansell, 1904.

State of New York. *Documents of the Assembly of the State of New York, One Hundred and Twenty-Fifth Session*. Albany: J. B. Lyon, 1902.

———. *Revised Statutes of the State of New York*. Albany: Banks Brothers, 1859.

State of Washington. *Session Laws of the State of Washington, Eleventh Session*. Olympia: E. L. Boardman, 1909.

———. *Session Laws of the State of Washington, Sixteenth Session*. Olympia: Frank L. Lamborn, 1919.

State of Wyoming. *The Census of Wyoming, 1905*. Cheyenne: N.p., 1905.

———. *The Census of the State of Wyoming, 1915*. Cheyenne: N.p., n.d.

———. *Wyoming State Census, 1925*. N.p., n.d.

Steinberg, Allen. *The Transformation of Criminal Justice, Philadelphia, 1800–1880*. Chapel Hill: University of North Carolina Press, 1989.

Stevens, Herbert. *Vigilantes Ride in 1882*. Fairfield, Wash.: Ye Galleon Press, 1975.

Storti, Craig. *Incident at Bitter Creek: The Story of the Rock Springs Massacre*. Ames: Iowa State University Press, 1991.

Takaki, Ronald. *Strangers from a Different Shore: A History of Asian Americans*. Boston: Little, Brown, 1989.

Taylor, Quintard. *In Search of the Racial Frontier: African Americans in the American West, 1528–1990*. New York: W. W. Norton, 1998.

Thomson, Bailey, and Patricia L. Meador. *Shreveport: A Photographic Remembrance*. Baton Rouge: Louisiana State University Press, 1987.

Thompson, E. P. "'Rough Music': Le Charivari Anglais." *Annales: Economics, Societies, Civilization* 27 (March–April 1972): 286–87.

Tolnay, Stewart E., and E. M. Beck. *A Festival of Violence: An Analysis of Southern Lynchings, 1882–1930*. Urbana: University of Illinois Press, 1995.

———. "When Race Didn't Matter: Black and White Mob Violence against Their Own Color." In *Under Sentence of Death: Lynching in the South.* Ed. W. Fitzhugh Brundage. 132–44. Chapel Hill: University of North Carolina Press, 1997.

Traub, Stuart H. "Rewards, Bounty Hunting, and Criminal Justice in the West, 1865–1900." *Western Historical Quarterly* 19.3 (August 1988): 287–301.

Tunnell, Ted. *Crucible of Reconstruction: War, Radicalism, and Race in Louisiana, 1862–1877.* Baton Rouge: Louisiana State University Press, 1984.

Tuttle, William M., Jr. *Race Riot: Chicago in the Red Summer of 1919.* New York: Atheneum, 1970.

U.S. Bureau of the Census. *Tenth Census of the United States.* Washington, D.C.: Government Printing Office, 1882.

———. *Eleventh Census of the United States.* Washington, D.C.: Government Printing Office, 1892.

———. *Twelfth Census of the United States.* Washington, D.C.: Government Printing Office, 1901.

———. *Thirteenth Census of the United States.* Washington, D.C.: Government Printing Office, 1913.

———. *Fourteenth Census of the United States.* Washington, D.C.: Government Printing Office, 1922.

———. *Fifteenth Census of the United States.* Washington, D.C.: Government Printing Office, 1932.

Vandal, Gilles. "Black Violence in Post–Civil War Louisiana." *Journal of Interdisciplinary History* 25.1 (Summer 1994): 45–64.

———. "The Policy of Violence in Caddo Parish, 1865–1884." *Louisiana History* 32.2 (Spring 1991): 159–82.

———. "Politics and Violence in Bourbon Louisiana: The Loreauville Riot of 1884 as a Case Study." *Louisiana History* 30.1 (1989): 23–42.

———. *Rethinking Southern Violence: Homicides in Post–Civil War Louisiana, 1866–1884.* Columbus: Ohio State University Press, 2000.

Vyzralek, Frank E. "Murder in Masquerade: A Commentary on Lynching and Mob Violence in North Dakota's Past, 1882–1931." *North Dakota History* 57 (1990): 20–29.

Waldrep, Christopher. *The Many Faces of Judge Lynch: Extralegal Violence and Punishment in America.* New York: Palgrave Macmillan, 2002.

———. *Night Riders: Defending Community in the Black Patch, 1890–1915.* Durham, N.C.: Duke University Press, 1993.

———. *Roots of Disorder: Race and Criminal Justice in the American South, 1817–80.* Urbana: University of Illinois Press, 1998.

———. "War of Words: The Controversy over the Definition of Lynching, 1899–1940." *Journal of Southern History* 66.1 (2000): 75–100.

———. "Word and Deed: The Language of Lynching, 1820–1953." In *Lethal Imagination: Violence and Brutality in American History.* Ed. Michael Bellesiles. 229–58. New York: New York University Press, 1999.

Walker, Samuel. *Popular Justice: A History of American Criminal Justice.* New York: Oxford University Press, 1980.

Watkins, Ralph. "A Survey of the African American Presence in the History of the Downstate New York Area." *Afro-Americans in New York Life and History* 15.1 (January 1991): 53–79.

Watkin-Owens, Irma. *Caribbean Immigrants and the Harlem Community, 1900–1930*. Bloomington: Indiana University Press, 1996.

Webb, Clive. "The Lynching of Sicilian Immigrants in the American South, 1886 to 1910." *American Nineteenth-Century History* 3.1 (Spring 2002): 45–76.

Webb, Warren Franklin. "A History of Lynching in California since 1875." M.A. thesis, University of California at Berkeley, 1934.

Weinberg, Carl. "'The Tug of War': Labor, Loyalty, and Rebellion in the Southwestern Illinois Coalfields, 1914–1920." Ph.D. dissertation, Yale University, 1995.

Wells-Barnett, Ida B. *On Lynchings: Southern Horrors [1892]; A Red Record [1895]; Mob Rule in New Orleans [1900]*. Reprint, New York: Arno Press, 1969.

White, Deborah Gray. *Ar'n't I a Woman: Female Slaves in the Plantation South*. New York: Norton, 1985.

White, Richard. "Outlaw Gangs of the Middle Border: American Social Bandits." *Western Historical Quarterly* 12.4 (October 1981): 387–408.

Williamson, Joel. *The Crucible of Race: Black/White Relations in the American South since Emancipation*. New York: Oxford University Press, 1984.

Wilson, Bruce A. *Late Frontier: A History of Okanogan County, Washington, 1800–1941*. Okanogan, Wash.: Okanogan County Historical Society, 1990.

Wood, Gordon S. *The Radicalism of the American Revolution*. New York: Vintage Books, 1993.

Works Progress Administration, Federal Writer's Project. *The Italians of New York*. 1938. Reprint, New York: Arno Press, 1969.

Wright, George C. "By the Book: The Legal Executions of Kentucky Blacks." In *Under Sentence of Death: Lynching in the South*. Ed. W. Fitzhugh Brundage. 250–70. Chapel Hill: University of North Carolina Press, 1997.

———. *Racial Violence in Kentucky, 1865–1940*. Baton Rouge: Louisiana State University Press, 1990.

Wright, Richard. *Native Son*. 1940. Reprint, New York: Perennial, 2001.

Wyatt-Brown, Bertram. *Southern Honor: Ethics and Behavior in the Old South*. New York: Oxford University Press, 1982.

York, Dena Lynn Winslow. "'They Lynched Jim Cullen': New England's Only Lynching." Ph.D. dissertation, University of Maine, 2000.

Zangrando, Robert L. *The NAACP Crusade against Lynching, 1909–1950*. Philadelphia: Temple University Press, 1980.

INDEX

Adams County, Iowa: lynching in, 52
Alaska: lynching in, 101
Albany County, Wyoming: lynching in, 56–57, 89
American Indians: lynching of, 86–87, 95, 96, 207n96
Ames, Jesse Daniel, 225–26n90
Asotin County, Washington: lynching in, 53–54, 136–37
Association of Southern Women for the Prevention of Lynching (ASW-PL): contribution to the decline of lynching, 146, 225–26n90
Audubon County, Iowa: lynching in, 52, 58, 111
Avoyelles Parish, Louisiana: lynching in, 43
Ayers, Edward L., 200n5, 204n51

Bakersfield, California: lynching in, 32, 65–66, 85–86
Baldus, David, 151
Bancroft, Hubert Howe, 5–6
Basin, Wyoming: lynching in, 108
Bedford, Iowa: lynching in, 87
Bienville Parish, Louisiana: lynching in, 49, 72, 118, 224n77
Black, Paul Walton, 25, 58
Blanchard, Gov. Newton: response to lynching, 142–45, 224n74, 224n76, 224n77, 224n79
Bossier Parish, Louisiana: capital punishment in, 217n119; lynching in, 15, 68–69, 71, 200n4
Bramel, Judge C. W.: and rough justice views, 105, 108, 212n43
Brasseaux, Carl, 215n103
Bremer County, Iowa: lynching in, 46, 58

Brennan, Justice William: on race, history, and capital punishment, 152
Brown, Richard Maxwell, 5, 55, 185n2, 198n101, 214n71
Brundage, W. Fitzhugh, 5, 191n1, 191–92n3, 193n24, 193n30, 216–17n116, 225–26n90

Caddo Parish, Louisiana: lynching in, 68, 118, 145, 200n4, 224n70
capital punishment: in California, 137; contemporary death penalty as a legacy of lynching, 149–53; contemporary debate surrounding, 12, 149–53, 226n9; debate over in Wisconsin, 114–15, 215n89; historical distribution by American region, 186n5; in Iowa, 112–14, 131, 221n31; in Louisiana, 120–21, 141, 146–47, 202n33, 204–5n66, 205n67, 225n88; in Louisiana's Sugarland, 79–80; in the Mississippi Delta of Louisiana, 73; in New York State, 123–29, 218n6, 219n7, 220n10, 220n11, 220n13; in Pennsylvania, 218n6; reform of, 5, 7–8, 11, 80; and supporters of lynching, 4; in Washington, 136; in Wyoming, 105–7, 109, 133–34
Carbon County, Wyoming: lynching in, 47, 54, 56–57, 62–63, 89
Carey, Gov. Joseph: political philosophy of, 222n45; and the reform of capital punishment, 134–35; response to lynching, 89, 104
Carrigan, William D., 85
Casper, Wyoming: lynching in, 28, 47, 108–9, 136

MICHAEL J. PFEIFER is a professor of
American history at the University of
Western Ontario, Ontario, Canada. He has
published articles on lynching and criminal
justice in *Western Legal History*, *Pacific
Northwest Quarterly*, the *Annals of Iowa*,
Louisiana History, and *Gateway Heritage*.

*The University of Illinois Press
is a founding member of the
Association of American University Presses.*

---

*Composed in 9.5/12.5 Trump Mediaeval
at the University of Illinois Press*

*University of Illinois Press
1325 South Oak Street
Champaign, IL 61820-6903
www.press.uillinois.edu*